After Ca

New Directions in International Studies

Patrice Petro, Series Editor

The New Directions in International Studies series focuses on transculturalism, technology, media, and representation and features the innovative work of scholars who explore various components and consequences of globalization, such as the increasing flow of peoples, ideas, images, information, and capital across borders. Under the direction of Patrice Petro, the series is sponsored by the Center for International Education at the University of Wisconsin–Milwaukee. The center seeks to foster interdisciplinary and collaborative research that probes the political, economic, artistic, and social processes and practices of our time.

For a list of titles in the series, see the last page of the book.

After Capitalism

HORIZONS OF FINANCE, CULTURE, AND CITIZENSHIP

Edited by
Kennan Ferguson and Patrice Petro

RUTGERS UNIVERSITY PRESS
New Brunswick, New Jersey, and London

Library of Congress Cataloging-in-Publication Data

Names: Ferguson, Kennan, 1968– editor. | Petro, Patrice, 1957–editor.
Title: After capitalism: horizons of finance, culture, and citizenship /
edited by Kennan Ferguson and Patrice Petro.
Description: New Brunswick, New Jersey: Rutgers University Press, 2016. |
Series: New directions in international studies | Includes bibliographical
references and index
Identifiers: LCCN 2015037351| ISBN 9780813584270 (hardcover: alk. paper) |
ISBN 9780813584263 (pbk.: alk. paper) | ISBN 9780813584287 (e-book (epub)) |
ISBN 9780813584294 (e-book (web pdf))
Subjects: LCSH: Capitalism. | Democracy. | Citizenship.
Classification: LCC HB501 .A455 2016 | DDC 330.12/2—dc23
LC record available at http://lccn.loc.gov/2015037351

A British Cataloging-in-Publication record for this book is available
from the British Library.

Visit our website: http://rutgerspress.rutgers.edu

Manufactured in the United States of America

CONTENTS

Part III: Belonging

ACKNOWLEDGMENTS

This volume emerged from a conference held in April 2014 at the Center for International Education at the University of Wisconsin–Milwaukee (UWM). As with previous conferences at the center, our aim was to showcase the work of new and established scholars, in this case by exploring the cultural, political, geographical, and organizational parameters of a world "after capitalism." We are grateful to everyone who participated in the conference and want to acknowledge the inspirational and groundbreaking lectures presented both at the conference itself (many of which are included here) and earlier in the year with a series of distinguished lectures at the Institute of World Affairs. Thanks to the leadership of Jeffrey Sommers, we were able to engage in discussions about capitalism's past and futures with James Kenneth Galbraith, Yanis Varoufakis, and Mark Blyth. The editors are grateful for the outstanding logistic and administrative support provided by Eric Herhuth, project assistant and doctoral student at UWM, who assisted with the coordination of the conference. The editors would also like to extend their profound gratitude to Mark Brand, also a project assistant and doctoral student at UWM, who has done an exceptional and meticulous job of helping to prepare this volume. Finally, the editors would like to express our continuing gratitude to Leslie Mitchner, editor-in-chief at Rutgers University Press, for her ongoing support for the series in which this book is a part and for her unwavering commitment to the importance of interdisciplinary, international, and imaginative scholarship.

After Capitalism

Introduction

PATRICE PETRO AND KENNAN FERGUSON

Capitalism has a beginning; must it have an end as well? If so, what comes after? Will capitalism cease and be replaced by another social and economic system?

A considerable literature is emerging on the problems endemic to capitalist economies. For many years the presumption remained that capitalism might only need some minor corrections (a safety net for vulnerable citizens or a slightly redistributive tax structure) in order to continue indefinitely. Those who rejected capitalism outright usually saw in it a rejection of the hard-won truths of tradition (the conservative critique, which called for a return to precapitalist times) or an unfortunate but necessary stage toward a predetermined outcome (the Marxist tradition, which called for movement toward a revolutionary overthrow). Recently, however, a large range of thinkers have argued that capitalism's inherent tendency is toward instability (one of Marx's central ideas) but that such an instability may lead in uncertain and complex directions. From Thomas Piketty's analysis that capital's natural tendency is to accumulate for the few at the expense of the many, to Nick Srnicek and Alex Williams's call to accelerate the conflicts of capitalism, to Paul Mason's vision of a free-flowing internet economy, a consensus is emerging among some scholars that capitalism itself is unsustainable.[1] The economic disasters in the Eurozone, the continuance of small-scale networks of trade and truck, and the emergence of life lived in digital forms, all point to the need for new, emergent conceptualizations of capitalism.

The modern system called capitalism ought not to be confused with certain of its aspects, such as private property or free trade. Many systems and locations have used free trade as part of their economies; a market in ancient China or in medieval Italy, for instance, would have both individual ownership of certain materials and monetary and goods exchanges. Capitalism as such emerges only in a specific historical period (though one hotly debated by economic historians) when capital itself emerges. Capital—the term for the abstract value that has the ability to reproduce itself—is distinct from such historically ubiquitous sites of production such as land or human labor.

Thus, the modern social system that seems so natural to its inhabitants proves neither ahistorical nor immutable. It is this insight that both unifies this volume of essays and underpins the contributors' ability to imagine capitalism's "after," and whether the spatial and temporal dimensions of this event refer to capitalism's appearance or disappearance. In the modern world, as forms of capital have multiplied to include intellectual property, social capital, and even symbolic representations (such as trademarks), the power of capitalism seems only to have grown. But its reliance on such abstractions also has the potential to weaken its hold on the world, as legal and political formulations may sometimes be speedily replaced by other formulations.

Capitalism's emergence entailed a considerable degree of violence. As David Harvey puts it, the "transformation of labour, land and money into commodities rested on violence, cheating, robbery, swindling, and the like. The common lands were enclosed, divided and put up for sale as private property. The gold and silver that formed the initial money commodities were stolen from the Americas. The labour was forced off the land into the status of a 'free' wage labourer who could be freely exploited by capital when not outright enslaved or indentured. Such forms of dispossession were foundational to the creation of capital."[2] Some of the essays in this volume expand on Harvey's assessment of "accumulation by dispossession" and argue that capitalism's continued violence is a necessary aspect of its persistence. And, as a large number of fictional representations of the end of the (capitalist) world hint, its disappearance could be a violent event as well.

This violence occurs from an attempt to correct the moral, ethical, or financial imbalances of a particular economy. Such imbalances can be measured only against alternatives: a more just world, a fairer economy, even a utopian dream. In each case, alternatives are imagined and then brought into being through argument, critique, and experimentation. It is this process, imagining alternative political-theoretical horizons, that the contributors herein address. In their hands, the idea of capitalism as a system encourages alternative thoughts, not only about the future but about other locations in the present-day world.

The concepts of "After Capitalism" that emerge in this volume raise a series of questions. First, where and when are capitalism's limits? What are the geographical, temporal, and organizational parameters of its operations? Even though debate remains over the precise time and place it began, the abstraction of capital in a market economy clearly has a human beginning, one tied to modern historical and global forms and networks of production. Second, does capitalism operate as a historical period, which must end, or as a human tool, which will endure while being transformed into new and unexpected modes? If the latter, what happens when (or if) capitalism ceases? Its overcoming may be necessarily a global phenomenon, but it may be that reconsiderations or attacks from different cultures and nation-states and indigenous peoples will cause and react to its disappearance in divergent ways. Economists, scientists, and historians attentive to periods of crisis such as the Great Depression or global climate change or the exigencies of the recent euro crisis see the political dissolution of capitalism as a recurrent possibility, with a different mode of production arising that could be either better or worse than the current order. Third, and finally, what forces in the world have the power to continue beyond or after capitalism, and what intellectual processes are best suited to conceptualizing such a time? What happens (politically, economically, socially, or environmentally) to a nation or a region after capitalism is established where it had not existed before (for example, in China, or Cuba, or the states of the former Soviet Bloc)? Building alternative conceptions of capitalism's temporal nature requires both imagination and intellectual distance. Perhaps capitalism has never truly existed but remains always in a mode of futurity, an idealized form that serves both to mask power and to invoke other potential futures. Elements of speculative fiction, economic imagination, and transglobal human relationships prove central to thinking through these possibilities.

One might even imagine that locales in our contemporary world exist after capitalism. Certainly the media sphere (including film, television, and the internet) regularly and persistently imagines such worlds, whether in reality television shows or science fiction fantasies, which in turn raise questions about dilemmas of representation itself. To borrow from Fredric Jameson: "The problem of representation today eats away at all the established disciplines like a virus, particularly destabilizing the dimension of language, reference and expression (which used to be the domain of literary study) as well as that of thought (which used to be that of philosophy). Nor is economics exempt, which posits invisible entities like finance capital on the one hand, and points to untheorizable singularities like derivatives on the other. And as for political theory, the traditional question—what is the state?—has mutated into something unanswerable with its post-contemporary version, where is the state?—while the former thing called power, as solid and tangible, seemingly, as a gold coin, or at least as a dollar bill, has become the airy plaything of mystics and physiologists alike. It is the problem of representation which has wrought all this destabilized confusion, and it can be said to be history itself which has deregulated it, so that if the dilemmas of representation are postmodern and historical, it can also be said that history as such has become a problem of representation."[3]

Each of the contributors to this volume attempts to imagine the unimaginable and represent the unrepresentable in an effort to ascertain the time and place where capitalism both is and is not. This is a demanding project. Fredric Jameson famously wrote (while attributing the idea to someone else) that "it is easier to imagine the end of the world than to imagine the end of capitalism."[4] It is the goal of this volume to attempt this difficult imagining by exploring concepts of austerity, credit, and risk as well as representations of ruination, homelessness, transformation, and multiple sovereign practices. The essays in this collection attempt this in three distinct but overlapping ways, by addressing political economics ("Financialization, Creditocracy, and Austerity"), representation and imaging ("Media/Art"), and geopolitical localities ("Belonging").

The first section, "Financialization, Creditocracy, and Austerity," begins with an analysis of those thinkers who have imagined the period after capitalism, with a particular emphasis on the quasi-utopic ideal where the workplace no longer serves as the fundament of selfhood. Geoff Mann examines the presumptions of Marx, Schumpeter, and especially Keynes to excavate capital's role in a world no longer defined and determined by the system called "capitalism." By redefining the goal of capitalism from *productivity* (as most historical and contemporary theorists imagine it) to that of *prospective yield*, Mann notes how the power behind capitalism will continue without capital as its driver. The emergence of the world into human engagement has always been a process, not a substance; yield in a noncapitalist form will therefore remain as an intrinsic but not determining aspect of a more humane, less destructive, economic system. As Mann points out, "Economic growth (accumulation, development, and so forth) remains at the heart of all conceptions of capital, from the Marxist to the new neoclassical synthesis, to the Chicago School. In most cases, the relation between capital and growth is basically tautological, so central has it become to our understanding of positive economic change. Growth is understood to be impossible without capital, and the power of growth as the great legitimizer of political economic order has underwritten virtually every half-way successful mode of economic organization—capitalist and noncapitalist, it is worth emphasizing—of the last century, if not longer." Thus, it is growth and threats to growth that are at the heart of much historical and contemporary thinking about capital. But Mann cautions against relying on growth as the means to achieve a more stable social order; it is, he points out, difficult to imagine that "we will be able to consume or produce our way out of our current ecological predicaments."

Andrew Ross takes up where Mann leaves off, summarizing the historical transition from industrial to financial capitalism, recounting the recent history of the debt resistance movement and highlighting the Occupy Student Debt Campaign, which he helped to found. Our relationship with the finance industry, he explains, has turned into "something like a term life contract" so that today we live in what he calls a *creditocracy*. Ross explains: "Creditors' profits come from extending our debt service as long as they possibly can. After all, if we pay down our debts, we are no longer serviceable to the banks. The goal is to keep us on the hook until we die, and even beyond the grave in the case of student debts that are co-signed by parents or grandparents." Education debt, in particular, which cannot be relieved even in bankruptcy, he explains, is not only central to our creditocracy but also a form of wage theft, since debts are wages of the future. "Whereas strife over wages was central to the industrial era," Ross concludes, "the grand conflict of our times is shaping up as the struggle over debt, and any just resolution calls for a level of organizing at least as momentous as the labor movement in its heyday." For Ross, the end of capitalism comes in the form of the ouroboros snake, an economic system eating its own tail.

Returning in a different way to the extraordinary expansion of the finance sector in the last forty years and more, Ivan Ascher locates analogies between today's advanced capitalist societies and European societies some five hundred years ago. The sudden enclosure of the commons in England, he points out, created a population that had little choice but to flee the countryside in order to survive. As they moved to the cities, expropriated peasants were met with extraordinarily harsh laws against vagabondage, and as a result there emerged a new population of individuals disciplined for the rigors of factory work and industrial labor. In recent decades, likewise, the demise of the welfare state in both Europe and the United States has had dislocating effects, confronting people with new forms of uncertainty and risks that up until then had been addressed collectively. The grand bargain of the welfare state was that the workers agreed not to strike, and capital in exchange conceded a larger share of its profits (through better wages and more secure long-term employment contracts). Like Ross, Ascher explores the collapse of that grand bargain and the concurrent development of new techniques and strategies for risk and wealth management via financialization and credit. He explains that the credit card—with its combined promise of freedom and security—best embodies the promise, the dangers, and the revolutionary character of the new, neoliberal, and financialized order: "One's purchasing power is no longer simply dependent on the number of bills one has in one's wallet, but is increasingly dependent on one's borrowing power or one's credit—which credit each of us has to negotiate as an individual." Social relations that once formed the basis of the commons have thus been undone, as populations that relied on means of protection held in common now turn to the financial instruments of capital—insurance companies, pension funds, and credit card providers—as the new forms of security. In this reading, capitalism has been replaced by a multiplication of Ross's creditocracy by a system of inherent risk and precarity.

The histories and processes of financialization explored by Ross and Ascher are taken up in a geopolitical economic specificity by Jeffrey Sommers, who turns his attention to the small Baltic state of Latvia to understand larger patterns of historical and global political economy in the post-Soviet, post-2008 world. Latvia, Sommers explains, was at the epicenter of the global economic crisis when the financial shock hit in September 2008. It had one of the world's biggest real estate bubbles in the run-up to the crisis, and the world's most severe collapse in GDP following the 2008 financial shock: "In the wake of the crisis the country also implemented one of the world's most aggressive austerity policies in response. In doing so, it received global acclaim from bankers, international financial institutions, policymakers, and opinion framers, which made Latvia a central focus of international attention." Although austerity policies crippled the country, its proponents "celebrated Latvia as the plucky country that through hard work and discipline showed the way out of the financial crisis plaguing so many countries." Represented as "a veritable Protestant morality play to a global audience of policy and opinion makers demonstrating austerity's effectiveness," what actually emerged was debt penury and the very structures of serfdom from which Latvians thought they had escaped in the nineteenth century.

The essays included in the second section of the volume on "Media/ Art" expand upon the analyses offered in the first, only here changes in political economy become visible in a different way: through entertainment industries and avant-garde practices. Where Sommers's discussion of austerity policies examines a nation, Patrice Petro identifies it as affecting our most intimate and domestic realms. "Austerity media," which emerged in the wake of the 2008 financial crisis, literalized consumption and an ideology of asceticism in popular entertainment. Looking at both contemporary reality television and fictional programming, she shows how austerity narratives are cheaply produced (hence, industrially austere), how they interact with the crises of nonfictional economies (hence, both offer and validate narratives of austere living), and how they promote an ethos of individuality and self-help (hence, ideologically aligned with austerity policies). We are witnessing, she claims, a collapse of distinctions not only between subject and object but also between mental illness, depression, hoarding, and excessive accumulation. Hoarding, as a symptom of excessive consumption, emerges from this reading as a distinctly modern illness and material practice, revealing that "we have too much information, but no ability to process it; too much stuff, and nowhere to store it; too much feeling, and no way to express it." Moreover, she claims that this state of affairs is pathologized and gendered as female or feminine, "despite the reality of the real hoarders in our midst (the banking industry and corporations) and the very real poverty among men and women and families after 2008."

Sherryl Vint also looks to contemporary media practices to discern how reality now is often depicted as science fiction. "Science fiction film," she argues, "foregrounds the gap between reality and representation, the difference between the imagined world of the mise-en-scène and the social world of the viewer. Through their fantastic settings, science fiction films become a privileged site for interrogating the troubled relationship between representation and reality under capitalism." Exploring the concept of capitalist realism (which promotes the cynical belief that there is no outside or beyond to capital), she demonstrates how the unrealistic conclusions to the problems of capitalism staged in some science fiction films can actually "become a way of showing us the similarly unrealistic 'pervasive atmosphere' of capitalist realism, encouraging us to penetrate this barrier and consider alternative possibilities for thought and action." From fictionalized worlds that literalize the spatial and temporal dynamics of postcapitalist relationships to the metafictions of mock documentaries that perform the unrealities of contemporary dystopias, Vint finds in popular films a critical perspective oriented against the received verities of our times.

Marcus Bullock expands this analysis, looking beyond utopian and dystopian responses to capitalist inevitability by foregrounding the human reality behind the statistics about economic stagnation and ever-expanding unemployment. Beginning with a reflection on self-immolation (which is on the rise among men in industrial societies, both rich and poor nations, and in allegedly stable democracies as well as ruthless dictatorships), Bullock underscores the human aspect of austerity policies and practices: "while the unemployment of a million people is a statistic, the unemployment of one person is a tragedy. But this misses the point of that simpler and yet deep question of human value to which we have already alluded. Why is it such a tragedy?" More than just material privation, the hardship of losing a job and living with unemployment is fundamentally about intangible social value. "People do not self-immolate just because they find themselves short of cash. The difference between a paycheck and an unemployment benefit check often doesn't always run so very high in dollars or euros. The real difference is paid out in the intangible social value of respect." To get at this loss of social value, Bullock explores avant-garde projects (Gustav Metzger's Auto-Destructive Art Movement of the 1950s), the writings of authors such as Nietzsche, Kafka, and Walter Benjamin, and the philosophical and theoretical consequences of unemployment in the past and today.

Esther Leslie examines a different relationship between the tangible, the legible, and social value through a focus on the technology of liquid crystal. Like art, technological innovation recombines the material world with a more ineffable remaking of the world. The indeterminate state of liquidity and crystallinity, Leslie argues, allows for a new kind of nonmechanistic machinery: the tactile smoothness of the iPhone, the transparent opacity of the video screen. Technology builds a new access into humanity, where "capitalism can reach right into our emotions, defy nature, shape our whole being, and, in that circuit, replicate the authority of capitalism itself." Via the metaphor of crystallization, Leslie traces a long history of making material reality out of social relations; in the metaphor of liquidity, she sees a parallel history of the dissolution of the ostensibly solid into the fungibility of financialization (building on Marx and Engels's famous statement in the *Communist Manifesto* that "All that is solid melts into air, all that is holy is profaned, and man is at last compelled to face with sober senses his real conditions of life, and his relations with his kind"). The combination of these modalities, she argues, results in new forms of emergence. Liquid crystal capitalism, she argues, is nonetheless deeply "contradictory, producing images and forms for capital, but also providing the material of its dreams, its oppositions, and its breakdowns. It invades our dreams, forms our myths, our gestures and movements." Leslie thus concludes the second section by pointing to how liquid crystal, as an art form and a technology, embodies the promise and threat of capitalism's future.

The third section of this volume, "Belonging," identifies a number of particular geospatial localities wherein the temporal questions concerning capitalism's aftermath have been realized. The authors in this section explain how the iterations of capitalism and its effects have been experienced and remade throughout the world. Cuba, for example, saw many of the worst effects of capitalism in the early twentieth century and has since attempted to overcome its consequences. But, as Christina Venegas argues, transitions from one anti-capitalist model to another have been ongoing and constantly changing. By tracing both law and the presentation of economic situations in Cuban film, Venegas examines an array of presumptions of the island's futures. The "resulting alteration of the socialist-conceived cultural space has occurred without any rejection of socialist ideals or deliberate embrace of capitalist cultural values," Venegas shows. "The disintegration of the institutional form of film culture in Cuba and the energies originally located within this central concept are flowing into the nation's larger malleable halfway space." From familial escape to empty agriculture to postapocalyptic landscapes to zombie apocalypse, Cuban filmmakers have reinvented a series of representational futures for postcapitalist life.

Like the Cuban revolution, Iran's rejection of the West was motivated by a sense of nationalism, but in this case with a religious overlay. Rather than a return to a pre-capitalist utopia, as it is often understood in the West, the Iranian project attempted to build an alternative economic space, a "third way" between capitalism and socialism. As Niki Akhavan shows, the ideals of such a project quickly met the competing forces of monopoly, distribution, and religion. The Iranian state's relationship with various forms of media, therefore, has been both instrumental (what can television or radio do for the state) and oppositional (as forms of media undermine or escape recognized authority). As much as the government can use law to mandate content, "media production almost inevitably requires interaction with foreign technologies and platforms. In short, cultural and media production are imbricated with foreign ideas and technologies." Thus the alternative to Western capitalism dreamed of by the revolution has not truly emerged, but other hybridized postcapitalist media forms remain, captured neither by Islamic theocracy nor by capitalism. This indeterminate and shadowy potentiality continues to emerge in variant forms.

Another postcolonial nation-state, India, similarly aspired to a set of identities and practices oriented around nationalist goals. And, like Iran, this autonomist project has found itself compromised by its continued engagement with the larger world. For A. Aneesh, this dynamic forces a reckoning with the contradictions at the heart of citizenship and belonging. The various solutions presumed by antinationalism, especially those of universalist human rights or global cosmopolitanism, have proved untenable; globalized capitalism may demand forms of citizenship beyond the singular nation-state, but the ascriptive ties to community and location that underpinned the force of nationalism have proved more resilient and capacious than universalists assumed. The contemporary solution, Aneesh notes, has been a pluralized and multiple conception of belonging: dual citizenships, staggered geographies, and nested belonging. This conception he calls the "virtual basket of rights," a set of claims and identifications that are shifting, social, commodified, and individualized all at once. Such a basket, "the composition of which keeps changing depending on one's institutional and spatio-temporal location," comports with a globalized system of claims and counterclaims of ethnicity, autochthony, mobility, and work. Its most overt form, Aneesh shows, is that of "dual citizenship," an ostensibly contradictory but common and workable system of doubled belonging and loyalty.

The final essay in this volume engages questions of postcapitalism and belonging from an international context internal to the United States. American Indian nations exist in a constantly contested relationship with the larger and more powerful North American governmentalities of Canada and the United States. Bernard Perley finds in their combination of traditional practices and anti-settler colonialism strategies a fugitive and resistant economic form, which he terms "coyote capitalism." By both highlighting the illegal genocidal histories of settler states and insisting on the legal reality of strategic grants of sovereignty, coyote capitalists transform capitalism into fugitive and creative forms. Even though "the colonial and settler society capitalists have historically imposed (and continue to impose) severe constraints on indigenous economic development efforts," the power inherent in the structures of colonial oppression can be turned against it. The casino, Perley shows, operates as an exemplary site of coyote capitalism, using legal rights and the excesses of imperial capitalism to transform and extract value from the dominant system to benefit Natives. Attempts to eradicate Indian identity, from military extermination to the tribal status termination of the twentieth century, have thus left traces of power that those who follow the trickster figure of the coyote can turn against settler colonialism, excavating postcapitalist life and even occasionally prosperity.

Each of these essays contends with the flows and forces within and against capitalism, taking into account not only its potential disappearance but the flotsam left in its wake. The concept "after capitalism" thus is meant to suggest a focus not simply on some utopian future once capitalism has passed from the scene but, rather, on following the spaces and traces of capitalism, a pursuing or going "after" capitalism in this sense. How do we best represent capitalism or its inevitable cycles of booms and busts, particularly given that history as such has become a problem of representation? For some, nothing better represents the ruinations of capitalism than that of contemporary Detroit. More compelling are the reasons for our contemporary fascination with images of first-world urban decline, and not just in the Motor City. For those from more prosperous cities, spaces of ruination appear to tell a history—or at least evoke a vague sense of historical pathos—absent in other, wealthier cities. Indeed, one of the notable features of this Detroit boom and bust is the fact that few of the people driving it actually live there. In a country perennially plagued with a historical amnesia, ruins are rare permanent reminders of a history unsuited to the war memorials and equestrian statues that dot the national landscape.

Another reason for the fascination with Detroit's decline is less about history, though, and more about the future. Today, Detroit, to use an overused but appropriate metaphor, is "ground zero" of the collapse of the finance and real estate economy in America. Detroit has been hit as hard as any city by the foreclosure crisis and by unemployment and, so, embodies the looming jobless future, or more precisely, our worst fears about that future.

Each essay in this volume examines in its own way how political economy, representational practices, and questions of citizenship and belonging are necessary to rethinking capitalism's past and potential futures. The transition from industrial to finance capital, the demise of the commons, the emergence of new forms of financial extraction through derivatives, student loan debt, credit cards, and the impact of post-2008 austerity measures inform all of the contributions here, whether the topic at hand is rethinking economic theory, Marx's writings, unemployment, hoarding, "capitalist realism," liquid crystal capitalism, or coyote (trickster) capitalism, among many other topics. Some of the essays in this volume assume that capitalism will shift and grow as the world changes, and that capital's capacity to change and absorb even its own critics will continue to give it an almost infinite flexibility. Others presume that capitalism, like all economic systems, will come to an end, although its traces and effects will continue to shape the world's makeup and climate as well as the humans that (hopefully) remain after its disappearance. And still others see in alternative locations and histories a hidden world that is already postcapitalist or even continues outside of capitalism's reach. The fissures and cracks in the ostensibly smooth operations of capital have, these latter authors argue, already been caused by (or filled with) these noncapitalist systems, thus offering alternative possibilities for thought and action.

Notes

1 Thomas Piketty, *Le Capital au XXIe siècle* (Paris: Seuil, 2013); Nick Srnicek and Alex Williams, "#Accelerate: Manifesto for an Accelerationist Politics," in *#Accelerate: The Accelerationist Reader*, ed. Robin Mackay and Armen Avanessian (London: Urbanomic, 2014), 347–361; Paul Mason, *Postcapitalism: A Guide to Our Future* (London: Allen Lane, 2015).

2 David Harvey, *Seventeen Contradictions and the End of Capitalism* (London: Profile Books, 2011), 57–59.

3 Fredric Jameson, *Representing Capital: A Commentary on Volume I* (London: Verso, 2011).

4 Fredric Jameson, "Future City," *New Left Review* 21 (2003): 76.

Part I

Financialization, Creditocracy, Austerity

1

Capital, after Capitalism

GEOFF MANN

What of capital—after capitalism? What, if anything, might the category describe, and what role might it play in the organization and reproduction of our societies and ways of life? These questions force us to turn directly to the category of capital; they force us to ask ourselves what exactly we mean by capital, to consider how it has been conceived and put to work in the past, and to reflect, if speculatively, on what it might or might not be able to do in conditions in which it is no longer hegemonic.

I would reject all suggestions that this task is anything less than urgent, that it is mere scholarly fiddling while Rome burns. The strained and creaking world we live in compels us to think differently about capital, to question and unsettle its apparently natural place in the political economic and cultural firmament. Indeed this is already happening all over the globe, inspired by the ongoing accumulation of capital's manifest predations and failures. Having arrogated the right to mediate many of our fundamental relations with each other and with the ecosystems upon which we depend, it has proved itself patently inadequate.

So what is capital, and what, if anything, will it be after the pedestal of capital*ism* topples? This is admittedly to open something of a Pandora's box, and I want to be quick to allay fears I am about to take up a definitional disquisition. As Joseph Schumpeter once said, "the theory of capital does indeed enjoy a reputation for this kind of thing that is rivaled by few other fields. People kept on asking the meaningless question: What is

Capital?"[1] It is tempting to find some solace in that remark: "What is capital?" is a meaningless question. Don't waste your time on it. Then again, this is Schumpeter talking and even he did not take his own advice. Neither should we. What follows, therefore, is a reflection on the status of capital, in conversation with some of the work that has most influenced political economic theory. My hope is to show that there is in fact an alternative way to think about capital embedded in (some of) the political economic canon, one grounded in John Maynard Keynes's concept of *yield*. If so, then to ask of capital—after capitalism—is to inquire into the end of yield, a possibility potentially as hopeful as it is terrible.

Does Capital Need Capitalism?

It is probably unsurprising that Schumpeter's point was not so much to suggest that a theory of capital was a fool's errand but, rather, that we need not trouble ourselves with a careful investigation of its dynamics or its specificities. Instead, he proposed we simply think of it as anything that is "requisite of production," an idea he argued is actually at the root of most "common sense" thinking on capital, among both political economists and everyday businesspeople.[2] David Ricardo, for example, said capital is "that part of the wealth of a country which is employed in production, and consists of food, clothing, tools, raw materials, machinery, etc., necessary to give effect to labour."[3]

Schumpeter even went so far as to claim that Marx—who one might imagine would be among those who had wasted their efforts subtly refining a theory of capital—would, instead, have been "all for" the "requisite of production" conceptualization of capital. Schumpeter claimed that the author of *Capital* "added nothing to this except that, in obedience to his principle of amalgamating economics and sociology [!], he confined the term capital to those things of this class that are owned by capitalists—the same things in the hand of a workman who uses them are not capital." As anyone familiar with *Capitalism, Socialism, and Democracy* knows, Schumpeter had a rather conflicted relationship with the insertion of sociological categories such as property into the science of economics, but ultimately, he did adopt a variation on Marx's ideas of constant and variable capital, concluding that the "structure of capital" can be usefully described as comprised of "wage capital," "technological capital," and a "coefficient, descriptive of the quantitative relation between the two." Indeed, "it was left to Marx to point this out in so many words and introduce such a concept explicitly," that is, the organic composition of capital.[4]

Setting aside the fact that, in the end, this sure looks like a specific theory of capital, through the lens provided by this categorical construction, the question "What of capital, after capitalism?" might seem pretty straight-forward. We would just answer (as Schumpeter probably would have) that whatever the after-states of capital*ism* end up looking like, capital itself will (perhaps even must) persist. Capital, as least as currently understood (as a set of material inputs to production, if not as the class that controls those inputs), can hardly be expected to just disappear. It might be after "capital-ism," that is, after a mode of production in which capital is hegemonic—but surely whatever isms eventually characterize our world will require capital, however subordinate.[5] This is interesting, especially since Schumpeter was so famously pessimistic regarding the long-term prospects for capital*ism*, given the self-destructive nature of its so-called monopoly form.[6]

This stance—the analytic separation of a transhistorical capital from a historically limited capitalism—is certainly not idiosyncratic to Schum-peter. Richard Duncan, for example, has recently laid out a plan for the future of capital in a world that he says is in fact already no longer capital-ist. In the twenty-first century context of what he calls "creditism," capital as "requisite to production" is no longer capable of reproducing contem-porary economic life. The self-expanding reproduction of capital, driven primarily via relations of production and exchange, has reached its limits, and state-backed credit is the sole force that can keep the relations of pro-duction in motion. In his schema, the creditist state has no choice but to arrogate to itself a kind of super-Keynesian role as the producer of money and the coordinator of investment. The alternative—leaving markets to do the work along "traditional" capitalist lines—is impossible, a guarantee of disaster.[7]

In Duncan's account, the postcapitalist future is no less reliant on capi-tal, at least of a Schumpeterian variety. This kind of thinking has influen-tial precedents notably in the work of John Maynard Keynes himself. In 1930 Keynes published an essay entitled "Economic Possibilities for Our Grandchildren," a pep talk for the British public in those troubled times. "We are suffering just now," he declared, "from a bad attack of economic pessimism," based on "a wildly mistaken interpretation of what is happen-ing to us." The "slump," he promised, was merely a brief bump in the road on the journey to a quasi-Utopian abundance, "only a temporary phase of maladjustment": "All this means in the long run *that mankind is solving the economic problem.* I would predict that the standard of life in progressive countries one hundred years hence will be between four and eight times as high as it is to-day. . . . This means that the economic problem is not—if we look to the future—*the permanent problem of the human race.*"[8] The achievement of such momentous prosperity was less a material or politi-cal task than a principally technical challenge. The question was not if, but when: "The *pace* at which we can reach our destination of economic bliss will be governed by four things—our power to control population, our determination to avoid wars and civil dissension, our willingness to entrust to science the direction of those matters which are properly the concern of science, and the rate of accumulation as fixed by the margin between our production and our consumption; of which the last will easily look after itself, given the first three."[9] Such optimistic prognoses might seem surprising coming from the person who famously said "in the long run we are all dead." But Keynes himself was extraordinarily confident in the probability of this coming "economic bliss," and in the rational way in which its attainment might be organized. It is no exaggeration to say that he actually thought it would be relatively straightforward, as long as the right people were in charge and had the power to do as they saw fit. As he declared in a national radio address in the early 1930s, "the economic problem is not too difficult to solve. If you leave it to me, I will look after it."[10]

Saving Capital from Capitalism

Now, bringing up Keynes in a discussion of what comes after capitalism might seem somewhat ironic. There is a very common assumption that whatever illusions of transformational grandeur he may have enjoyed, Keynes's rose-colored predictions were in no way a critique of capitalism, and his quasi-utopian future was in no way noncapitalist. Certainly, Marxist critics have long been saying of Keynes (basically since the publication of *The General Theory of Employment, Interest, and Money* in 1936) that (in the words of Eric Hobsbawm) he had "come to save capitalism," but this judgment is now widely shared across the ideological field.[11] Some go so far as to suggest not only that he wanted to save capitalism but that he offered an energetic endorsement, a celebratory reminder not to forget how excellent capitalism truly is.[12]

This understanding of Keynes as capitalism's great champion is both inaccurate and quite misleading. It elides perhaps the most important question regarding Keynes's political economy—a political economy in which, like all others worthy of the name, the emphasis should be on the *political*. The crucial question is both *what* Keynes was trying to save and what he came to save it *from*. He and many others had been arguing loudly for what later came to be called "Keynesian" policies (i.e., demand management via state intervention and public works) since not long after the Versailles Treaty of 1919.[13] Neither he nor the others needed the *General Theory* to get there: the policies we call "Keynesian" are all more or less logical or obvious responses to falling profits, rising unemployment, and social unrest. At the time, many (though by no means most) "orthodox" economists advocated these responses along with Keynes, which is to say, therefore, that "saving capitalism" cannot describe anything distinctive about his efforts, since virtually every economist in Europe and North America was on the same rescue mission.

Keynes's main concern was bigger than capitalism: it was the legitimacy and stability of the social order. As he said in 1924, "No man of spirit will consent to remain poor if he believes his betters to have gained their goods by lucky gambling. . . . The business man is only tolerable so long as his gains can be held to bear some relation to what, roughly and in some sense, his activities have contributed to society."[14] But while it might be the sanctity of capitalism that everyone else thought this delicate situation put at stake, for Keynes that was a problem of a second order. For him capitalism was only one part—and perhaps not even the most important or enduring part—of something much more worthy of saving: civilization. "Civilization," he said in 1938, is "a thin and precarious crust, erected by the personality and will of a very few, and only maintained by rules and conventions skillfully put across and guilefully preserved."[15]

One might read these words and think, "Oh, he said civilization, but he really meant capitalism, or at least *capitalist* civilization." But Keynes was different from today's economists who, like Paul Krugman, snicker derisively at the word "capitalism," convinced—or, rather, desperate to believe—that it just states the obvious about an immutable and universal human nature. Keynes, in contrast, talked explicitly about capitalism, and especially "individualistic" capitalism, all the time.

Moreover, if you get the chance to read the *General Theory* today, you will find there not only very little of what now goes by the name "Keynesian" (it is largely a theoretical book about money and monetary dynamics and is very far from the manual for fiscal stimulus many take it to be) but a vision of the future that is in many ways not really all that capitalist. It is definitely not socialist or communist or anarchist. But Keynes is absolutely unequivocal on the matter of economic bliss: it is a world beyond rent, beyond what he called the "love of money," and beyond scarcity. I would suggest that this does not sound like a straightforwardly capitalist world, or at least it does not sound like a world organized by capitalism as I understand it.[16] I would also suggest, certainly, that his plan for getting there (wherever "there" is) is impossible; but saving "capitalism"—at least as it has been described by either its greatest champions or its greatest critics—was not his ultimate goal.

Instead, we have to place Keynes's thought and politics in his fundamental concern for the future of (bourgeois) civilization. When we do, Keynesianism, or at least Keynes's variety of it, is best described as an attempt to save capital—as "requisite of production," as relation, as process, and as a class—from capitalism. For a variety of reasons both purposeful and unintended, capital, despite capitalism, is for Keynes the lever of civilization.[17]

If Schumpeter was a glass-half-empty or glass-mostly-empty person, Keynes's analysis stands as a "glass-mostly-full" plan to exempt capital from the inexorable fates that the 1930s intimated for capitalism.

If so, then the question one might want to ask him is "Why?" What good is capital in a postcapitalist world? And the answer—to Keynes and to many others, both then and perhaps especially now—is somewhat unsurprising: growth. Economic growth (accumulation, development, and so forth) remains at the heart of all conceptions of capital, from the Marxist to the new neoclassical synthesis, to the Chicago School. In most cases, the relation between capital and growth is basically tautological, so central has it become to our understanding of positive economic change. Growth is understood to be impossible without capital, and the power of growth as the great legitimizer of political economic order has underwritten virtually every half-way successful mode of economic organization— capitalist and noncapitalist, it is worth emphasizing—of the last century, if not longer.

Indeed, today, with the question of civilization very much back on the radar, it is growth and the threats to growth that animate the most influential and the most compelling analyses of the current conjuncture. From Mark Blyth's critique of austerity to Thomas Piketty's diagnosis of accelerating inequality, from every call for a "Green New Deal" to the endless if no less necessary stream of radical critiques of financialization: in all cases growth is taken as the principal, if not the only, means by which to achieve a more just and stable social order.[18]

If, then, as Immanuel Wallerstein wrote just before he died, "capitalist civilization has reached the autumn of its existence," the question for many, just as it was for Keynes, seems to be how to save civilization, *sans* capitalism.[19] And the answer (at least from outside the houses of orthodoxy, and sometimes from within them) is almost always not capital*ism* but capital—greener, maybe, more evenly distributed or less politically powerful, perhaps more entrepreneurial or more socialized. But the way out of our current crises often seems to be the very thing we once thought got us here in the first place: capital.

If we return very briefly to the definitional debate, this leads us back to the classical conception of capital one might find reading someone like Walter Bagehot (the founding editor of *The Economist*) from the 1870s. On these terms the word "capital" describes the assets or resources one can choose to *do something "productive"* with: invest, build, speculate, grow.[20] This is a conception of capital that made sense to Ricardo, Schumpeter, Keynes, and many others. The question, though, is less about what capital can or cannot do and more about the worldly conditions of possibility that allow or grant an asset its status as capital. It is fair to say that, for the overwhelming majority of economic analyses, this key question never arises. Capital just is, and capital is as capital does in a naturally capitalist world.

Marx, however, begged to differ. While the "something-you-can-do-something-productive-with" sense always partially animated his discussions of capital, he refused the idea that an asset's status as capital is "natural" or axiomatic and rejected the assumption that capital is merely comprised of *things*, whether they be material, like money, tools, and natural resources, or immaterial, like skills or technique. Instead, as is often said, Marx said capital is not a thing but a relation or "process" (M-C-M), specifically, a process of the circulation of value. For some Marxists, this "processual" conception of capital is among Marx's greatest and most innovative contributions. David Harvey claims it "marks a radical departure from the definition you'll find in classical political economics, where capital was traditionally understood as a stock of assets (machines, money, etc.), as well as from the predominant definition in conventional economics, where capital is viewed as a thing-like 'factor of production.'"[21]

On these grounds, the capitalist is merely a "conscious bearer of this movement."[22] And yet, if we maintain our focus on Marx's thoughts on the matter, it must be admitted that the category remains not only a little blurry, it is not confined to so dialectically pure a dynamic. As I mentioned, Marx and many Marxists also clearly (and justifiably) not only speak of capital as the class of capitalists but, and perhaps more importantly, think of capital as a stock of assets, something "owned and controlled by a specific social class."[23] Capital as a stock of assets would certainly suggest a bit more thing-ness than sometimes Harvey wants to admit or than "relation" seems to allow. The categorical overlaps and polyvalences leave the conceptual framework a little wobbly.

Perhaps surprisingly, I think we can get some help here from Keynes (if unwillingly, which was his position on all things Marx, whom he dismissed but did not read and never understood). Help is forthcoming because, on the matter of "capital is as capital does," Keynes also begged to differ. One of Keynes's bugbears was the common belief among capitalists and the capitalist state (and not only them) that what drove capitalist political economy and the capitalist entrepreneur was the search for "productivity" or "productive investment." Keynes thought such assumptions entirely unfounded. The mistake, he said, "comes from believing that the owner of wealth [—the one usually known as the capitalist—] desires a capital-asset *as such*, whereas what he really desires is its *prospective yield*."[24]

We could read this as Marxist, that is, as the use of orthodox language to state what Marx had made clear almost a century earlier: yield = surplus value, and the imperative to realize surplus value, to valorize as such, is the motor of the capitalist engine. If so, Keynes is merely unconsciously acknowledging the debt to Marx he spent his life disavowing. But there is more going on here, and Keynes hit on something crucial. In the same passage of the *General Theory*, he suggests that at least part of the basis for his critique of "productivity" lies in the fact that, as he thought everyone knew but somehow forgot, "there is always an alternative to the ownership of real capital-assets, namely the ownership of money and debts."[25]

The End of Yield?

The concept of "yield" is crucial to understanding what is at stake here, in Keynes's reluctantly radical but not-necessarily-Marxist analysis of the category of capital. Capital on his account is *not* a set of "assets" that produce but a set of processes and relations that "yield." I suppose one might link this wisdom to Marx by contending that there may once have been a time when these were closer to the same thing, when—although I doubt it—the circulation of any given capital required something we might call "production."[26] In fact, this is something that Keynes's avatar Thomas Piketty emphasizes to great if controversial effect: he defines capital as "the set of nonhuman assets that can be owned and exchanged on the market," a definition he adopts because "all forms of capital always play a double role, in part as factor of production and in part as store of value."[27] Consequently (and this is what distinguishes Piketty's contribution from the unwittingly Keynesian foundations on which it rests), "capital is not a fixed category: it reflects the state of development and the social relations that reign in a given society."[28]

Piketty is no radical, but there is wisdom in this analysis. We err if we hew too close to capitalist reason's own "productivity" story. Capital is defined not by its transhistorical capacity to generate growth but, as Piketty says, by the specifics of its time and place. Capital describes not so much the relations through which the world *produces* surplus. Rather, to take up the unwillingly radical analysis Keynes unintentionally bequeathed us, capital describes the relations through which the world yields itself up— often through processes in which the actors are unaware they have been valorized, and increasingly via dynamics that are themselves in many ways impossible to subsume (climate, ecosystems, etc.). There is no longer, if there ever was, a need for the production of surplus *qua* something "extra" or new, but more properly only that which—at least in the short term—the world must make do without.

Consequently—and, for present purposes, lastly—we must ask if there is any such left: What remains that the world can do without? This question has both relative and absolute dimensions. And surely, we might argue that "absolutely," there is a lot of surplus to pare before we are down to the bone. That, I think, is hardly the point, even if austerity imposes such conditions on more and more people. Rather, one might reasonably suggest that we are fast approaching a time when there is little more to yield, no more principal upon which to draw.

The most influential and attractive orthodox response to our rapid approach to such a threshold is captured in the common call for "green" business or capitalism, underwritten by an ecological or green Keynesianism. The advocates of such a "Green New Deal" are spread across what are usually much less agreeable camps, from orthodox policy insiders like Lawrence Summers to critics like Susan George.[29]

There are, however, two things we can say about these plans. First, it is startlingly obvious that basically nothing has come of them. Second, it requires no particular expertise to work out the logic behind the plans, which seem both intuitive and appealing. The state jumps back in with both feet, and Keynesian stimulus not only reprimes the pump but does it "greenly," modified to spur carbon-reducing employment and investment growth. This thinking underwrites such disparate efforts as the Green European Foundation's Green New Deal, the Stern Report, and the Obama administration's short-lived cash-for-clunkers program. The problem, however, is that, in theory and practice, Keynesianism is ultimately dependent on material throughput, even if in green energy. Since it is difficult to imagine we will be able to consume or produce our way out of current ecological predicaments, it is not impossible that "green Keynesianism" is an oxymoron. In the policy work of most of Keynes's greatest champions today among economists (Joseph Stiglitz is an exception), one would hardly know that the world is facing any more of a crisis than that acknowledged by mainstream economists and policymakers.

This moment—the "end of yield," or more precisely the end of the conditions of possibility for capitalist yield—would by definition mark the end of capital. (Interestingly, it is also the ultimate perfection of capital in orthodox theory, in which there is no profit.) In that eventuality, however uneven, the place of capital after capitalism would be determined less by what capital "does" in a postcapitalist era, and more by its aftereffects, the social and ecological echoes of the search and demand for yield. In other words, capital may outlive capitalism for quite a while. Or we may soon see the end of its reign. Either eventuality will demand that we do our utmost to ensure that the end of capitalism prepares the ground for something better—freer, more secure, more just, less violent and arbitrary. Those efforts will entail a great deal of experimentation and failure. The answers are not obvious, and no matter how logically or strategically sound the analysis is, no matter how well it can anticipate and organize, it can neither guarantee success nor prevent failure.

Capitalism is likely to leave us with a catastrophe, but its culpability will not provide cover; an ineffective response will move no one. If so, then the "emancipation" of labor with the end of capital is in no way a guarantee of freedom. Nor, however, does it necessarily mean the end of wealth, or of development, and in that there is great hope.

Notes

1 Joseph Schumpeter, *History of Economic Analysis* (Oxford: Oxford University Press, 1954), 632.
2 Ibid., 632, 634.
3 David Ricardo, *Principles of Political Economy* (Cambridge: Cambridge University Press, 1951), 1:95.
4 Schumpeter, *History of Economic Analysis*, 634–635.
5 Ricardo disagreed: he said this distinction was "not essential . . . the line of demarcation cannot be accurately drawn" (*Principles of Political Economy*, 31n). For Ricardo, all capital is essentially distinguishable by one factor, its "time distance between investment and the emergence of the corresponding consumer good, time is the element that unifies all its specific forms" (*History of Economic Analysis*, 636, 637).
6 Schumpeter, *History of Economic Analysis*, 423–424. "The reasons for believing that the capitalist order tends to destroy itself and that centralist socialism is . . . a likely heir apparent I have explained elsewhere. Briefly and superficially, these reasons may be summed up under four heads. First, the very success of the business class in developing the productive powers of this country and the very fact that this success has created a new standard of life for all classes has paradoxically undermined the social and political position of the same business class whose economic function, though not obsolete, tends to become obsolescent and amenable to bureaucratization. Second, capitalist activity, being essentially "rational," tends to spread rational habits of mind and to destroy those loyalties and those habits of super- and subordination that are nevertheless essential for the efficient working of the institutionalized leadership of the producing plant: no social system can work which is based exclusively upon a network of free contracts between (legally) equal contracting parties and in which everyone is supposed to be guided by nothing except his own (short-run) utilitarian ends. Third, the concentration of the business class on the tasks of the factory and the office was instrumental in creating a political system and an intellectual class, the structure and interests of which developed an attitude of independence from, and eventually of hostility to, the interests of large-scale business. The latter is becoming increasingly incapable of defending itself against raids that are, in the short run, highly profitable to other classes. Fourth, in consequence of all this, the scheme of values of capitalist society, though causally related to its economic success, is losing its hold not only upon the public mind but also upon the "capitalist" stratum itself. Little time,

though more than I have, would be needed to show how modern drives for security, equality, and regulation (economic engineering) may be explained on these lines."

7 Richard Duncan, *The New Depression: The Breakdown of the Paper Money Economy* (Singapore: John Wiley, 2012).

8 John Maynard Keynes, *Collected Writings* (Cambridge: Cambridge University Press, 1971–1990), 9:364–366. It turns out, at least in income per capita terms, that Keynes was right. Average per capita incomes have more than quadrupled since 1930; but neither our world nor our daily life—even in the richest societies on the planet—looks much like what he expected.

9 Ibid., 373.

10 John Maynard Keynes, *Collected Writings* (Cambridge: Cambridge University Press, 1971–1990), 28:34.

11 Eric Hobsbawm, "Goodbye to All That," *Marxism Today* (October 1990): 18–23 (quote, 20); also Antonio Negri, *Revolution Retrieved: Writings on Marx, Keynes, Capitalist Crisis, and New Social Subjects* (London: Red Notes, 1988); Martin Wolf, "Keynes Offers Us the Best Way to Think about the Financial Crisis," *Financial Times*, December 23, 2008, at http://www.ft.com/cms/s/0/be2dbf2c-d113-11dd-8cc3-000077b07658.html#axzz3qYMyraCe/.

12 Roger Backhouse and Bradley Bateman, *Capitalist Revolutionary: John Maynard Keynes* (Cambridge: Cambridge University Press, 2011).

13 Roy Harrod, *The Life of John Maynard Keynes* (New York: Harcourt Brace, 1951), 350; Friedrich A. von Hayek, *The Collected Works of F. A. Hayek*, Vol. 9: *Contra Keynes and Cambridge* (Chicago: University of Chicago Press, 1995), 6–8.

14 John Maynard Keynes, *Collected Writings* (Cambridge: Cambridge University Press, 1971–1990), 4:29.

15 John Maynard Keynes, *Collected Writings* (Cambridge: Cambridge University Press, 1971–1990), 10:446–447.

16 Compare Bernard Maris, *Keynes, ou l'économiste citoyen*, 2nd ed. (Paris: Sciences Po, 2007), 8, 93–97.

17 Keynes, *Collected Writings*, 9:258. "The bourgeois and the intelligentsia who, with whatever faults, are the quality in life and surely carry the seeds of all human advancement."

18 Mark Blyth, *Austerity: The History of a Dangerous Idea* (Oxford: Oxford University Press, 2013); Thomas Piketty, *Le Capital au XXIe siècle* (Paris: Seuil, 2013); Edward Barbier, *A Global Green New Deal: Rethinking the Economic Recovery* (Cambridge: Cambridge University Press, 2010).

19 Immanuel Wallerstein, *Historical Capitalism* (New York: Verso, 2011), 141.

20 Walter Bagehot, *Lombard Street: A Description of the Money Market* (New York: Charles Scribner's Sons, 2011).

21 David Harvey, *A Companion to Marx's Capital* (New York: Verso, 2010), 88–89.

22 Karl Marx, *Capital, Vol. 1* (New York: Vintage, 1977), 254.

23 Neil Smith, "Capital," in *The Dictionary of Human Geography*, ed. R. J. Johnston et al. (London: Wiley, 2000), 56.

24 John Maynard Keynes, *Collected Writings* (Cambridge, Cambridge University Press, 1971–1990), 7:212 (emphasis in original).

25 Ibid.

26 Geoff Mann, "Value after Lehman," *Historical Materialism* 18, no. 4 (2010): 172–188.

27 Piketty, *Capital au XXIe siècle,* 82, 85. See also Geoff Mann, "A General Theory for Our Times: On Piketty," *Historical Materialism* 23, no. 1 (2015): 1–35.

28 Piketty, *Capital au XXIe siècle*, 84.

29 Joseph Stiglitz, "Climate Change and Poverty Have Not Gone Away," *The Guardian*, January 7, 2013, at http://www.theguardian.com; Susan George and Walden Bello, "A New, Green, Democratic Deal," *New Internationalist*, January 1, 2009, at https://www.tni.org/en/article/a-new-green-democratic-deal.

2

Restoration of the Rentier and the Turn to Lifelong Extraction

ANDREW ROSS

In the course of the 1980s, the "shareholder revolution" put pressure on corporate managers to focus, exclusively, on maximizing shareholder value. The insurgency was billed as a remedy for a sclerotic corporate culture incapable of responding to the falling profits and restructuring initiatives of the 1970s. But at root the shareholder revolution was an attack on the assumption, widely accepted in the 1950s and 1960s, that corporations were accountable to a wider range of stakeholders; to their workers, to the communities that hosted their facilities, and even to the national interest. The new, surgical focus on shareholder returns and profit optimization translated into an all-consuming fixation on short-term results, as measured by quarterly earnings. The fallout from this reorientation of priorities typically involved mass layoffs (invariably producing a bump in stock value), plant closures, asset-stripping, abandonment of communities with deep historical ties to the companies in question, and the wholesale transfer of operations offshore. A corporate culture increasingly programmed in this way to respond to pressure from financial markets had little capacity for long-term planning, and for CEOs, whose bonuses were tied to stock performance, there was no incentive to think beyond the next quarterly report.

The "tyranny of short-termism," as McKinsey's global managing director put it, looked to be in for a long, absolutist reign, and it was a prospect that worried business economists obliged to put the best public face on corporate conduct.[1] Yet the galloping financialization of all sectors of society—private and public, corporate and personal—tells a different story. Extraction of profit from financial contracts has a much longer temporal cycle. Most loans mature on a multi-year basis, and the thirty-year mortgage is still a standard in the housing market. As far as household debt goes, the creditor class increasingly favors a pattern of lifelong financial extraction, in which debts are never fully paid down and debtors generate a steady stream of income as they struggle to make payments over long periods of their precarious working lives. Indeed, our overall relationship with the finance industry, as this essay will explore, is turning into something like a term life contract.

Moreover, finance is the capitalist sector that is growing most rapidly and returning the most profit to its beneficiaries, suggesting that it will become, if it is not already, the dominant operational engine of twenty-first-century capitalism. As capitalism exhausts its capacity for profit-taking in the present, it is generating ever more paper claims on the future, and so it is the long-term contingent future, not the next three months, that holds the key to the treasure chest. Whatever credence was given to the "euthanasia of the rentier" (Keynes's remedy for the dysfunctional capitalist system in 1936) has lost its steam over the last thirty years, though it remains a potent slogan for those who believe that democratic practice will further erode if the power of the creditor class continues to go unchecked.

Thanks to Thomas Piketty (and his collaborator Emmanuel Saez), a lot of attention has been focused recently on wealth accumulation at the top. The income data they have gathered shows that the primary source of accumulation for the 1 percent now comes in the form of economic rents (from debt-leveraging, capital gains, manipulation of paper claims through derivatives, and other forms of financial engineering).[2] The corresponding accumulation of household debt (you can't have one without the other) has been neglected, however, despite evidence that it continues to increase, posing a threat to the capacity of democracies to protect their citizenry from economic harms imposed by the creditor class.

For a while, there seemed to be some good news on this front. Overall household debt in most industrialized countries was on the decrease from its sky-high levels just before the financial crash. In the United States debt service, which reached more than 14 percent of after-tax income by the end of 2007, had fallen to 10.5 percent by April 2013.[3] Much of the deleveraging was due to low interest rates and to a reduction in mortgage debt, though it is not clear how much of the decrease came from banks' writing off delinquent loans rather than from faithful repayment. In the third quarter of 2013 this decline ended, and mortgage debt started to rise again, by $56 billion. The fourth quarter showed a 1.9 percent leap in mortgages and 3.9 percent in nonhousing household debt. Auto loans and credit card balances also started to move upward, and the trend continued through the first quarter of 2014 with an advance of 1.1 percent, taking overall U.S. household debt to $11.65 trillion. Similar figures were recorded for most of the industrialized economies, though none could compare with the United States' outlier figures on the student debt burden—which has not abated at all in the six years since 2008 and, in the course of 2014, surpassed $1.3 trillion with default rates averaging a million a year.

If these numbers continue to rise, as it seems likely, then it's clear that the bottom of the debt deflation trend turned out to be not very deep. Once people are persuaded it is safe to start borrowing again, then interest rates will be hiked—an invitation for the banks to stop hoarding their cash reserves and embark on a new season of predatory lending. This invitation to the banks is backed by the proved willingness of governments to bail them out even in the face of high rates of personal default and mass immiseration among the citizenry. Such assurances that the banks will always be made whole are critical to any creditor's calculation that higher levels of debt service are sustainable. The gap between the deflated bottom and projected, or aspirational, levels of rent extraction is now large enough for them to jump back into the lending game, an outcome that no amount of quantitative easing has been able to bring about.

Equally serviceable is the gathering consensus among economists (even those critical of neoliberalism) that the so-called debt overhang from the 2008 crash has largely been resolved and that not only is it safe to begin borrowing again but also it is necessary if GDP-driven growth is to get back to business as usual. This is not particularly good analysis nor is it good advice. A debt overhang is one of these dodgy concepts that economists use to rationalize an otherwise unsustainable or high-risk condition. And as for GDP-driven growth, all the evidence shows that any such economic program is a recipe for ecological collapse.

Rise of Creditocracy

Today we live in the kind of society—I call it a creditocracy—where pretty much everybody is up to their neck in debt that can never be repaid, nor is it supposed to be. The gut liberal response to this is to say, "That's not fair, no one should have debts that can never be repaid, and besides, why would banks want that?" This is to miss the point entirely. It's important to understand that our creditors don't want us to pay off our debts entirely—for the same reason that credit card issuers don't want us to pay off our credit card balance every month. Customers who do this diligently are known in the industry as "deadbeats," because they appear to get credit for free. The ideal citizens in a creditocracy are the revolvers who cannot make ends meet, and who pay the minimum along with merchant fees and penalties every month, rolling over their credit from month to month.

Creditors' profits come from extending our debt service as long as they possibly can. After all, if we pay down our debts, we are no longer service-able to the banks. The goal is to keep us on the hook until we die, and even beyond the grave in the case of student debts that are co-signed by parents or grandparents. Not surprisingly, there has been a marked genera-tional shift in the debt burden toward the elderly. In the postwar model of life-cycle lending, it was more or less assumed that middle-class borrow-ers would earn the right, in their senior years, to live debt-free, and it was a source of pride among the elderly, especially debt-abhorrent Depression babies, to have never paid a finance fee. That is no longer the case, and not just because debt-tolerant boomers have entered the ranks of the retired. Patterns of capitalist profit in industrialized economies have shifted and are more tied to lifelong financial extraction.

The major banks are bigger and more profitable than before the 2008 crash. The exposure of American banks to derivatives alone has increased to $232 trillion, almost one-third more than before 2008 when the esca-lation of these risky bets helped to bring on the financial crash. The big six U.S. banks collectively are carrying a debt load of $8.7 trillion. With that combination of debt overhead, exposure to dodgy derivatives, leverage over the national economy, and continued weak regulatory oversight, there is a very high risk of a repeat of the 2008 meltdown. Indeed, many industry insiders believe that an equally ruinous relapse is already in the making. Legislators are all but powerless to bring the banks to heel. U.S. Attorney General Holder himself acknowledged publicly in testimony to the Sen-ate Judiciary Committee that when banks acquire so much concentrated power, it is "difficult for us to prosecute them . . . if you do bring a criminal charge, it will have a negative impact on the national economy, perhaps even the global economy."[4]

Holder's admission that the government lacked the wherewithal to pun-ish bankers for their widely publicized record of extortion was a significant milestone, particularly for a democracy that has long struggled to contain the damage inflicted by plutocrats in its midst. But the ability of Wall Street barons to hold the government in thrall is nothing new.[5] In a 1933 letter, Franklin D. Roosevelt wrote: "The real truth of the matter is, as you and I know, that a financial element in the large centers has owned the gov-ernment ever since the days of Andrew Jackson."[6] Owning lawmakers may be a venerable prerogative for American financiers, but the rise of a full-blown creditocracy is more recent. Financialization had to creep into every corner of the household economy before the authority of the creditor class took on a sovereign, unassailable character.

In other words, it is not enough for every social good to be turned into a transactional commodity, as is the case in a rampant market civilization. A creditocracy emerges when the cost of access to each of these goods, no matter how staple, has to be debt-financed, and when indebtedness becomes the precondition not just for material improvements in the quality of life but for the basic requirements of life. Financiers seek to wrap debt around every possible asset and income stream, placing a tollbooth on every revenue source, ensuring a flow of interest from each. Furthermore, when fresh sources of credit are routinely needed to service existing debt (neatly captured in the 1990s bumper sticker "I Use MasterCard to Pay Visa"), we can be sure we are entering a more advanced phase of creditor rule.[7]

This kind of arrangement—borrowing to cover existing debt service—was formally institutionalized in the so-called debt trap of the 1970s and 1980s, which put paid to the development aspirations of so many global Southern countries. IMF loan installments were offered, not to support social or economic development but specifically to ensure Northern creditors would continue to see debt service on their older loans. When the debt trap migrated to the North, the same formula got a good airing during the Eurozone crisis, especially in Greece, where the "rescue package" offered by the troika was expressly aimed at making German, French, and Swiss bankers whole.

For the working poor, this kind of permanent indebtedness is a very familiar arrangement and has long outlived its classic expression under feudalism, indenture, and slavery. Each of these systems of debt bondage gave birth to successor institutions—sharecropping, company scrip, loan sharking—and their legacy is alive and well today on the subprime landscape of fringe finance, where "poverty banks" operate in every other storefront on Loan Alley. But the bonds generated by household debt have also spread upward in recent decades and now affect the majority of the population, tethering two generations of the college-educated. In the United States, 77 percent of households are in serious debt, and one in seven Americans is being, or has been, pursued by a debt collector.[8]

Even those without personal loans are debtors, because public debts, especially municipal obligations, have been structured in such a way that the service costs to Wall Street are now routinely passed on to all of us in the form of austerity policies. And what about the beneficiaries? The tipping point for a creditocracy occurs when "economic rents" are no longer merely a supplementary source of income for the creditor class but have become the most reliable and effective instrument for the amassing of wealth and influence. In that respect, a full-blown creditocracy may be considered distinct from earlier forms of monopoly capitalism in which profits from production dominated.

There are many ways of illustrating this historic development. Consider the balance of power between banks and government. In 1895 (and again in 1907) J.P. Morgan was called upon to save the U.S. Treasury from default, yet the shoe was on the other foot by 2008 when the Treasury was forced to bail out JPMorgan Chase, and few doubt it would be obliged to do so again today. The shift is also displayed in how corporations make profits. Jumbo firms like GE and GM that commanded the economy on the strength of their industrial production have become much more dependent for their revenue on their firm's finance arms. Companies are no longer regarded primarily as worthy recipients of productive loans for tangible outputs but, rather, as targets for leveraged buyouts, to be loaded down with debt and ruthlessly used to extract finance fees and interest. The difference between Mitt Romney's career at Bain Capital and his father's at the American Motor Company neatly summarizes the transition from industrial to financial capitalism.[9] As for ordinary individuals, we are now under constant financial surveillance by the major credit bureaus (Equifax, Experian, and TransUnion) whose credit reports, scores, and ratings of our conduct as debtors control the gateways to so many areas of economic need and want. Operating outside of public oversight, these agencies answer only to the requirements of the creditor class, and the profiles they assign to us are like ID tags, marking our rank and class in the present and in the years to come since they are used to predict future behavior.

We know that more and more of the 99 percent are suffering from undue debt burdens—financial claims that can never be repaid—but is it so clear who belongs to the class of creditors? Following Margaret Thatcher's promotion of "pension fund capitalism," the pension funds of workers have been drawn into the financial markets. Indeed, these funds now hold a significant portion of the public debt, especially municipal debt, currently being used as a justification for pushing through austerity policies. In a formal and legal sense, the workers are creditors, and they stand to lose if the debts are written off indiscriminately in a bankruptcy proceeding. In accord with the "popular capitalist" mentality encouraged by Thatcher and her neoliberal successors, their investments, like all others, are exposed to risk. Indeed, pension funds managers are forced to make speculative investments to meet their long-term promises (as much as 8 percent in annual returns) to contributors, and so they entrust the money to Wall Street hucksters looking to charge high fees and offload high-risk derivatives. Corporate pension funds are routinely looted by corporate raiders, and state pension funds have become an especially ripe target for employers or governments looking to borrow cash or to turn them over to hedge funds and private equity funds.

Investing savings for retirement has little bearing on workers' primary identity as waged labor, though contradictions clearly arise when the investments are handled by Wall Street funds that inflict damage on workers' interests in general. Even if the annuities do turn out as promised, decades hence, the recipients have not been generating their main income from investment as is the case for the principal beneficiaries of a creditocracy. Workers who are part of the "real" economy and whose household debts have risen while their wages stagnated do not really inhabit the same world as the players who live off unearned income in the undertaxed world of financial engineering. For sure, the diversification of pension funds and the growth of 401(k) retirement plans mean that many more of us who do productive work are tied into the world of finance than was once the case. But this circumstance has not substantially altered our sense of being in the world, and it is far outweighed by our ensnarement, like everyone else we know, in the bankers' debt trap.

Banks, hedge funds, private equity firms, and other entities that operate in the shadow banking system have an interest in gathering influence and immunity for themselves, but they are first and foremost tools of accumulation for their owners, clients, shareholders, and direct beneficiaries. As such, their business is to grab as much of the economic surplus as they can by keeping everyone else in debt for as long as possible. The fact is that debts, especially at compound interest, multiply at a much faster rate than the ability to repay. Original lenders know this fact, which is why they sell on the loans as fast as they can.

Democracy and Debt

Managing the lifelong burden of debt service is now an existential condition for the majority, but what about its impact on citizenship? How can a democracy survive when it is on the road to debt serfdom? The history of the struggle for political liberty is closely tied to the growth of credit. As James MacDonald has argued, the democratic institutions of liberal societies were able to survive and flourish because government bonds made it possible to borrow cheaply, especially in times of war.[10] But today's bond markets, which are globally networked and susceptible to speculative bets from hedge funds, are more likely to "judge," "discipline," and "reward" policymakers than to faithfully serve their ends. Central banks increasingly act to ensure the solvency of banks—and not sovereign governments struggling with public deficits. The right of creditors to be made whole now routinely overrides the responsibility of elected national representatives to carry out the popular will, resulting in "failed democracies" all over the world. Everywhere we look, officials are being pressured to use governments as collection agents for foreign bondholders or to pass on the costs of bankers' speculative investments to the most vulnerable populations. This is not just an economic arrangement. It is also a relationship of power, with devastating impact upon popular sovereignty. Even Mario Monti— the placid technocrat appointed in 2012 as Italian prime minister in order to dampen popular opposition to financial power—spoke out against what he called the emergence of "creditocracy" in Europe. He was referring specifically to how sovereign governance was being circumvented by the priority given to foreign bondholders, as represented through the big German, French, Swiss, and Dutch banks.

The historical record shows that a society unable to check the power of the creditor class will quickly see the onset of debt bondage; democracies segue into oligarchies, credit becomes a blunt instrument for absorbing more and more economic surplus, and rents are extracted from nonproductive assets. Are we heading down this path, once again? Or is it just loose talk? Many commentators are saying as much when they point to the revival of debtors' prisons, speak of student debt as a form of indenture, and compare banking practices, on Wall Street as well as on Loan Alley, to the most extreme forms of usury. So, too, the revival of interest in a debt jubilee, not only in developing countries but here in the global North, is evocative of macro-solutions hatched in the ancient world by rulers who were so desperate to restore the balance of popular power in their favor that they abolished all existing debts, freed debt slaves, and returned land to original owners.

This kind of talk is indicative of the extremity of the current debt crisis. All the evidence shows that drastic relief measures are needed, and that a new kind of non-extractive economy, benefiting from what Keynes called the "euthanasia of the rentier," ought to be built. Pursuing that alternative path—to a society guided by the productive use of credit—may be the only way to salvage democracy. But for establishment economists, even those who question the credo of neoliberalism, there is no crisis, only a debt "overhang" that needs to be reduced to manageable levels before the normal pattern of debt-financed growth can reassert itself.

There is no easy return to that debt-growth formula. After incomes stagnated in the 1970s, respectable growth rates could only be achieved through a series of speculative asset bubbles. Each time the bubble burst, we could see how the formula rested on an insubstantial foundation. As far as lasting prosperity goes, we can say that much of the growth was fake, producing only phony wealth, and that future efforts to inflate prices will end the same way. But from an ecological perspective, this pattern is entirely unsustainable. There now exists a mountain of scientific evidence, beginning with the seminal 1974 report *Limits to Growth*, that testifies to the calamitous impact of GDP-driven growth on the biosphere. Restoring business as usual, once that pesky "overhang" disappears, can only be a recipe for eco-collapse.

As with any unjust social arrangement, a creditocracy has to be stripped of its legitimacy in the public mind before its actual hold on power is dissolved. How far along this road have we come? Given the battering that bankers have taken over the past five years, it's a testament to their self-projected mystique that they still command even a fraction of their standing as indispensable members of society. Every other day brings a fresh headline about their misconduct and profiteering as swindle after swindle is uncovered. The judicial investigations multiply, producing few convictions (and only of junior employees) but an ever-longer roster of fines, refunds, and other penalties. Some of the settlements to end the criminal and civil charges are massive. JPMorgan Chase, for example, negotiated a $13 billion settlement with the U.S. Justice Department over packing mortgage-backed securities with dodgy home loans. Notably, less than $3 billion was claimed in fines and only $4 billion in relief for homeowners, while more than $6 billion was allocated for investors who suffered losses.[11] Bank of America settled for $17 billion under similar terms. But the profits of these banks and their peers are so large that such penalties are shrugged off as the cost of doing business. Public trust, the crucial quality that banks have customarily relied on in order to trade, has long been decimated; we have come to regard their ingenious financial products as little more than scams, and we know that the bill for all of their risky conduct will likely end up with us. Yet the banks retain their cachet as essential institutions, and most important, their lobbying firepower ensures that legislators will look out for their interests.

In *The Bankers' New Clothes*, Anat Admati and Martin Hellwig argue that "there is a pervasive myth that banks and banking are special and different from all other companies in the economy. Anyone who questions the mystique and the claims that are made is at risk of being declared incompetent to participate in the discussion."[12] Finance, we are encouraged to believe, is too complex for lay people to understand. One of the outcomes of this mystique is that too many of us are trapped in the payback mind-set. Though we may be more and more aware of the irresponsibility and fraud of big creditors who won't pay their own debts, and who offload all their risky loans to others, we still accept that it is immoral to fail to repay our debts to them. Of course, there are lawyers, courts, and police standing at the ready to enforce this payback morality, and a ruined credit score to live with in the case of a default. But these are instruments of coercion; they serve as backups if the mechanism of consent falters. When the psychology of the debtor shifts, as it is now slowly doing, from resignation to reluctance, or even resistance, then the authority of the creditors' self-interested moralism begins to lose its sway. Then, and only then, are we able to question honestly whether we owe anything at all to people and institutions that—were it not for the figment of the banker's new clothes— would rightly be seen as engaged in extortion.

Abolishing the Debt Sentence

More public education is needed about how creditor rule is upheld and it is in this spirit that we must make the case for the refusal of household debts. When a government cannot protect its people from the harms inflicted by rent extractors and when debt burdens become an existential threat to a free citizenry, then the refusal to pay is a defensible act of civil disobedience. For those aiming to reinvent democracy, this refusal is nothing short of a responsibility. The case for debt cancellation in developing countries has already been made by groups within or allied to the Debt Jubilee movement.[13] These advocates have devised moral and legal arguments for repudiating the external debts of governments and have had some success in delivering relief for some of the world's poorest populations. Public debts in the global North are now at the core of the austerity policies being implemented, from the battered periphery of the Eurozone to the beleaguered cohort of ex-industrial cities like Detroit and Baltimore. The process of questioning which of these debts is legitimate and deserving of repayment—and which are unfair impositions to be rightfully rejected—is already underway.[14] Now is the time to extend this initiative to household debts, especially those taken on simply to gain access to basic social goods.

In what follows, I summarize some of the arguments underpinning the case for debt refusal. These arguments have been developed in the debt resistance movement, whether aimed at cancellation of sovereign debt on the global South or at household debt in the affluent countries of the North. Most appeal to broad moral principles as opposed to quantifiable rules, but there is no reason these principles could not be applied in a way that would produce some hard numbers.

- Loans that either benefit the creditor only or inflict social and environmental damage on individuals, families, and communities, should be renegotiated to compensate for harms.
- The sale of loans to borrowers who cannot repay is unprincipled, so the collection of these debts should not be honored.

- The banks and their beneficiaries, awash in profit, have done very well; they have been paid enough already and do not need to be additionally reimbursed.
- Even if household debts were not intentionally imposed as political constraints, they unavoidably stifle our capacity to think freely, act conscientiously, and fulfill our democratic responsibilities.
- Extracting usurious, long-term profits from our short-term need to access subsistence resources is immoral; no less so in the case of vital common goods such as education, health care, and public infrastructure.
- Each act of debt service is a nonproductive addition to the banks' balance sheets, and a subtraction from the "real" economy that creates jobs, adequately funds social spending, and sustains the well-being of communities.
- The credit was not theirs to begin with—it was obtained through the dubious power of money creation, thanks to fractional reserve banking and to the "magic" of derivatives.
- Obliging debtors to forfeit future income is a form of wage theft, if the debts were incurred simply to prepare ourselves, in mind and body, for employment.
- Given the fraud and deceit practiced by bankers and the likelihood that they will not refrain from such antisocial conduct, it would be morally hazardous of us to reward them any further.

The foregoing is not an exhaustive list but it is a start, and I offer it with an invitation to add other items. Through the reasoned combination of these moral arguments with more practical principles of measurement, it will be possible to determine which debts should be refused and which should be honored. Most important of all, debtors who stand together—with the spirited support of a broad movement behind them—can make the strongest moral case. Negotiating with creditors on an individual basis might win some personal relief but will not alter, let alone supplant, the norms of conduct that sustain a creditocracy.

Once the public psychology around debt has decisively shifted away from automatic compliance with payback morality, how will the new mind-set translate into action? When there is no prospect of debt relief issuing from the government, debtors will have to take it for themselves, and by any means necessary. Millions annually default on their household debts and are personally punished for the outcome. A collective default, in the form of a mass debt strike, seems unlikely from our current vantage point, though there is little doubt it would have a sharp political impact. Organizing around debt is not easy—each debtor's situation is like a fingerprint—but the conditions for the emergence of a debtors' movement have seldom been more auspicious. Even though we cannot predict at this point what form it will take, which pathways it will pursue, and which tactics it will adopt, the need for such a movement is self-evident. For those who like neat distinctions, the historical moment can be summarized as follows: Whereas strife over wages was central to the industrial era, the grand conflict of our times is shaping up as the struggle over debt, and any just resolution calls for a level of organizing at least as momentous as the labor movement in its heyday.

The rejection of existing illegitimate debts is not enough, of course. In and of itself the business of wiping the slate clean will not alter the continuing use of debt-leveraging to redistribute wealth and constrain democracy. Debt cancellation is only the first step. An alternative economy, run on socially productive credit, has to materialize if the control over economic planning by Wall Street and other banking centers is to be decisively loosened. To most people, that is a daunting prospect because it evokes some colossal overhaul of the current system that could only be achieved through the capture of state power. Yet many of the institutions and practices that support an alternative economy already exist and are thriving in their own right.

Mutualist, nonprofit, commons-based, and community-oriented, their economic impact is already much larger, in the aggregate, than is typically acknowledged. Credit unions, workers' cooperatives, and community-supported agriculture are well established and expanding in membership everywhere, while more experimental practices involving time banks, social money, and community currencies are being tried out in places like Greece and Spain, where the mainstream economy has collapsed. Building on these existing commonist initiatives may be easier than halting the neoliberal privatization of the public sector, but for some social goods (education, health care, infrastructure, and energy among them), public provision is still critical. An alternative economy should be a mixed one, public and commonist. Whatever the ratio of the mix there should be no place and no need for most of the reckless rent-seeking activity that feeds the financial services industry.

A successor economy cannot sustain itself without new forms of political expression and association. Historically, creditors needed a representative government to ensure the citizenry would agree to the repayment of public debts—as borrowers, absolute monarchs had been fickle about their obligations. "Since the Renaissance," Michael Hudson observes, "bankers have shifted their political support to democracies. This did not reflect egalitarian or liberal political convictions as such, but rather a desire for better security for their loans."[15] Democratic governments proved more reliable clients, though they still defaulted on sovereign debts on a regular basis—more than 250 times since 1800, according to one estimate.[16] But today's legislators are more and more exposed as helpless in the face of creditors' demands and incapable of checking the power of high finance over policy-making. Too many younger people now see the current exercise of representative democracy as a rotten end-game. It has stopped being meaningful, and not just because of the hijacking of power on the part of the creditor class. Younger activists have been practicing democracy in different ways—often labeled horizontalist—since the late 1990s. The leaderless process in decision-making and action is now a default mentality for at least one generation, as are the social customs of cooperative networking and mutual aid.[17] Perhaps we should no longer refer to these as experimental practices, "prefigurative" of a more humane future. Among the politically aware, they have become quite normative and are likely to work their way into the main currents of civil society in the years to come. When this happens, we will see if the impersonal relations of money debt can actually be transformed into warm social bonds—mutually nourishing debts, in other words, that we owe each other in the exercise of our freedoms.

Coda—A Brief Movement Memoir

In the years since the financial crash, many debt resistance initiatives sprang up. Most of them were directed at lobbying legislators, yet the payoffs were minuscule. No effective financial regulation, no program of debt relief, and no justice enacted on Wall Street for bankers' malfeasance. In light of the paralysis of the political class, other small-scale efforts were aimed instead at self-empowerment through collective action. In the conclusion to this chapter, I will briefly summarize those in which I have participated.

In November 2011 I helped to found the Occupy Student Debt Campaign, which aimed at mass student debt refusal. In its boisterous heyday Occupy was the signal moment for student debtors to come out publicly and throw off the personal shame and trauma that envelops those who cannot repay what they owe. Our campaign set itself the goal of organizing one million debtors committed to a collective default. But the time was not yet ripe for organizing around debt—not that it is ever easy to do so. Even so, one million student debtors did default over the course of that year, but purely on an individual basis so there was little to no political impact as a result.

In the summer of 2011 Strike Debt, a broader coalition focused on all kinds of household debt, was formed. We compiled and widely circulated the *Debt Resisters Operations Manual*, which offered advice to debtors of all kinds about how to reduce their obligations and evict the power of creditors from their lives.[18] In the fall, Strike Debt launched the Rolling Jubilee (roll-ingjubilee.org), a crowdfunded project that purchased distressed debt for pennies on the dollar through the secondary market. Instead of collecting on the loan portfolios it bought, the Rolling Jubilee wiped out the debt-ors' obligations. Over the next two years we abolished almost $15 million of medical debt. From the outset the Rolling Jubilee was designed as a public education project (not a solution to the household debt crisis) in order to highlight the injustice of having to go into debt to access vital social goods like health care and education. Knowing how little collection agencies have paid for debts transforms the conversation debtors have with them about what they should repay.

In the summer of 2014 we bought and abolished almost $4 million of debt owed by students at Everest College (part of the stumbling, for-profit Corinthian College network) at the discounted rate of three cents on the dollar.[19] Corinthian targeted the most vulnerable populations, going after student recruits who were overwhelmingly minority, female, and low income, including war veterans from Iraq and Afghanistan, for whom the chain could extract a rich flow of post-9/11 GI bill funds. Elected officials who allow higher education to be used as a vehicle for profit ignored all the warning signs that a sordid scam was afoot in the Corinthian network.[20]

Education debt is seldom sold at a deep discount, primarily because it cannot be discharged through bankruptcy and is therefore more lucrative than other kinds of lending. We searched for and bought the Everest debt to make a point about the inequities of debt-financed education in a high-profile way. As a result almost three thousand students were off the hook, and a much bigger buy in January 2015 brought relief to thousands more. Yet many more of their peers are still in a deep hole, carefully and deliber-ately prepared for them. The students recruited by colleges like Corinthian may be among the most callously duped, but institutional abuse of the fed-eral loan program extends far beyond the for-profit sector. More reputable universities are no less complicit in the tight nexus between the DOE and the Wall Street banks that has delivered a generation or two of our students into a condition that some see as akin to indenture.[21] That is a strong word but, insofar as it describes the need to go into debt in order to labor, it may be an accurate one.

The Rolling Jubilee was a short-term project, and we closed the fund in December 2013 to move on to direct organizing. In the summer of 2014 we helped Everest College students to self-organize, offering legal services and IT and media support, along with financial advice aimed at having all of their debts discharged. This is a pilot for our debtors' union project, called the Debt Collective (debtcollective.org), which was launched along with the September announcement of the student debt buy. The fledgling union—the Everest Avengers—took on the Department of Education in public hearings in the fall of 2014 and prepared its members to declare a debt strike.

Organizing a debtors' union is different from organizing around wages. For most people debts are the wages of the future, to which creditors lay claim far in advance. Education debt, in particular, can be viewed as a form of premature wage theft, and debtors who organize to defend their common interests are in a position to engage in a form of collective bargaining. The debtors movement that so many want to join will require new forms of organizing and action, just as arduous and momentous as the labor movement in its heyday. In and of itself, it will not be a sufficient response to twenty-first century capitalism, but it may be a necessary one.

Notes

1 Quoted in Steve Denning, "Why Can't We End Short-Termism?" *Forbes*, July 22, 2014, at http://forbes.com.

2 Thomas Piketty, *Capital in the Twenty-First Century* (Cambridge, MA: Harvard University Press, 2014). "Striking It Richer: The Evolution of Top Incomes in the United States," a series of data reports by Emmanuel Saez and Thomas Piketty, outlines how the 1 percent have captured income growth. The first in the series was "Income Inequality in the United States, 1913–1998," *Quarterly Journal of Economics*, 118, no. 1 (2003): 1–39, at http://eml.berkeley.edu/~saez/pikettyqje.pdf. The most recent update can be found at http://elsa.berkeley.edu/~saez/saez-UStopincomes-2012.pdf, showing that the top 1 percent earners captured 95 percent of the income gains since the recession officially ended. Also see Josh Bivens and Lawrence Mishel, "The Pay of Corporate Executives and Financial Professionals as Evidence of Rents in Top 1 Percent Incomes," *Journal of Economic Perspectives* 27, no. 3 (2013); Edward N. Wolff, "The Asset Price Meltdown and the Wealth of the Middle Class" (New York University, 2012), accessible at https://appam.confex.com/appam/2012/webprogram/Paper2134.html.

3 Many of the arguments, and a good deal of the content, for this article are drawn from Andrew Ross, *Creditocracy and the Case for Debt Refusal*, available at http://www.orbooks.com/catalog/creditocracy/.

4 Andrew Ross Sorkin, "Realities behind Prosecuting Big Banks," *New York Times*, March 11, 2013, at http://dealbook.nytimes.com/2013/03/11/big-banks-go-wrong-but-pay-a-little-price/?_r=0/.

5 See Nomi Prins, *All the Presidents' Bankers: The Hidden Alliances that Drive American Power* (New York: Avalon, 2013).

6 Franklin D. Roosevelt to Col. Edward Mandell House (21 November 1933) in *F.D.R.: His Personal Letters, 1928–1945*, ed. Elliott Roosevelt (New York: Duell, Sloan and Pearce, 1950), 373.

7 As quoted in Robert Manning, *Credit Card Nation: The Consequences of America's Addiction to Credit Cards* (New York: Basic Books, 2000), 27.

8   According to an August 2013 report from the Federal Reserve Bank of New York, almost 15 percent of all credit reports—covering an estimated 30 million consumers—displayed collection items from debt collection. In other words, one in seven Americans has experienced being pursued by debt collectors. *Quarterly Report on Household Debt and Credit* (August 2013) accessible at http://www.newyorkfed.org/.

9   Matt Taibbi, "Greed and Debt: The True Story of Mitt Romney and Bain Capital," *Rolling Stone*, August 29, 2012, at http://www.rollingstone.com/politics/news/greed-and-debt-the-true-story-of-mitt-romney-and-bain-capital-20120829/.

10   James MacDonald, *A Free Nation Deep in Debt: The Financial Roots of Democracy* (New York: Farrar, Strauss, and Giroux, 2003).

11   Peter Eavis and Ben Protess, "Considering the Fairness of JPMorgan's Deal," *New York Times*, October 21, 2013, at http://dealbook.nytimes.com/2013/10/21/considering-the-fairness-of-jpmorgans-deal/.

12   Anat Admati and Martin Hellwig, *The Bankers' New Clothes: What's Wrong with Banking and What to Do about It* (Princeton, NJ: Princeton University Press, 2013), 2.

13   See Damien Millet and Eric Toussaint, *Who Owes Who? 50 Questions about World Debt* (London: Zed Books, 2004); Damien Millet and Eric Toussaint, *Debt, the IMF, and the World Bank: Sixty Questions, Sixty Answers* (New York: Monthly Review Press, 2010).

14   François Chesnais, *Les dettes illégitimes: Quand les banques font main basse sur les politiques publiques* (Paris: Liber, 2012).

15   Michael Hudson, "Democracy and Debt: Has the Link been Broken?" *Frankfurter Algemeine Zeitung*, December 5, 2011, accessible in English at http://michael-hudson.com/2011/12/democracy-and-debt/.

16   Carmen Reinhardt and Kenneth Rogoff, *This Time Is Different: Eight Centuries of Financial Folly* (Princeton, NJ: Princeton University Press, 2009).

17   Marina Sitrin and Dario Azzelini, *They Can't Represent US! Reinventing Democracy from Greece to Occupy* (New York: Verso Press, 2013); David Graeber, *The Democracy Project: A History, a Crisis, a Movement* (New York: Spiegel and Grau, 2013); Michael Hardt and Antonio Negri, *Declaration* (New York: Hardt and Negri, 2012); A. J. Bauer, Cristina Beltran, Rana Jaleel, and Andrew Ross eds., *Is This What Democracy Looks Like?* (New York: Social Text, 2012), accessible online at http://what-democracy-looks-like.com.

18   Strike Debt, *Debt Resisters Operations Manual* (San Francisco: PM Press, 2014), downloadable at http://strikedebt.org/drom/.

19   Nona Willis Aronowitz, "Shame to Outrage: Group Takes Action against Student Debt Crisis," *NBC News* September 16, 2014, at http://www.nbcnews.com/news/education/shame-outrage-group-takes-action-against-student-debt-crisis-n204926/.

20   Molly Hensley-Clancy, "Documents Show What the Department of Education Knew about Corinthian College's Financial Situation," *Buzzfeed*, August 5, 2014, at http://www.buzzfeed.com/mollyhensleyclancy/documents-show-what-the-department-of-education-knew-about-c#.en4rJwJ791/.

21   Jeff Williams, "Student Debt and the Spirit of Indenture," *Dissent* 55, no. 4 (2008): 73–78.

3

The Subprime Subject
of Ideology

IVAN ASCHER

Toward the end of *Capital*'s first volume (most of which proceeds—however ironically—within the idiom of classical political economy), Marx finally changes register and distances himself explicitly from the bourgeois economists whose work he has been critiquing all along.[1] In particular, Marx takes a swipe at those economists who seem to treat the existence of the "free worker" and his confrontation with the capitalist as an eternal and natural fact, or (per Adam Smith's formulation) as the result of some "previous accumulation" now long forgotten. As Marx puts it with his usual verve, this "primitive accumulation plays approximately the same role in political economy as original sin does in theology. Adam bit the apple, and thereupon sin fell on the human race." The origin of this sin "is supposed to be explained when it is told as an anecdote about the past. Long, long ago there were two sorts of people; one, the diligent, intelligent and above all frugal élite; the other, lazy rascals, spending their substance, and more, in riotous living. . . . Thus it came to pass that the former accumulated wealth, and the latter sort finally had nothing to sell except their own skins."[2]

Against this naïvely benign if thoroughly ideological account of how the division of society into two classes came to be (an account that, he seems to imply, serves only to legitimate the continued exploitation of workers by capitalists), Marx offers in the book's final chapters a fuller account of the violent processes through which this primitive accumulation in fact occurred. "In actual history, it is a notorious fact that conquest, enslavement, robbery, murder, in short, force, plays the greatest part, in the tender annals of political economy."[3] First starting in the fifteenth century, through a series of both illegal and legal means, peasants were dispossessed of the land to which they had had access. Coupled with the dissolution of bands of feudal retainers, this expropriation of the peasants gave rise to a "free, unprotected and rightless proletariat [that] could not possibly be absorbed by the nascent manufactures as fast as it was thrown upon the world."[4] The result was that people were turned "in massive quantities into beggars, robbers and vagabonds," who all but flooded the nascent towns of Western Europe. There, as Marx puts it, a "bloody legislation" was put in place "at the end of the fifteenth and during the whole of the sixteenth centuries," which sought to criminalize vagabondage and eventually made possible the creation of a new industrial working class.

Looking back on the history of capitalism since the time of Marx's writing, it is hard not to be struck by the fact that the violence Marx so vividly describes—a violence he seems to think belonged squarely to the prehistory of capital—has in fact been part and parcel of its entire history. As David Harvey has argued, it may be more helpful to speak no longer of a "primitive accumulation," lest one think of it as a process that has been completed once and for all, but instead of an "accumulation by dispossession"—a process that is clearly unfolding to this day wherever noncapitalist societies are being brought into the fold or wherever there is a "deepening" of advanced capitalism at the expense of "traditional" forms of capitalism.[5] As Saskia Sassen documents, such a process can just as easily be found in developing countries that have been ravaged by years of debt-servicing regimes as in the United States, where financial innovations over the last twenty years have resulted in the destruction of millions of households and led to the "expulsion" of people from their traditional "capitalist encasements."[6]

In the following pages I, too, make a case for returning to Marx's analysis of early modern Europe as a way to help us understand our own predicament, but I do so with a slightly different emphasis and set of concerns. Specifically, where Harvey, Sassen, and others have found in Marx's analysis of "primitive accumulation" a way to underscore the remarkable continuities in the history of capitalism and, in particular, the relentless violence that capitalism seems to visit upon the most vulnerable populations, my aim here is chiefly to reflect on the discontinuous nature of contemporary capitalism. More specifically, if I turn in the following pages to Marx's analysis of the emergence of capitalism, it is with an eye to what it might teach us about the transformation of Anglo-American capitalism in the last forty years—a transformation characterized both by a dramatic rise of the financial sector and by the concurrent emergence of a distinctly neoliberal subject and set of relations. As Michael Hardt notes in a slightly different idiom, there is a "strange symmetry that links biopolitical production to the technologies of finance and the governance of neoliberalism." The present chapter is one attempt at exploring this symmetry.[7]

My argument, simply put, is that advanced capitalist societies have undergone changes in recent decades that are in many ways analogous to those undergone by European societies some five hundred years ago. At that time the sudden enclosure of the commons in England created a population that had little choice but to flee the countryside in order to survive. As they moved to the cities, these expropriated peasants were met with harsh laws against vagabondage, and as a result there emerged over the years a new population of individuals suitably disciplined for the rigors of factory work and the industrial labor market. Likewise in recent decades, I argue, the end of Keynesianism and the demise of the welfare state in both Europe and the United States have had similarly dislocating effects, confronting people with new forms of uncertainty and risks, which until then they had shouldered collectively. Many people have become vagabonds as a result of this process, and much as in the sixteenth century, their poverty has been largely criminalized. More significantly, perhaps, a great many of them have been forced to seek alternative forms of protection—if not in the cities *per se*, as in the story that Marx tells, then in the world of finance; or to put it differently, in the *City* itself.

Thus the collapse of the Bretton Woods monetary regime had the effect that many companies and countries that once relied on the stability of a fixed exchange rate turned to the nascent derivatives markets to manage their newly discovered risks. Similarly, when employers in the United States ceased to contribute to pension plans or to offer their employees health insurance, millions of American workers found themselves facing the risks of old age and ill health not as a community but as individuals, through the use of pension funds or private health insurance plans. The result has been an extraordinary expansion of the financial sector and of financial markets.[8] But what kind of larger social transformation does this represent? What kind of new relations does it augur? The financialization of Anglo-American capitalism may be shown to entail an enclosure of the market itself, which in turn remains inseparable from the emergence of new, distinctly neoliberal relations. These relations are such that people are not only disciplined and conditioned as individuals capable of alienating their labor-power in exchange for a wage but are also constructed as individuals and populations whose credibility or ability to be trusted must be similarly measured, abstracted, and exchanged.[9]

The Golden Age of Actually Existing Capitalism

The story begins not in the fifteenth or sixteenth century but in the latter half of the twentieth at a time when, in countries such as Britain, France or the United States at least, life was not without its charms or without a certain form of solidarity.[10] The working class was still exploited by capital, to be sure, but for the most part the conditions Marx had described in the 1860s no longer obtained. Already by the end of the nineteenth century in fact, partly because of the ruthlessness of these conditions and partly because of Marx's "ruthless criticism" thereof, the "market society" constructed in the eighteenth century had become largely discredited. As Karl Polanyi explains it, the effects of *laissez faire* on the population had been so devastating—and the crises it created so severe—that something of "society" eventually rebelled and measures were devised to shield those most vulnerable from the vagaries of the market.[11] In France, Britain, and Germany specifically, the late nineteenth and early twentieth centuries saw the establishment of something like a "social state," and by the 1930s even the United States could be seen to reconsider its commitment to the "free market" that had defined the period of the Roaring Twenties.[12] By the middle of the century, most of the national economies of Western Europe and the United States had been significantly reorganized around political compromises that involved formerly competing actors, and the basic schemes that had once protected the indigent had been transformed into full-blown "welfare states."

To put it schematically, the bargain went like this: workers agreed not to strike, and capital in exchange conceded a larger share of its profits than before—not only through better wages and through more secure long-term employment contracts but also through a variety of new benefits such as health, retirement, and unemployment insurances. This allowed workers to enjoy higher living standards and simultaneously ensured that capitalists would find a broad consumer base. Most significantly, perhaps, it meant that people in what is now called the global North were spared from having to go through the market to meet their every need. They benefited instead from the existence of a commons of sorts, meaning that life in the welfare state had largely been "de-commodified," as Gøsta Esping-Andersen put it, and that the *société ouvrière* of the nineteenth century (as Robert Castel called it in his account of nineteenth-century France) had largely transitioned into a *société salariale*. Workers were no longer living and working under conditions of utter precarity; instead, their condition as salaried workers afforded them a modicum of security and protection, which allowed them in turn to look beyond their next paycheck and build a better future for themselves and their communities.

And Beyond

To the extent that life in advanced capitalist societies did in fact correspond to the idyllic portrait just sketched (and for the most part it admittedly did not, save perhaps for a privileged minority of white men with "traditional" families), it was not thanks simply to the domestic political bargains brokered by the state between capital and labor. To a significant extent, these arrangements and the Keynesian policies that accompanied them were themselves predicated on an international bargain that had been struck toward the end of the Second World War, also under the influence of John Maynard Keynes. It was Keynes, after all, who had been the main architect of the Bretton Woods monetary system—a system of fixed exchange rates in which the United States (which by then held nearly 80 percent of the world's gold reserves) not only agreed to the convertibility of other currencies into dollars but agreed to the convertibility of dollars into gold, at a fixed exchange rate of 35 dollars per ounce. As Geoff Mann explains, this was a system in which capitalist monies could be freely exchanged without any need for frantic trading, and this in no small part because the currencies and the corresponding economies also had the "backstop" of the World Bank and International Monetary Fund—two institutions that had been established to help the reconstruction and transformation of economies after the war.[13] There too it was the richer countries, especially the United States, that contributed disproportionately; but there too the arrangement was deemed advantageous to all if only because it helped create stable trading relationships and a potential market for U.S. goods. By mid-century, something of new commons had been established on both a national and an international level—a commons that allowed individuals and communities to partake in all aspects of capitalist production and exchange with the confidence that, while the means of production were privately held, the system of exchange itself was available to all.

By the early 1970s, unfortunately, the political basis for both the international monetary system and the national welfare states of many advanced capitalist economies began to fray, as the United States found itself increasingly unable or unwilling to meet the global demand for gold—leading Richard Nixon in 1971 to decide to suspend the convertibility of dollar into gold. On one level the policy change proved remarkably successful because it exported inflation and spread the cost of the war in Vietnam around the world.[14] The more lasting consequence of the decision, however, lay in the dismantling of the system of mutualization of risks that had characterized the Bretton Woods system, which itself had the effect of introducing—or reintroducing—an element of uncertainty in economic life that had not existed since 1944. Without the anchor provided by the dollar's convertibility to gold, countries and companies that had been involved in international trade were now confronted with the uncertainties and risks associated with fluctuating exchange rates—risks they would very quickly have to manage by turning to the newly burgeoning markets in financial derivatives.[15]

Domestically, too, the compromise between labor and capital was becoming strained. Starting in the 1960s and continuing in the 1970s labor had grown strong enough that, when growth started to slow, capital found itself unable to reduce labor costs without cutting into profits, which grew frustrating. As Harvey explains it, capital had encountered a limit, and it was not until the late 1970s—in 1979, to be precise—that it found a way to circumvent this.[16] In October 1979, indeed, then chairman of the U.S. Federal Reserve Paul Volcker resolved to allow interest rates to rise in the hopes that this would break the back of inflation. Once again, the strategy worked; inflation dropped from 13 percent in 1980 to 3 percent in 1983; but once again, the true significance of the "Volcker shock" extended well beyond the immediate reduction of inflation. Not only did the shock dramatically increase the size and importance of bond markets, it also sounded the death knoll for Keynesian policy-making and for the societal bargain that had underpinned it.

In the years that followed (thanks in large part to the work of Margaret Thatcher and Ronald Reagan, among others), the social relations on which this so called Golden Age of capitalism was predicated and the mutualizing of risk that it made possible were largely undone. The capitalist class was allowed to disengage from the commitments to which it had been bound for the previous thirty years. And as the welfare state was gradually dismantled, so a process was set in motion that gradually brought about both the dramatic expansion of the financial sector and the emergence of what we now recognize as a specifically *neo*liberal society, in which individuals are not only free to make promises in their own name but, in the process, are made to alienate something of their own credibility in exchange for the ability to borrow.

The Great Risk Shift and the Rise of Finance

Taking the case of the United States as our exemplar, it is easy to see that employers in the 1980s and 1990s decided they wanted "out of the social contract"; not only did they "mostly get what they want," as Jacob Hacker aptly puts it, but risk as a result was shifted "back onto workers and their families."[17] Or as we might also put it, the means of social protection that were once held in common were suddenly enclosed, with the effect that populations that were formerly cared for now had to seek alternative forms of protection—whether in the world of private insurance or in finance more generally.[18]

To wit: after the passage of Medicare and Medicaid in 1965, as Hacker explains, "health coverage peaked at roughly 90 percent of the population, with approximately 80 percent of Americans covered by private insurance."[19] This coverage was for the most part arranged through private insurers and private medical care providers (in Europe it might have been provided by and through the state), but it was nonetheless among the basic benefits that came with being gainfully employed. Since the 1970s, however, employers have increasingly given up on providing this benefit. Insurance companies were more than happy to pick up the slack, but since employers were no longer willing to engage in the practice of broad risk-pooling, it was the individual employees who were left to negotiate contracts on their own, choosing among plans that seemed tailored to their needs but were, most importantly, tailored to their individual risk profile.

The story is much the same in the case of old-age insurance—or what most of us, perhaps naïvely, still call "retirement" or "social security." In 1980, over 80 percent of medium and large firms provided their employees with "defined benefit" pension plans (by 2003, Hacker notes, the share is less than one-third).[20] The pension was often modest, but it had the advantage of being fairly certain, and unlike the pension funds or 401(k) plans that would eventually take their place these were "defined benefits" programs that depended neither on the employees' individual contributions (since the contributions were made by the employer) nor on the ups and downs of the stock market. Indeed, such pensions schemes in many ways served to protect people from the vagaries of the stock market . . . until a change in the U.S. tax code allowed for a shift away from defined benefits to defined contributions.[21] Today, rare is the employer who can provide the kind of retirement benefits that General Motors once provided its employees at the Rouge plant; but it is not unusual for the employees of Wal-Mart to have access to a 401(k)—allowing them to invest a share of their modest income in financial markets.[22]

Last but not least, as U.S. workers have seen their wages decline and their jobs become more precarious since the 1980s, they have also found it easier than ever to apply for and obtain credit. Indeed as Harvey and others demonstrate very clearly, no sooner did capital succeed in dismantling the labor unions than it realized it had also succeeded—however inadvertently—in destroying its own consumer base.[23] Credit was thus extended to those workers whose purchasing power had been so severely weakened, such that—while it was becoming difficult for workers to find employers who might be willing to offer them long-term contracts, it was increasingly easy for them to find lenders who were interest in a lasting relationship.

Indeed, lenders proved eager to provide people with so-called revolving credit—that is, lines of credit that would last indefinitely provided the borrower was willing and able to make a small minimum payment every month.

The Bloodless Legislation against the Expropriated

If we were to recast the story told so far strictly in terms that Marx himself might have recognized, we might say that, where the late nineteenth and early twentieth centuries saw the establishment of a new commons of sorts as social insurance schemes were developed and life in capitalist societies was significantly decommodified, so the late twentieth and early twenty-first centuries witnessed its dramatic "enclosure"—not only in the sense that this commons was simply privatized (though in many cases it was), but in the sense that the social relations that had formed the basis of this commons were systematically undone. As a result, populations that had relied on the means of protection being held in common found themselves having to devise alternatives and, in particular, having to turn to the *City*— to its insurance companies, pension funds, and credit card providers—for new forms of security. But what exactly are the conditions that awaited this "free and rightless" proletariat? What hardships have they had to endure, to what forms of discipline are they now being subjected, and with what potential consequences?

In the story that Marx tells, the displaced populations of Europe were met with the harshest possible laws regarding vagabondage. Those who were caught begging were branded on their back or on their forehead and enslaved and those who sought to escape their masters were liable to be killed.[24] Surely the newcomers to the City have been more fortunate; there is no branding, no enslavement, and in many cases they are greeted with open arms as financial services and credit cards are foisted on them without their even asking. But does this mean that violence is altogether absent or that no form of power is at work? Clearly the rules that govern contemporary credit relations are less "bloody" than the ones that were passed in early modern Europe. But are they any less crucial in the construction of today's neoliberal subject?

Consider, for instance, the all-too-ordinary case of a young college graduate who, having just finished her studies the University of Washington (a wise investment in her future, she no doubt thought), decided to move to New York City in search of an apartment and a job.[25] As her profile in the *New York Times* explains, she was lucky enough to find both, but the wages she earned as a nanny proved insufficient to cover both the rent and her monthly student loan payments, which were now coming due. The loan payments alone were in the neighborhood of $1,000 a month and so, quite sensibly, she prioritized her rent. She missed a first loan payment, and thirty days later her inattention to detail was—apparently—reported to a credit bureau. Another thirty days passed without a payment, and her negligence had now become a problem; her credit score had been docked several points—as had her father's, who had kindly co-signed her loan applications only a few years earlier. If it happens again (and it will), their scores will likely fall below 660 or 620 (if they haven't already), at which point they will be deemed *sub-prime* by the financial industry, meaning they will either be denied credit altogether or the terms on which they are offered credit will be so egregiously high they will wish they had never applied for a loan.

Unlike the branding of the vagabond so vividly described by Marx, the branding of the subprime does not sear the flesh. As a result, it is also not visible—indeed in many cases the subprime borrower herself may not even understand why her loan application has been denied or why the interest rates for her existing loans have shot up to unprecedented levels. In this regard, the pressures experienced by present-day borrowers whose credibility is constantly being evaluated may be closer to the pressures experienced by workers (who worry that they might be fired) than the pressures felt by the displaced peasants of the sixteenth century (who worried that they might be branded a slave). After all, just as the worker is likely to see his wage diminish or disappear altogether if he is deemed less productive than others, so the borrower whose credit history shows him to be less "safe" than another is likely to be saddled with fines or higher interest rates, if his loan application is not purely and simply denied. In both cases individuals are placed in competition with one another, and in both cases the threat of being punished—while allowing them to maintain their formal freedom—nonetheless serves to discipline them into a specific kind of behavior.

That said, however, the mechanisms by which people are disciplined as borrowers are also markedly different from the ways they are disciplined as workers. The worker, in principle, is paid for the work he has already accomplished (that is, for his past productivity); the borrower, by contrast, is granted a credit score that reflects his estimated risk as a borrower in the future. The score itself is ostensibly based on his past performance as a borrower—and in this it does resemble the wage—but what is being estimated is the *future* liability he poses for the lender. Moreover, whereas two workers who are equally productive should in principle receive similar wages, it is quite conceivable that two individuals who borrow the same amount and repay their debts with the exact same regularity but differ in other regards (say, in terms of where they live or where they buy their food) should nonetheless receive different credit scores. And the reason for this discrepancy, need it be said, could simply be that, in these particular respects, they were deemed to belong to different populations with differing levels of credit risk.

It is not simply the case, then, that borrowers are pitted against each other as workers already are; it is also the case that the terms of this competition are particularly opaque and, arguably, perverse. For instance, I find it somewhat disturbing that the mere fact that I might be making my credit card payments on time is sufficient to make someone else's record look worse by comparison. What is more, I also have to acknowledge that the person whose risk profile earns them an interest rate higher than mine (deservedly or not) is effectively the person whose monthly payments are insuring our lender against the possibility—however slim—that *I* might actually default, regardless of my outstanding record so far. Officially, of course, her high premium may seem justified by the fact that *she* is considered to be a risk to the lender. But the reality is that the payments she is making are used to protect our lender against the consequences of *my* possible default. And finally, though I may hate to admit it, it is also quite possible that my relatively good credit score depends less on the fact that I have proved myself true to my word than on the fact that others who share my zip code (or my penchant for buying wild bird seeds) have made me look like a relatively safe bet.[26]

Admittedly, the peculiar system I am describing was not devised with the express purpose of exploiting whatever historical inequities characterize any given society. In fact, it is worth acknowledging that it is technically illegal in the United States for lenders to discriminate on the basis of ascriptive categories such as race, gender, or age lest they be tempted to presume that a certain type of person—say, an African American person—is less creditworthy than any other. This would be acting on prejudice, and laws have been put in place to prevent it. That said, however, so long as the lender can empirically demonstrate that a certain kind of person—or more precisely, a person that engages in a certain kind of *behavior*—has a higher probability of default, so the lender can in all good conscience require them to pay higher interest rates than others pay even if, as individuals, they themselves have never defaulted in the past. What this means, unfortunately, is that while individual lenders may not be allowed to bring *their own prejudices* to bear on a lending decision, the regulations governing the use of credit scores do little to remedy the already decisive effects on people's lives of prejudices both past and present.[27]

Ultimately, it is tempting to say that, as techniques for credit scoring are perfected, lenders hardly even *need* to inquire whether an applicant is Black or White to discriminate among racial groups. The material they are allowed to gather—which material indirectly reflects what social conditions the applicant is living under—tells them all they need to know, and the social fact that is a person's race is therefore already embedded in (and amplified by) the terms of the lending decision. What is more, to the extent that an individual's risk profile comes to determine the terms on which they are allowed to borrow, so the more "objectively" risk is measured, so the more objective it becomes—that is, the more it comes to *govern* social life reflexively, which then most likely amplifies what social patterns already exist but does so under cover of scientific neutrality.

Paper or Plastic and Cash or Credit?
Life in an Enclosed Market

I have described the financialization of contemporary capitalism as if it had somehow been inflicted by external forces onto the most vulnerable populations, rather like the enclosures movement described by Marx. The fact is, however, that the gradual replacement of wages by credit—like the replacement of employer-sponsored pensions by pension funds, or the gradual erosion of state- or city-sponsored security services in favor of private alternatives—did not take place without significant popular support. Although many of us may find ourselves longing for the days of the welfare state, it is also undeniable that the neoliberal promise of the 1980s and 1990s was, and for many people remains, very enticing indeed. From the invention of the 401(k) (which allows individuals to plan their own retirement as they wish, contributing as little or as much as they want, reaping the benefits of a bustling stock market without having to rely on a bureaucratic inefficient state to manage their future) to the proliferation of private insurance and protection schemes (which allow individuals to tailor their coverage to their specific needs and risk profiles), the 1980s and 1990s saw the development of countless new techniques and strategies for risk and wealth management that broadly appealed to a population increasingly unable (even unwilling) to depend on their government. But more than any other technology, it is perhaps the *credit card*—with its promise of freedom and security combined—that best embodies the promise, the dangers, and the revolutionary character of the new neoliberal and financialized era.[28]

As myriad advertising campaigns have made clear over the years, the credit card is both an instrument of freedom and a source of security. Whether one is in a foreign country (or in a country so radically transformed by neoliberalism that it is no longer recognizable), a credit card offers its holder the promise of protection if anything should go wrong—which is no doubt why American Express reminds us not to "leave home without it." Likewise, the fact that Visa is "everywhere [one] want[s] it to be" allows one to move about the market freely, even if one is barely employed or living from paycheck to paycheck. Most remarkable of all, perhaps, the technology of the credit card empowers a person to determine when to borrow and when to pay and, in so doing, to decide for herself on the true value of things. Thus MasterCard, most famously, allows its users to decide what things are truly *worth it* and what things are not and in this regard, undoubtedly, it is truly "priceless."

At the same time, as many card holders have discovered, it is easy to get entangled in the mesh of this credit card safety net. The ability to borrow afforded by the card does seem often to compound people's vulnerability, leading not to greater freedom or autonomy but to increased levels of indebtedness and, as a result, ever-greater dependence on capital. But what is less often acknowledged than the sheer increase in the level of debt is the fact that the generalization of the credit card effectively amounts to a new form of enclosure—an enclosure of the *market* itself, so to speak, the consequences of which are yet to be fully grasped or theorized.

Consider for a moment "the market" as it existed, if not in Marx's time, at least in his imagination. As Marx puts it in *Capital*, when commodities go to market, they are accompanied by their guardians. There, the guardians recognize each other as representatives of their commodities, representatives who are equal before the law—equally entitled to alienate their property (and to receive property in return). One of them may have little to his name—indeed, he may have nothing to sell other than his own labor power, while the other has an overabundance of money he is looking to invest, but formally the encounter is one of equals.

Although he does not dwell on this, Marx acknowledges that in this encounter both the seller and the buyer of labor-power can count on the existence of a state to protect their private property, just as both can count on the existence of a universal equivalent to mediate the encounter. So long as these conditions obtain, the capitalist can expect the worker to perform the tasks that are demanded of her, and the worker in turn can expect to receive a wage (however modest) in exchange for her labor-power. What is more, both worker and capitalist can trust that the money they exchange—whether when the worker gets paid or when she goes to purchase the goods she herself has produced—will be recognized as such and allow the transaction to occur.

Fast-forward from the mid-nineteenth century to the present-day United States, however, and what do we find? Today's capitalist, to be sure, still expects the worker to work and the worker in turn still expects to be paid, and both continue to expect that their money will be recognized on the marketplace. But much has changed in the last 150 years, and the seemingly immediate encounter between the buyer and the seller has grown more complex. For one thing, our present-day worker will rarely be paid in cash; more likely than not, her earnings will be deposited in a bank account—which increasingly she is *required* to have in order merely to be hired. For another, when she leaves work and goes to the market, what is it she encounters? In recent years, especially in the United States, many transactions that once involved only cash have become mediated by credit. Whether they are paying for repairs to their car or ordering items of clothing from an online retailer, U.S. consumers are increasingly having to produce their credit card or their credit card information—which means they also have to produce themselves as creditworthy customers—before they can even engage in the most quotidian of market transactions.

The experience of using a credit card, admittedly, will often seem less complicated than that of using cash—and in many ways it may even seem more *immediate*. Whether I am using it at the local Starbucks, for instance, or using it online to replenish my stash of Nespresso capsules, the convenience of the credit card is nearly undeniable: a swipe of the card or a stroke of the keyboard and *voilà*, I have my fix. And yet it almost goes without saying that on close inspection, the institutional setup that enables my coffee addiction is considerably more intricate. For one thing, though I may *think* that it is I who paid for my coffee, the truth of the matter is that my bank purchased it on my behalf—effectively fronting me the money for a few weeks while I maintain my habit. (I need only read the small print on the paper slip the barista has handed me to be reminded that I have merely agreed to reimburse my lender "as per the terms of the cardholder agreement.")

That is not all. The merchant, too—whether it be Starbucks, Nestlé, or the owner of a franchise—may feel similarly pleased that he now has money in the bank that he can use as he wishes. But while this may be true, it is only because *his* bank (the so-called acquiring bank) has agreed to deposit "my" money into his account and in doing so is taking risk for which it shall have to be compensated.[29] After all, what if the barista serves me an iced hazelnut macchiato in lieu of the mocha frappuccino® I ordered? Or more plausibly, what if instead of the five hundred Arpeggio capsules I wanted I am mistakenly sent fifty Volluto decaffeinated capsules? Surely I would request a refund and the bank would have to pay me back. The merchant's bank, presumably, will therefore charge him a premium for its services—lest it find itself having to return the money unexpectedly. On both sides of such an ostensibly simple transaction both the customer and the merchant are merely *borrowing* money, where before they seemed to be only exchanging commodities. Goods and services are still exchanged and the presence of the state is still required, but in order merely to engage in this exchange of commodities, customers and merchants now have to be evaluated *as borrowers.* The customer is evaluated for her fitness to borrow the amounts she needs to make her purchases; the merchant is similarly evaluated for his fitness to borrow the amounts his business generates in credit card transactions.

In sum, where only a few years ago buyers and sellers could meet at the marketplace and use a currency that was available to all, we are increasingly finding that the marketplace *itself* has been enclosed. One's purchasing power is no longer simply dependent on the number of bills one has in one's wallet but is increasingly dependent on one's borrowing power or one's *credit*—which credit each of us has to negotiate *as an individual.* And what this means in turn is that, much as nineteenth century workers in order to survive had to present themselves before their employer as free workers, that is, as individuals whose labor-power could be not only measured and abstracted but freely alienated in exchange for a wage, so today we are further required to present ourselves as credible borrowers or investors of a sort, that is, as individuals whose capacity to take risks—their capacity to make promises or their general "probability," as I have called it elsewhere—can similarly be measured and appropriated in exchange for a specific line of credit.[30]

Conclusion

If there is one lesson to be learned from the exercise just completed, what might it be? Nineteenth-century political economists feigned to believe that the existence of the free worker and of the wage relation between him and the capitalist was an eternal and God-given fact. Man has a natural "propensity to truck, barter, and exchange one thing for another," as Adam Smith put it, and that was that. Marx exposed this for the lie it was and highlighted along the way the extraordinary violence that made possible the emergence of these relations and that made it possible for "labor-power," as a result, to become a commodity in its own right (albeit a "fictitious" one, as Polanyi would later observe).[31]

Today in the United States in particular we are similarly encouraged to think of ourselves as natural-born choosers, rational actors with the ability and desire to make our own decisions and accept the consequences thereof. We may each have our idiosyncratic preferences and temperaments, whereby some of us are risk-averse while others are risk-seeking, but overall it is understood that we all have the same capacity and right to determine what risks to take and what commitments to make. We have property in our own person, so to speak—just as in the time of John Locke—and this entitles us not only to alienate our own labor-power. It allows us also to make promises in our own name and, more precisely, to alienate our credibility to anyone who might have an interest in acquiring it.

The fact is, however, that while we may still be asked to believe that to be the natural condition of mankind, nobody is really fooled. Even the apostles of neoliberalism, in fact—*especially* the apostles of neoliberalism, I should say—all but acknowledge that this neoliberal *homo probabilis*, this "entrepreneur of the self" on which the capitalist mode of prediction depends does not exist in the wild: it had to be bred.[32] Or to borrow from Simone de Beauvoir: one is not born but, rather, *becomes* an entrepreneur of the self. But under what terms and what conditions? If the emergence of the liberal individual of the nineteenth century can be traced in part to the enclosure of the land that occurred two or three centuries prior, today's neoliberal individual similarly finds his origins in another kind of enclosure, namely, the enclosure of the twentieth-century welfare state and the market itself. And if, in the story recounted by Marx, it was the threat of enslavement followed by the threat of unemployment (or, as he euphemistically put it, "the silent compulsion of the market") that made possible the emergence of the "free worker," so in the story told here, something of the same threat still obtains—not only because the threat of unemployment still remains, nor simply because debtors' prisons have returned, but most generally because, as Boisguilbert once remarked, it is as easy to "ruin a poor person" as to enrich him.[33]

Notes

1 On the change of tone in Marx's writing, see David Harvey, *A Companion to Marx's Capital* (London: Verso, 2010), 279.

2 Karl Marx, *Capital: A Critique of Political Economy, Vol. I*, trans. Ben Fowkes (New York: Vintage, 1977), 873.

3 Ibid., 874.

4 Ibid., 876, 896.

5 David Harvey, *The New Imperialism* (Oxford: Oxford University Press, 2003), 137. Marx's analysis of the "so-called primitive accumulation" has been a source of inspiration for countless readers at least since Rosa Luxemburg. Harvey's recent reinterpretation of Marx is one the most widely cited, but recent scholarship also includes Werner Bonefeld, "The Permanence of Primitive Accumulation: Commodity Fetishism and Social Constitution," *The Commoner* 2 (2001); Jim Glassman, "Primitive Accumulation, Accumulation by Dispossession, Accumulation by 'Extra-Economic' Means," *Progress in Human Geography* 30, no. 5 (2006): 608–625; Jason Read, "Primitive Accumulation: The Aleatory Foundation of Capital," *Rethinking Marxism* 14, no. 2 (2002): 24–49; Silvia Federici, *Caliban and the Witch: Women, the Body and Primitive Accumulation* (New York: Autonomedia, 2004); Massimo de Angelis, *The Beginning of History: Value Struggles and Global Capital* (London: Pluto Press, 2007); Kalyan K. Sanyal, *Rethinking Capitalist Development: Primitive Accumulation, Governmentality and Post-Colonial*

Capitalism (London: Routledge, 2007); Sandro Mezzadra, "The Topicality of Prehistory: A New Reading of Marx's Analysis of 'So-called Primitive Accumulation,'" *Rethinking Marxism* 23, no. 3 (2011): 302–321; Saskia Sassen, *Expulsions: Brutality and Complexity in the Global Economy* (Cambridge, MA: Harvard University Press, 2014); Glen Sean Coulthard, *Red Skin, White Masks: Rejecting the Colonial Politics of Recognition* (Minneapolis: University of Minnesota Press, 2014); Pierre Dardot and Christian Laval, *Commun: Essai sur la révolution au XXIe siècle* (Paris: La Découverte, 2014).

6 See Saskia Sassen, "A Savage Sorting of Winners and Losers: Contemporary Versions of Primitive Accumulation," *Globalizations* 7, no. 1 (2010): 23–50.

7 Michael Hardt, "Falsify the Currency," *South Atlantic Quarterly* 111, no. 2 (2012): 369.

8 On the rise of finance post–Bretton Woods, see Giovanni Arrighi, *The Long Twentieth Century: Money, Power, and the Origins of Our Time* (New York: Verso, 1994); for accounts of the political origins of American financialization, in particular, see Greta Krippner, *Capitalizing on Crisis: The Political Origins of the Rise of Finance* (Cambridge, MA: Harvard University Press, 2012); Gerald Davis, *Managed by Markets: How Finance Re-shaped America* (Oxford: Oxford University Press, 2009).

9 On debt and discipline more generally, see Mahmud Tayyab, "Debt and Discipline," *American Quarterly* 64, no. 3 (2012): 469–494; Ananya Roy, "Subjects of Risk: Technologies of Gender in the Making of Millennial Modernity," *Public Culture* 24, no. 1 (2012): 131–155; Mark Kear, "Governing *Homo Subprimicus*: Beyond Financial Citizenship, Exclusion, and Rights," *Antipode* 45, no. 4 (2013): 1–21; Paul Langley, "Equipping Entrepreneurs: Consuming Credit and Credit Scores," *Consumption Markets & Culture* 17 (2014): 448–447.

10 Geoff Mann is to be credited for the clever turn of phrase in the subheading. See *Disassembly Required: A Fieldguide to Actually Existing Capitalism* (Oakland, CA: AK Press, 2013).

11 Karl Polanyi, *The Great Transformation* (Boston: Beacon Press, 1944).

12 See Christophe Ramaux, "Quelle théorie pour l'état social? Apports et limites de la référence assurantielle. Relire François Ewald 20 ans après *L'État providence*," *Revue française des affaires sociales* 1, no. 1 (2007): 13–34.

13 Geoff Mann, *Disassembly Required: A Fieldguide to Actually Existing Capitalism* (Oakland: AK Press, 2013), 117.

14 Ibid., 126.

15 See Edward LiPuma and Benjamin Lee, *Financial Derivatives and the Globalization of Risk* (Durham: Duke University Press, 2014).

16 See David Harvey, *A Brief History of Neoliberalism* (Oxford: Oxford University Press, 2005), 23.

17 Jacob S. Hacker, *The Great Risk Shift* (Oxford: Oxford University Press, 2006), 7.

18 See Pat O'Malley, "Uncertain Subjects: Risks, Liberalism and Contract," *Economy and Society* 29, no. 4 (2000): 460–484.

19 Jacob S. Hacker, Statement before the Committee on Senate Health, Education, Labor and Pensions, January 16, 2007, OUPblog, at http://blog.oup.com/2007/01/jacob_hacker_ad/.

20 Hacker, *The Great Risk Shift*, 14.

21 On the changes to the tax code and the subsequent rise of pension funds, see Davis, *Managed by Markets: How Finance Re-shaped America*, 132.

22 Max Haiven, "Walmart, Financialization, and the Cultural Politics of Securitization," *Cultural Politics* 9, no. 3 (2013): 245.

23 See, for instance, Susanne Soederberg, *Debtfare States and the Poverty Industry: Money, Discipline and the Surplus Population* (London: Routledge, 2014); David Harvey, *The Enigma of Capital and the Crises of Capitalism* (Oxford: Oxford University Press, 2010), 17.

24 Unlike value, which famously "does not have its description branded on its forehead" (Marx, *Capital*, 167), the enslaved vagabond under Henry VI, if he is "absent for a fortnight," is liable to be "condemned to slavery for life" and to be "branded on forehead or back with the letter S; if he runs away three times, he is to be executed as a felon" (Marx, *Capital*, 897).

25 Natalie Kitroeff, "Young and in Debt in New York City," *New York Times*, June 6, 2014, at http://www.nytimes.com/2014/06/08/realestate/student-loans-make-it-hard-to-rent-or-buy-a-home.html.

26 See Charles Duhigg, "What Does Your Credit-Card Company Know about You?" *New York Times Magazine*, May 12, 2009, at http://www.nytimes.com/2009/05/17/magazine/17credit-t.html?pagewanted=all/.

27 For a discussion of the various ways in which lenders and credit rating agencies are able to "discriminate" among borrowers, see Martha Poon, "Statistically Discriminating without Discrimination," Centre de Sociologie des Organisations, January 25, 2013, at http://www.cso.edu/fiche_rencontre.asp?langue=en&renc_id=362/. See also Marion Fourcade and Kieran Healy, "Classification Situations: Life-Chances in the Neoliberal Era," *Accounting, Organizations and Society* 38 (2013): 559–572; Stephen Ross and John Yinger, *The Color of Credit: Mortgage Discrimination, Research Methodology, and Fair Lending Enforcement* (Cambridge, MA: MIT Press, 2002); Danielle Keats Citron and Frank Pasquale, "The Scored Society: Due Process for Automated Predictions," *Washington Law Review* 89, no. 1 (2014): 1–33. On the racialized parameters of the subprime crisis, specifically, see Gary A. Dymski, "Racial Exclusion and the Political Economy of the Subprime Crisis," *Historical Materialism* 17 (2009): 149–179; Angie K. Beeman, Davita Silfen Glasberg, and Colleen Casey, "Whiteness as Property: Predatory Lending and the Reproduction of Racialized Inequality," *Critical Sociology* 37, no. 1 (2010): 27–46.

28 See, among others, Johnna Montgomerie, "The Financialization of the American Credit Card Industry," *Competition and Change* 10, no. 3 (2006): 301–319.

29 For a description of "What You Need to Know about Credit Card Processing," see Paul Downs's post by the same title on the *New York Times* website, March 25, 2013, at http://boss.blogs.nytimes.com/2013/03/25/.

30 See Michel Feher, "Self-Appreciation; or, The Aspirations of Human Capital," *Public Culture* 21, no. 1 (2009); also Annie McClanahan, "Bad Credit: The Character of Credit Scoring," *Representations* 126, no. 1 (2014): 31–57.

31 Adam Smith, *An Inquiry into the Nature and Causes of the Wealth of Nations* (Chicago: University of Chicago Press, 1976), 17; Polanyi, *The Great Transformation*, 68–76.

32 On the changing morphology of the *homo economicus* and the rise of the "entrepreneur of the self," see Michel Foucault, *The Birth of Biopolitics: Lectures at the Collège de France, 1978–1979*, trans. Graham Burchell (New York: Palgrave Macmillan, 2008); Thomas Lemke, "'The Birth of Bio-politics': Michel Foucault's Lecture at the Collège de France on Neo-liberal Governmentality," *Economy and Society* 30, no. 2 (2001): 190–207; Wendy Brown, *Edgework: Critical Essays on Knowledge and Politics* (Princeton, NJ: Princeton University Press, 2005); Christian Laval, *L'homme économique: Essai sur les racines du néolibéralisme* (Paris: Gallimard, 2007); Jason Read, "A Genealogy of *Homo-Economicus*: Neoliberalism and the Production of Subjectivity," *Foucault Studies* 6 (2009): 25–36; Andrew Dilts, "From 'Entrepreneur of the Self' to 'Care of the Self': Neo-liberal Governmentality and Foucault's Ethics," *Foucault Studies* 12 (2011): 130–146; Angela Mitropoulos, *Contract and Contagion: From Biopolitics to Oikonomia* (Wivenhoe: Minor Compositions, 2012), 148.

33 Pierre Le Pesant de Boisguilbert, *Mémoires,* in *Correspondance des contrôleurs généraux des finances* (1874), 2:531, referenced in Robert Castel, *From Manual Workers to Wage Laborers*, trans. Richard Boyd (New Brunswick: Transaction Publishers, 2003), 88. See also Linda Coco, "Debtor's Prison in the Neoliberal State: 'Debtfare' and the Cultural Logics of the Bankruptcy Abuse Prevention and Consumer Protection Act of 2005," *California Western Law Review* 49, no. 1 (2012); Genevieve LeBaron and Adrienne Roberts, "Confining Social Insecurity: Neoliberalism and the Rise of the 21st Century Debtors' Prison," *Politics & Gender* 8 (2012): 25–49.

4

Social Democracy
and Its Discontents

The Rise of Austerity

JEFFREY SOMMERS

History repeats itself, the first time as tragedy, the second time as farce, as Karl Marx noted of France's two truncated revolutions later usurped by dictatorships. In a third instance of revolution disappointed, we have the collapse of the Soviet bloc, where liberation was followed by the tragedy of austerity policies and accompanying social decay. The revolutions of 1989–1991 that supposedly cleansed the Soviet bloc of bureaucratic rule were intended to align the states of East Europe with the "West" but in the end merely replaced them with the central planning of financial institutions in the "really existing democracies." Thus was born the "New Europe," as Donald Rumsfeld termed the East, whose crescendo of ever more extreme neoliberal economic policies ended with a crash in the financial crisis of 2008. This was followed by the imposition of austerity policies previously unmatched in their severity. The epicenter of this new economics and their "anti-society" policies (bearing in mind Margaret Thatcher's statement that "society" does not exist and her society euthanizing policies) were the three Baltic states. Among these, Latvia imposed the most radical austerity program—capturing the attention of global policy and opinion makers as a solution to the world's crisis economies and providing defenders of the current order an example showing, in contrast to Greece, that austerity works.

In presenting an attractive alternative to "really existing socialism" a generation back, the West projected an image, if not reality, of social democracy as a counter—model to Soviet communism. When citizens of the Soviet bloc turned their ear to the United States in 1980s they heard echoes of the order created during FDR's rule and the social movements of the 1930s. Thus, people in the Soviet bloc conflated the still existing mass-based prosperity of the United States, forged in the New Deal, with the University of Chicago free-market rhetoric being introduced into public policy discourse during Reagan's America. Moreover, the anti-statism of the Reagan/Thatcher era was far more appealing to anti-Soviet activists who often became political leaders in the post-Soviet bloc. While the foundations of the New Deal were being rapidly eroded by Thatcher's policies beginning in the late 1970s, closely followed by Reagan's starting in the early 1980s, the contours of this new order in its full economic outlines only became fully visible by the twenty-first century.

Indeed, the high tide for social democracy was reached at the peak of Soviet power. This timing was no coincidence. As Finland's postwar president Urho Kekkonen reputedly remarked, "the Soviet Union created a worker's paradise [long pause], just not in the USSR, but in Finland." What was meant, of course, was that the ideological, if not military, threat of an alternative to economic liberalism had focused Western Europe's political and economic elites on the project of creating a sustainable capitalist order based on a "social compact" with the then strongly organized working classes. In short, it was the existence of the Soviet bloc in the East that created a reasonably civilized capitalism in the West. Absent that ideological alternative from the East, the contradictions of capital accumulation present in the late nineteenth and early twentieth centuries reappeared with new virulence and with them many of the same economic and social challenges that existed before the "short 20th century" (1917–1989/91) returned with renewed force.

The peril of an ideological alternative to unrestrained capital provided an opening for worker struggles in Western Europe to make economic and social gains following the establishment of the USSR and even more so during the Cold War. In the case of Germany, Scandinavia, and much of Western Europe generally (not to mention Japan and the United States, to a certain extent), this took the form of economies that balanced power among labor, industry, and government. Finance capital opposed this arrangement, but given the larger realities of the time, there was little choice but to reach an accommodation. This model proved ephemeral as the collapse of the Soviet bloc acted as a solvent washing it away. The economic crisis of the 1970s and subsequent weakening of the Soviet bloc, however, created a channel for the return of liberalizing currents that by the late twentieth and early twenty-first centuries had swept away many of the gains of the preceding era of Europe's Social Model. A generation after the Soviet collapse figures such as Mario Draghi, the president of the European Central Bank, in 2012 doubled down on austerity and declared Europe's Social Model dead—or in his words, "already gone."[1]

Liberal capitalism, devoid of these external and internal political threats, is now free to discard corporatist compromise with labor and seems incapable of producing stable social relations, let alone conditions for ensuring the reproduction of society.[2] Contra the previous contention of Francis Fukuyama that liberalism constituted the "end of history," we see that history remains restless and still quite in motion.[3] Liberalism does not organically evolve toward social democracy but, instead, toward the dictatorship of capital and the concentration of financial power, as was observed in the mid-nineteenth-century and again in 1920s Europe, and as it appears today as well.[4] Indeed, rather than social democracy, liberalism's last stop (if there is one) seems to be located in austerity and ever-widening inequality.[5]

Labor finds itself in a weakened position. Even among some of the world's wealthiest economies, millions find themselves now part of what Guy Standing calls a *precariat* of people living in informal or nonemployment whose day-to-day existence is tenuous at best.[6] Meanwhile, another group constitutes what Charles Woolfson has termed an *austeriat*, those who because of austerity policies are thrown into unemployment and virtual destitution that drive them to emigrate. The return of these conditions in the twenty-first century is removed from the experience of nearly all Europeans except its most elderly inhabitants with memories of the interwar years.[7] Many Europeans have experienced the widespread return (undreamed of only a decade ago) of what Karl Marx described as *immiseration*, thus ignoring Adam Smith's caution that "no society can surely be flourishing and happy, of which the far greater part of the members are poor and miserable."[8]

Latvia: Laboratory for a New Order

In studying the case of Latvia, the totality of contradictions of our financialized neoliberal economic system can be observed in microcosm with the historical specificities of this small state in a remote corner of Europe that witnessed the biggest economic crash following the 2008 financial crisis and the harshest austerity policies imposed thereafter. More important, however, are general patterns of world history and global political economy significance in the changing outlines of cultural, economic, political, and social development made manifest in the experience of this small state. Latvia's geography and historical experience placed it in the crosshairs of radical experiments in austerity, revealing the means by which capital is seeking to preserve capitalism. In short, its experience reads like a blueprint (and indeed has been proposed as such by certain EU policymakers) for the larger global austerity project underway. What follows, in part, is an approach to understanding austerity that explains patterns of global capital accumulation revealed through the case study of Latvia.

How was it that this tiny, obscure, former Soviet republic, now on the periphery of the European Union and nearly forgotten for much of the twentieth century, came to merit so much attention and debate in the twenty-first century? Latvia is small but in the past punched above its weight in the international arena. It is situated on the eastern edge of the Baltic Sea, geographically across from—but in recent decades economically and socially worlds apart from—its rich Scandinavian neighbors. Among the notable historical figures who called it home under tsarist rule were Mark Rothko, Isaiah Berlin, Richard Wagner, and Sergei Eisenstein. The biggest city in Latvia is Riga, which, once part of the Swedish Empire, vied with Stockholm as its largest city. By the early twentieth century Riga was the largest handler of port traffic in tsarist Russia. Riga was also one of the empire's most industrialized cities and a grain producer of global note. Grain prices from the Baltic were routinely reported in outlets as far away as the *New York Times*, and fluctuations in the supply of its wheat had global impact on grain prices. Latvia was a major actor in the 1905 revolutions for social justice (or what Vladimir Lenin termed the "dress rehearsal" for 1917) against the German land barons under tsarist Russia. The area provided a greater share of votes for the Bolsheviks in the 1917 elections than any other region in the Russian Empire. Indeed, along with Finland, Riga contained per capita the largest concentration of socialists in tsarist Russia. The city also supplied Lenin's guard, the "Latvian Riflemen," who provided the chief defense forces (with a soldier-elected officer corps) for the early Union of Soviet Socialist Republics (USSR) before Leon Trotsky formed the Red Army.

From this past global prominence, Latvia faded into obscurity under its first period of independence declared from the Soviet Union in 1918. Latvia found itself unfortunately positioned dead center between the warring Soviets and Nazis, and the First Republic lasted until its occupation in 1940 during World War II by both. Latvia was forcibly incorporated into the USSR as a Soviet republic in 1940 and, after the war, was relegated to even further anonymity as a place the world forgot. In the late 1980s Latvia briefly recaptured world attention as it took a leading role, along with the two neighboring Baltic states with their Singing Revolutions, in massive popular protests against the Soviet rule. Thereafter, with the breakup of the Soviet Union, Latvia's economic reconstruction was typified by a strongly neoliberal orientation commonly observed in much of the Soviet bloc. With a strongly nationalist anti-Soviet stance, Latvia's policymakers rejected regulation of the market. They scorned industrial policy as "picking winners" in the economy and purposefully worked to let even potentially salvageable industries collapse. This was done for both ideological and political reasons—the latter to prevent Russia from having any pretext to return as Ivars Godmanis, the first prime minister of Latvia's Second Republic, argued was necessary.

In the wake of the collapsed manufacturing sector, Latvia's economy was financialized. This would have tremendous importance in both creating Latvia's largest economic crisis and also guiding its turn toward austerity policies. Offshore banking and transit of oil and colored metals from the East have been the largest drivers of Latvia's economy since the Soviet collapse. Organizing the economy along financial lines, the country focused activity on extraction of existing wealth from the natural resource endowment of the former Soviet republics to the east. This created economic vulnerabilities, which produced social vulnerabilities, as social supports were sacrificed in order to maintain profits in a system possessing only truncated agricultural and manufacturing sectors. Bereft of meaningful political challenges either from within (labor movements) or from without (international socialism), a frictionless space for austerity policies was created that would later come to be heralded by transatlantic financial planners as the "Latvian Miracle" proving that neoliberalism and austerity work. This would take on greater resonance when a successful example of austerity was sought by international financial institutions and policymakers. As the world's economy had been organized around regimes of low taxation and the extension of credit to square the circle, following the 2008 crisis an example was desperately needed to demonstrate that austerity was the "tool" to "repair" the system. This took on greater salience as Greece's economic and social calamity unfolded with accelerating speed despite the "Troika"-demanded austerity policies promising to fix Greece's potholed economy by 2012. By 2015 Greece's economy was more riddled with broken pavement than ever. Germany, in particular, was the chief advocate for Latvian austerity as the decisive solution for repair of the European Union's failing economies.

The Great Transformation: The Anatomy of Austerity and Spatial Fixes to the Global Economy

Austerity policies have their roots in the economic slowdown that began with the decline of profits in the global economy of the late 1960s and 1970s. This manifested itself in a global crisis of capital accumulation by the 1970s that brought the great economic gains of the post–World War II period to an end (parts of East Asia excepted). The basic causes were too much industrial capacity (ability to make too much "stuff"), ever-increasing labor costs (both wages and benefits), anticolonial movements, and resource shocks (oil, etc.). The result would be a period of experimentation, planning, and opportunism in the coming decades seeking to restore profits and stability. This required rolling back the challenges to profits and reorganizing the global system away from one based on national economic development toward one centered on financialization and outsourcing production to low-cost labor countries and integrating their output into global production chains. Addressing the crisis also required expanding markets for multinational corporations and reducing commodity prices. Reorganizing the global economy required sophisticated offshore financial structures in order to evade national capital controls for tax avoidance. Opening up the Soviet bloc as a new terrain for export of West European consumer goods and the import of commodities and capital from the former Soviet space made important contributions to the restoration of global profits and economic growth in the 1990s (already underway in the 1980s) and after. Latvia would play a key role in this process of finding a spatial fix for capitalism.

With the emergence of Latvia's Second Republic following the collapse of the USSR in 1991, Latvia came to play a vital role in the system as an offshore banking center to oligarchs emerging from the breakup of the Soviet Union. During both tsarist and Soviet periods, Latvia was among the most advanced industrial areas in their respective domains. This was especially the case during the Soviet period when Riga lost its significance as an international port. From polymers for the Soviet space program to metallurgy, to electronics, computers, and software, Latvia was a leading industrial and technological center within the USSR. Riga was roughly at parity with Helsinki in terms of development and living standards until about 1970.[9] In the 1970s and 1980s, however, the gap in wealth between Riga and West European cities grew as the USSR declined. Meanwhile, more Latvians traveled abroad on business or cultural exchanges, which permitted them to see the higher living standards enjoyed by the middle classes of the NATO bloc nations. Thus, the increasing wealth of the West, the stagnation of the East, and the still recalled experiences of Stalinist terror and deportations both during World War II and immediately after, all combined to propel forward a movement for independence from the USSR by the mid-1980s. This structure was reflected in much of the developing world. Local industrial production not integrated into global circuits of capital represented markets and natural resources removed from the global economy. Moreover, these local elites saw their earning potential circumscribed by the ideology of really existing socialism. Capital needed these markets and material for its spatial fix. Meanwhile, the local elite wished to be liberated from the restraints that socialism placed on their capacity to amass wealth.

Latvian independence occurred during the twin—yet related—movements of neoliberalism and Russian rejection of communism. From the Soviet side, a cleavage by the 1970s was emerging between the Communist Party and the KGB. The latter increasingly saw the former as inept and wasteful of Russia's resources. Chekists came to view themselves as a meritocratic elite whose careers rose on talent. Meanwhile, they perceived the Communist Party as corrupt, lazy, and possessing a misguided ideology. Yuri Andropov was the first of their number to assume control of the country in November 1983. He intended to introduce significant economic reforms that would create ten economic zones in competition with each other.[10] But he was sick, and he died within fifteen months without realizing much of his agenda. Meanwhile, Gorbachev's reforms of the 1980s saw the economy and social order generally unwind at an accelerated pace. It was during the chaos of the mid to late 1980s that KGB views hardened against the Communist Party and its ideology.

Certain factions of the KGB responded to this turmoil by quietly assuming control over state assets. The methods employed would have tremendous import, as the neoliberal model was spreading and seeking to divert the natural resources of the Soviet Union from domestic use to global markets. Oil, gas, and metals would be thrown onto global markets in a "spatial fix" to the global crisis of accumulation.[11] Global commodity prices would be driven down from their 1970s peak and were sustained at low levels into the 1990s. This was complemented by what David Harvey termed "accumulation by dispossession," in which many assets were transferred to Western ownership.[12] This was matched by corrupt privatization efforts that enabled a process of primitive accumulation to occur. These processes, however, rarely led to capital formation and modernization of the Soviet bloc economies. Instead, they merely disposed the public from ownership of nature's land rent and transferred it to local oligarchs and foreign investors. This process in part fueled and sustained the economic boom of that decade and worked to suppress raw material prices whose rise in the 1970s had been a significant cause of the economic crisis from that decade.

The Soviet Union needed a trained cadre of KGB specialists who could tap into the world of offshore banking. While increasingly bureaucratized the Communist Party, through a combination of inertia and the need to maintain appearances of still being a revolutionary state, financially supported political left movements the world over. This required making recourse to offshore banking structures. Chekists came to view these financial transfers as wasting Russia's national patrimony. Rather simplistically they (Vladimir Putin was among their number) maintained that Russia could find renewal if shorn of the naïve ideological imperatives of the Communist Party.[13] From their perspective, what was needed was more an Augusto Pinochet Chilean-like realism and less ideology. Thus, in the chaos of the late 1980s Chekists who managed the state's overseas bank accounts simply privatized them.[14] These accounts provided part of the initial seed capital that was used for privatizing many of the assets of the dissolved Soviet Union in the early 1990s. This, in turn, set up the offshore financial structures used to enable the spatial fix and continued reorganization of the global system.

This restructuring of global economy along financialized lines created a special role for Latvia as a major offshore banking sector in the New Europe. The country would be recast as a two-way conduit, transferring the vast equity of natural resources and production of metals from Russia, Kazakhstan, Ukraine, et al. to global markets. It then took the cash paid for those resources and washed it back from the East to banks and equity markets in London and New York, thus fueling London and New York's gentrified rise in the 1990s.

But, it's not enough merely to theorize how neoliberalism works, bereft of concrete examples. What is needed are examples of the really existing transformation of the system. Already a site for illicit transfer of Soviet oil and metals to world markets before independence in 1991, Latvia became a major destination for oligarch hot money liberated by the opening of the Soviet bloc to global capital and the spatial fix of the world system. The Latvian port of Ventspils was the largest export terminal for Soviet oil, providing foreign exchange that was an embezzler's dream. Figures such as the notorious Grigori Luchansky of Latvia (later persona non grata in several countries) cut his chops in corruption as a provost at the University of Latvia. He was relieved of his duties in the early 1980s for selling off university furniture on the black market. Luchansky graduated from these humble beginnings to become a billionaire. His climb to riches began by his selling off Soviet oil secured at state cost and then sold to world markets at global prices. His company Nordex (later headquartered in Vienna) became one of the world's most notorious money-laundering operations.[15] Also involved were Americans such as Luchansky's partner, the late Marc Rich (later pardoned by Bill Clinton). The Latvian government signaled its intentions to defend this offshore banking sector at all costs (including imposing austerity on its people after the 2008 financial shock) when it bailed out Latvia's biggest offshore bank, Parex, at the cost of slashing social expenditures. European Commission (EC) and International Monetary Fund (IMF) authorities gave a massive foreign loan for Latvia, which in part enabled the government to function after bailing out Parex and thus its correspondent (offshore) accounts and continued payment of above-market interest rates to "favored" (read: "well connected") customers. Indeed, the decision to use EU and IMF bailout funds was meant to bail out banks as needed and to ensure that Latvia met balance of payment obligations (foreign debts). Joaquin Almunia, the European commissioner for economic and monetary affairs, explicitly stated in a letter dated January 26, 2009, to Ivars Godmanis, Latvia's prime minister, that the money was *not* to be used to "promote export industries" or "stimulate demand" in the economy.[16]

Latvia's largest domestic bank before the 2008 financial shock, Parex, captured in miniature the rags to riches stories of the new rich that emerged from the breakup of the USSR and thus merits a description of its origins, in order to divine the character of this new post-Soviet elite and the new political economy it enabled. The bank was owned by two enterprising former Komsomol (communist youth league) members, Viktor Krasovitsky and Valery Kargin. They began their enterprise in the late 1980s, carrying bags of cash by train to trade on the very small arbitrage that existed on the value of the Soviet ruble between Moscow and Riga. They were then granted the first private currency exchange license in the Soviet Union. In short order they built one of the chief offshore banks handling billions of dollars of offshore accounts of oligarchs throughout the former Soviet Union.[17] Eventually, Parex grew to have branches throughout much of Europe and even Japan; their accounts and ATM cards became a favorite for West African warlords wanting to deposit cash with no questions asked. Meanwhile, Latvia's bank-regulating agency, funded by the financial sector, took a "don't ask, don't tell" attitude toward this sector—and still chiefly do.

Although not in the same league as London, New York, and Zurich as a kleptocratic capital flight center, Latvia has carved out a substantial niche in the global money-laundering tax evasion system that facilitated the development and maintenance of the spatial fix to the long crisis of global capital accumulation. According to *Bloomberg*, "As non-European inflows into Cyprus stagnate, about $1.2 billion flooded into Latvia in the first half of the year [2012]. Nonresident deposits are now $10 billion, about half the total, regulators say, exceeding 43 percent in Switzerland, according to that nation's central bank."[18] These are large amounts, given that Latvia only has 1.88 million people and $28.2 billion annual GDP, one-fourth of Switzerland's population and roughly only one-tenth of its GDP. But these deposits represent only a small share of the cash Latvia handled in transit to points west (mostly New York in the 1990s and then London post-9/11) via offshore "companies" designed to evade oversight and taxation. It was this economy that Latvia's people were forced to bail out by their government, and austerity was the instrument used to effect that action.

Thus austerity was not only a means to restoring this small Baltic state's economy to macroeconomic "balance." Placed in a broader political economy context, austerity was also a centrally important factor in maintaining the spatial fix to the long economic crisis of global economy since the 1970s. As an offshore banking and offshore "companies" center, the country facilitated capital flight from the entire former USSR.

New Europe and Latvia's *Austeriat*

Latvia was at the epicenter of the global economic crisis when the financial shock hit in September 2008, because it was one of the most (neo) liberalized economies on the planet. It had one of the world's biggest real estate bubbles in the run-up to the crisis, and it suffered the world's most severe collapse in GDP following the 2008 financial shock. In the wake of the crisis the country also implemented one of the world's most aggressive austerity policies in response. In doing so, it received global acclaim from bankers, international financial institutions, policymakers, and opinion framers, which made Latvia a central focus of international attention. Latvia had only one-seventh of metropolitan Detroit's GDP in the runup to the 2008 crisis. Yet this small country's deployment of arguably the world's most punishing austerity regime came to capture the attention of the global financial press and policymakers, as the country, contra all other examples, proved that austerity policies work. Austerity was the needed—and effective—tonic for what ailed the European Union, if not the entire global economy.

Austerity advocates declared a victory by 2012 in Latvia's battle against the European economic crisis, advocating Latvia as the model for Greece, Spain, and other "less disciplined" Southern European states to emulate. These "austerians" celebrated Latvia as the plucky country that, through hard work and discipline, showed the way out of the financial crisis plaguing so many countries. For austerians, Latvia represented a veritable Protestant morality play for a global audience of policymakers and opinion makers demonstrating austerity's effectiveness. Neoliberals, smarting from the failures of financialization and free-market dogmas both in the lead-up to the 2008 economic crisis and in the solutions they tendered for curing it, hoped the Latvian example could retread Thatcher's frayed "there is no alternative" tires for a European-scale austerity tour. Few writing on the subject unfortunately had the time on the ground to evaluate the economic and social costs of the Latvian model. Thus, Latvia could serve global economic policymakers as a tabula rasa on which to impose their austerity success narrative. While the Latvian government chose austerity, contrary to these austerians' account, most of its people decidedly did not. Feeling there was no acceptable political alternative available to them, many elected to emigrate, thus exercising the ultimate show of no confidence via what Albert O. Hirschman termed "exit" in his classic treatise *Exit, Voice, and Loyalty: Responses to Decline in Firms, Organizations, and States* (1970).[19]

Following the 2008 financial shock, austerity policies were prescribed in several countries (such as England, Ireland, Greece, et al.) but with no favorable result. The rigid monetary and fiscal policy prescriptions of the EC and the European Central Bank (ECB) represented the victory of economic thought known as the "freshwater" school of economics that by the Reagan years had come to dominate the United States. These ideas arose in the universities of the Great Lakes states in the American Midwest, hence the freshwater moniker. The doctrine held that government spending during economic downturns made economic crises worse. In effect, this policy represented a rejection of Keynesian interventions to mitigate business cycle downturns.[20] The embrace of such thinking by economic policymakers marked the final act in a long drama begun with the opening scene of the Maastricht Treaty in 1992 to create the euro, which after 2008 saw the coup de grace delivered to much of Europe's Social Model as austerity policies were imposed in many parts of the European Union in order to achieve a monetary union. Coincidentally, in 1939, Friedrich von Hayek wrote of how the pestilence of Europe's "developed states" could be controlled through federalism. In what reads like a blueprint for the European Union and the Maastricht Treaty and Lisbon Agreements, von Hayek detailed how a liberalized set of fiscal and monetary policies could be imposed to restore a pre–World War I liberalized Belle Epoque to Europe, thus ridding it of the "pox" of state economic planning and social policy.

The 2008 crisis made more visible the longtime liberalizing trends of European capitalism dating back to the Maastricht Treaty, which created Europe's currency union. Europe had begun following the U.S. lead on economics and business organization in the 1970s.[21] Freshwater economic doctrine, ironically, was most prominent in those countries that previously had possessed among the strongest social democratic economic and social policies. This Americanization of economic policy in Northern Europe accelerated during the 1980s in Germany and much of Western Europe in the face of their high unemployment and lackluster economic growth. By comparison, the United States' relatively strong economic performance after the early 1980s looked attractive to European leaders. Viewed from the other side of the Atlantic, it appeared as if it was economic liberalization sui generis that drove the U.S. economic recovery of the 1980s and 1990s. Thus, by the time the 2008 economic crisis hit, much of the Northern European economics profession and public policy community had taken on a strongly neoliberal orientation in marked contrast to their previous policy recourse to Keynesian countercyclical spending during crises.

Spending cuts in much of the European Union following the 2008 crisis were not delivering economic recovery, however. This risked the legitimacy of austerity policies on ideological grounds, while threatening the project of a European unified currency zone. The euro could only survive under conditions of austerity during an economic crisis given the need for strict fiscal limits and inflation limits. Thus, it was with relief—not to mention desperation—that an austerity "success case" was found in the small EU country of Latvia. The EC and the IMF publicized this austerity story with a public event in Riga on June 5, 2012, that celebrated the Latvian model. The IMF head, Christine Lagarde, proclaimed that Latvia "could serve as an inspiration for European leaders grappling with the euro crisis."[22] The IMF's chief economist, Olivier Blanchard, followed with a mea culpa admitting initially he thought the Latvian currency peg to the euro and internal devaluation and austerity measures program a "disaster," but now he saw success. To better appreciate Blanchard's remarks one must bear in mind that Latvia is one of the few countries following the 2008 crisis that actually attacked the IMF from the right on economic and social policy for having gone soft on austerity. In effect, Blanchard and the IMF declared, "our policies were too cautious on austerity, long live austerity!" For the IMF it reprised a familiar chorus harking back to their greatest hits of the 1980s and 1990s glory days of structural adjustment and conditionality. By contrast, at the national level, David Moore (the IMF's resident representative to Latvia at the time) maintained a more measured view on the wisdom of Latvia's ultra-austerity program. By 2015 the IMF, including Ms. Lagarde, had returned to this critique of austerity, even if Germany stubbornly refused.

A seat at the table of power routinely flatters pundits invited to these affairs. They dutifully report, rather than investigate, what they are told. On Latvia, The Economist provided its customary solidly written, factually rich, yet analytically weak reporting that gets anything of importance wrong, while it rhapsodized over the Latvia Miracle. Meanwhile, big names on the financial press circuit such as Chrystia Freeland (now also Canadian member of parliament) embarrassingly (for anyone who might have bothered to query the hotel bartender or the taxidriver on the ground for their views on Latvia) alleged, "the harsh Latvian plan worked because the whole country was committed to it."[23] This is reminiscent of the Red Cross inspections of the Theresienstadt showcase concentration camp when international inspectors, shown the orchestras and clean conditions, announced, "Everything in order." Of course, Latvia is no concentration camp, its people are not fascists and Riga, its capital, is indeed among Europe's most beautiful and (if one has a bit of money) livable cities. But others with less resources report that the country feels like a prison. The reality is that there are several realities, depending on one's social class and income. To declare the "whole country" was "committed" to anything in this society deeply divided by class and ethnicity is, at best, lazy reporting and, at worst, irresponsible journalism complicit in the societal devastation.

Latvia was and is not a model of austerity for Greece or any other country to emulate. The impression that neoliberal policy has been a success for its economics is debatable, and the claim that a majority of Latvians supported it is demonstrably false. Latvia's solid economic growth is billed as success, since its economy contracted by 25 percent following the 2008 crash. Its unemployment during the crisis soared above 20 percent as the shutdown of foreign capital inflows (mainly Swedish mortgage loans to inflate its real estate bubble) threatened Latvia with deep current-account deficits. The country had to choose between devaluation of its then independent currency (Latvia finally adopted the euro in 2014) and maintaining its euro peg during the crisis. There were inherent problems with either choice, and the ideological and interest-based manner in which the choices were made was disturbing.

The Macroeconomics of Austerity and the Myth of Its Public Support

The economic crisis in Latvia presented the opportunity to test in real time a heretofore never implemented economic policy called *internal devaluation*. What previously was merely an academic debate regarding a proposed alternative to deal with economic crises was now about to be tried out on real people. Internal devaluation had never been used in modern times because it was known to create significant economic pain. The thinking was that no political party could survive the fallout from its implementation. In short, if a population in an electoral democracy could be shown to accept internal devaluation and austerity, then really existing capitalism would not be under threat.

The standard practice for dealing with economic crisis had been to use currency devaluations. When economies are revealed to be weak and uncompetitive, with imports exceeding exports, then standard economic theory counseled reducing the value of one's own currency relative to other nations. The advantages are that this reduces the power to purchase foreign goods by making them more expensive while making one's own goods cheaper for export. This increases exports and rebalances the economy. Internal devaluation, by contrast, proposed a writ large reduction in living standards by slashing wages. Rather than merely targeting imports, internal devaluation makes all goods and services more expensive by decreasing wages and government benefits. The means to achieve this would be massive cuts to public employee pay (roughly 30 percent in Latvia's case) and massive reductions in public expenditures. This in turn would squeeze private sector businesses and lead them to reduce wages.

Why would any country do this to its own people, and why would the experiment be of such interest to policymakers at a North Atlantic–wide level? One reason was in order to proceed toward euro accession—a policy eagerly embraced by Latvia's elite but with a majority of its people against it, as shown in the polls. Latvia's bid to join the euro was improved by maintaining macroeconomic stability and a stable currency peg to the euro. Second, Latvia's policymakers (the head of Central Bank and many others in government) had big mortgages denominated in euros and not in the Latvian currency. For example, the head of the Central Bank, Ilmars Rimsevics, had a 750,000-euro mortgage worth roughly $1 million USD at the time of the crisis.[24] His salary was paid in the local currency, the lat. Any devaluation of the Latvian currency would have resulted in an increase of his mortgage payment (in proportion to the amount by which the Latvian currency was devalued). Third, the measure was popular with many Latvians, given that people had lost their savings multiple times to devaluations and banking crises since the collapse of the USSR.

Yet what enabled Latvia to survive the crisis was not its austerity policies but, rather, EU and IMF bailouts (a "credit card" of sorts). Relatively low public sector debt (9 percent of gross domestic product at the start of the crisis) also provided some protection from bond traders tempted to attack its currency. Latvia's problem, in short, was not government debt but *private-sector debt*, chiefly mortgages that were often secured not only by the collateral of the property itself but also by the personal liability of entire families daisy-chained into the loans as joint signatories. Indeed, on nonperforming loans, borrowers were still responsible for debt-service payments even after a mortgage they could no longer pay resulted in their property being confiscated by the bank. Thus, borrowers who missed a few payments sometimes had their homes sold off by the banks but were still responsible for the full payment of the mortgage thereafter. The net effect of these policies was to create a neo-serfdom where borrowers were prevented from ditching their mortgaged underwater properties. If they pulled up stakes and left, they would not only lose their property but also see their extended family's co-signers consigned to debt penury as well. Banks (like Germany for the Greek nation) insisted on these stringent repayment regimes, which replicated in effect the very structures of serfdom from which Latvians thought they had escaped in the early nineteenth century.

For this, the Swedes thanked Latvia for taking on a Stockholm Syndrome view of the crisis, thus having it fall on the sword of austerity to protect Swedish banks from collapse and the Swedish government and people from financing massive banking bailout. In short, the poor (Latvians) were subsidizing the rich (Swedes) in a pattern that has again come to be all too common under twenty-first-century neoliberalism.

In the past decade Swedish banks took their largest profits from their Baltic operations in a kind of Viking reprise of their Baltic raids of centuries past. The opportunities for windfall profits were enormous. The Baltic capital of Tallinn had Europe's best preserved "old city." Meanwhile, the other Baltic capital of Riga had the greatest density of Art Nouveau buildings in Europe. For bankers this presented a veritable El Dorado. At independence from the Soviet period in 1991, these properties were free of any debt. This presented an opportunity for Swedish banks to load these properties down with mortgages and to extract massive profits from properties previously unburdened by any debt.[25] The global "carrying trade" of U.S. dollars at low interest rates fueled the Baltic (and global) property bubble. Created to sustain the U.S. economy following the 2001 recession, the policy was orchestrated by the chair of the U.S. Federal Reserve, Alan Greenspan, and represented a surge of cheap money onto global markets looking for investment outlets. Meanwhile, the Baltic states joined the European Union in May 2004. This availability of so much low-cost investment capital and confidence in the future of these new EU property markets combined to inflate one of the world's largest property bubbles. Indeed, at its peak, the per square meter price of property in the once remote corner of the USSR seaside community of Jurmala equaled prices in Monaco. Trained to believe that the market prices assets correctly, few questioned the meteoric rise of property prices, which should have been recognized as being well in excess of any underlying economic fundamentals.[26] The coming real estate crash was inevitable, and the collapse of U.S. finance in September 2008 hit Latvia hard. As in much of the rest of the world but worse in Latvia, asset inflation (property bubbles, etc.) became a sink draining wealth that once went to workers and the middle class during the embedded liberalism of the post–World War II period. The highly volatile nature of these asset price spikes (manias) and bailouts has made for a capitalism prone to crises of growing intensity and frequency that threaten its very existence, as the late Hyman Minsky predicted it would in his classic *Stabilizing an Unstable Economy*. Nowhere was this more evident than in Latvia.

By November 2008 a run on deposits ensued at Parex bank and threatened to destroy not only Latvia's banking sector but Sweden's as well (a run on deposits was forming at Sweden's SEB bank in Latvia). Had this wound not been cauterized by a massive public bailout of Parex, Swedish banks in Latvia could have collapsed—with Scandinavian, if not Europe-wide, implications for which the Swedish taxpayer likely would have been on the hook. To be fair, the Latvians expected this gratitude to be returned by both euro accession in 2014 and continued Swedish liquidity supplied to the Latvian economy. This was done in due course, but whether either of these was good for Latvia is contestable. Thus, in the wake of the short twentieth century's collapse we saw the USSR's previously indentured populations under tsarist serfdom returned to subservience as the Baltic states were opened to Scandinavian financial exploitation.

While Latvia's people might formally own title to their land, for many this was rendered merely a simulacrum by their de facto landownership, because foreign banks not only owned the mortgages but, as previously mentioned, also held claims on the property of entire families as co-signatories to property.

What of the contention that Latvia's people supported austerity as necessary, if distasteful, and replicable as a model for saving financialized capitalism? Since the implementation of austerity, Latvia's parliament has polled approval ratings in the single or low double digits, yet the government has survived two elections. How is one to read this? Chiefly by ethnic politics. Harmony Center, a party with little harmony and no center, was the biggest party opposing the austerity model. The party (as with most in Latvia) had its quota of grabbers and neoliberals, albeit with a minority of sincere reformers. The party largely represents ethnic Russians and had no chance of winning, given its focus on rights for Russian speakers in a country where nearly every ethnic Latvian family had at least one relative sent to Siberia during the Stalin-era deportations. Other powerful parties were run by post-Soviet oligarchs. They were rightly seen as being in league with Russian interests. So the only political force with relatively clean hands (largely as a consequence of having been out of power) were the austerians. Most voters disliked their economic policy but were convinced they were best able to resist Russia's embrace. For many Latvian voters, economic issues came in a distant second to fear of Russia. Thus it was that a program of internal devaluation and austerity could be sustained in an electoral democracy. In sum, Latvia represents both one of the clearest examples of Donald Rumsfeld's vision for a "New Europe," which is really a return to a Europe of the nineteenth century. Latvia's post-Soviet neoliberal character was crafted by global processes at work in the global political economy during its post-1970s restructuring, yet its economic and political "solution" to the crisis was made possible only by very local and historically specific conditions not reproducible in most electoral democracies.

That said, contra claims of its hagiographers, Latvians strongly protested austerity. On January 13, 2009, in the dead of winter, ten thousand in Riga protested against austerity and corruption (I was there). Teachers, nurses, and farmers held demonstrations in the months following. The national police were called in to suppress protests over the closure of a hospital in Bauska, because authorities feared that the local police might not do what was "required." Police detained one economist for two days for his critical remarks on the economy, meanwhile there is evidence that a foreign economist in Riga critical of Latvian economic policy had his phone tapped. Latvia is by no means a police state, but neither is it innocent in matters of controlling public opinion either.

Latvia's policymakers in the main are neither saints nor sadists. Indeed, some policymakers genuinely cared about the country's future. Their then prime minister (and now European commissioner for the euro) who led the austerity charge, Valdis Dombrovksis, was by all accounts a comparative paragon of integrity—although, even here there existed a conflict of interest given that his spouse ran a property development company that would be adversely impacted by a currency devaluation. Dombrovskis came under the policy counsel of the Swedish economist and consultant Anders Aslund, who sought to salvage his place in history as one of the chief counselors to the failed shock therapy program in Boris Yeltsin's Russia. A policy victory for austerity in Latvia could clean the slate and rehabilitate his role in history, not to mention leading to lucrative policy contracts.

Too many of Latvia's policy elites, however, take a view of the poor that comes straight from the pages of Ayn Rand's *Atlas Shrugged*. This is especially true of Central Bank, which has dominated economic policy management since Latvia's independence in 1991. For Latvia's policymakers, the internal devaluation and austerity program became something of a vanity project. Coming of age during the 1980s when the USSR was crumbling and the U.S. neoliberal model was ascendant, policymakers fully internalized market fundamentalism as a rigid dogma counterposed to Soviet ideology. To see their austerity model heralded by the IMF and ECB was like a vindication of their worldview and a repudiation of the putdowns heaped on them by chauvinistic occupiers in the past.

While the 30 percent of the population who held mortgages were less free to exit the country, after the protests against austerity subsided, many Latvians resigned themselves to the country's austerity policies and left. Demographers estimate that two hundred thousand Latvians (roughly 10 percent of the population) have left Latvia in the past decade.[27] Moreover, birthrates declined from already low numbers. Thus, the austerity model could not be reproduced in most sizable countries as it would result in perhaps millions of emigrants with no country large enough to absorb them.

Why did so many leave Latvia if austerity were the economic success its advocates claim? Latvia experienced its full effects. Birthrates plummeted during the crisis, as is the case almost everywhere austerity programs are imposed. Latvia continues to have among Europe's highest rates of suicide, road deaths, and alcoholism. Violent crime was high, arguably because of prolonged unemployment and police budget cuts. Moreover, a soaring brain drain moves in tandem with blue-collar emigration, but this is lessening as the worst of the crisis has ended. In short, society itself is collapsing under the weight of the austerity policy.

The moral for Europeans is that the austerity model can work in highly circumscribed situations. A country has to be small enough (only a few million people) for other nations to absorb any émigrés seeking employment abroad. Such a country should be willing to have its population decline dramatically, especially its prime working-age cohort. In Greece, this could only worsen an already serious demographic challenge. Politically, it helps for the country to be a post-Soviet economy with a fully flexible, poorly unionized labor force. Above all, its cultural and policy elite needs to put an almost blind faith in "free market" central planners. The country must also have serious ethnic divisions that can distract voters from complaints against austerity. It's difficult to imagine how austerity on this magnitude could be sustained without all the above factors in play.

On balance, the Latvian model has done much harm. Demographically, in terms of its future, one can even argue that the country is being euthanized. That this point is even debatable hints at the huge costs and risks the country has undertaken with its neoliberal program since 1991 and deepening austerity following 2008. To be fair, one must also give the Latvian government their due. After the calamitous crash following 2008, their economy eventually returned to growth. Yet, much Latvian growth was linked to unsustainable clear-cutting of timber to satisfy West European demand. Other sectors grew too, such as food exports—as global grain prices were high between 2007 and 2013 and even now after some slight decline are still well above pre-2007 levels. There was also some rebound of the country's small manufacturing sector. Transit and the emergence of a new Silk Road are other growth areas. And, last of all, there was the revival of offshore banking and the servicing of "mailbox" companies for tax evasion.

One must also note that Latvia's options were restricted by the limitations imposed by Article 123 of the EU Lisbon Treaty. This removes currency autonomy and public credit creation for national development, thus transforming capitalism in Europe into a system guaranteeing private rent collection for banks. The treaty locks countries like Latvia into an embrace of private credit markets that forces governments to pay rents to bankers rather than financing their own development where possible. Regressive tax policies that place Latvia's tax burden on labor rather than on capital additionally hold production back more than anything. This makes the tax portion of labor's cost more expensive and prevents advantages that could accrue from lower labor costs without reducing labor's wages. Meanwhile, speculators get a free ride on taxes as labor picks up the tax bill.

Latvia's growth, however, is tenuous. It is exceptionally dependent on a rogue financial offshore industry that destroys wealth in other countries. Production is also disproportionately geared to exports, even for a small country. Thus, victory laps on recovery—let alone advocacy for others to follow the Latvian path—are premature at best and reckless at worst, given the social costs of austerity.

Austerity's Social Balance Sheet

Neoliberal reforms since independence failed to develop Latvia's post-Soviet economy. Following the 2008 economic crisis, implementation of austerity policies amplified the trend toward social decay and demographic devastation that has been characteristic of many post-Soviet countries. On the score of demography, Latvia suffered extensive population loss since freeing itself from Soviet rule. It could ill afford the departure of some 10 percent of its population, which left during the past decade, on top of the many who left in previous years. Many social indicators suggest neoliberal and austerity policies have damaged Latvian society, perhaps irrevocably.

One of the chief reasons given by Latvian nationalists for pursuing independence from the USSR was to defend against cultural entropy and against assimilation into Russia, or in short, to defend the nation. The Soviets permitted significant migration of peoples from other republics into Latvia, thus reducing the percentage of ethnic Latvians in its territory. This made Russian a lingua franca that over time was slowly displacing the Latvian language.

Nevertheless, despite the long-term threats to Latvian culture, the Soviets constructed an infrastructure that promoted family life generally. National cultures, such as Latvian, were supported by the government at generous levels, even if in everyday usage the Russian language was dominant. Family life was supported in many ways. A vast kindergarten infrastructure was put in place (now in short supply in the post-Soviet period) and more childcare was made possible by women who could retire early, at fifty-five, thus leaving grandmothers available for this service. The burden of childcare was largely upheld by women, and in the post-Soviet period of neoliberal and austerity policies, women still maintain the burden of childcare. Yet, without recourse to as many kindergartens or grandmothers on paid pension, there are far fewer resources supporting families today than under the previous regime. The result has been added strains on families, especially on women, and the reduction of live births by those who simply don't think it practical to support children.

Live births declined precipitously after the 2008 economic crash. Children conceived in 2007 before the "Baltic Tiger" economic boom went bust stood at 24,397. By 2011 annual births had dramatically fallen to 18,825, thus placing the very future of the country at risk.[28] Meanwhile, there were 27,045 long-term emigrants from Latvia at the start of the crisis in 2008. By 2010, two years of austerity policies contributed to 39,651 long-term emigrants departing.[29] Those leaving are likely to take their full families with them, thus making return migration less likely. It's not just low wages that are driving emigration but also uncertainty and unhappiness with work conditions. These sentiments are even more pronounced among university graduates, with all the implications this brings for the country's cultural, economic, and social health.

Latvian rates of reproduction (including for ethnic Latvians) in the Soviet Union were at replacement levels, if not slightly growing. Indeed, Latvia had 40,000 births in 1985 (during the Soviet period). This plummeted to 19,000 ten years later, after independence, and never climbed above 24,000, even at the height of the recent credit-fueled economic boom of the last decade.[30] To place these figures in further relief, while Latvian women were having just over 2.00 children in 1985 (again, replacement rates), this dropped to 1.12 children in 1998, and even during the economic boom years right before 2008 it never surpassed 1.40.[31] The problem of low birthrates is not just a post-Soviet one—although it is generally worse in countries that emerged from that system. While largely a European (perhaps France excepted) and East Asian challenge, the exceptionally small populations of the Baltic states make cultural extinction a real threat in this low-birthrate environment.

Inequality is another important marker of societal health, and on this score Latvia has the worst record in the European Union, with a current GINI coefficient of 35.2 and growing.[32] At roughly U.S. rates of inequality, this might not appear too bad, but the real rate is much bigger given that much of Latvia's economy is "off the books" and designed to under-report income for tax avoidance. Indeed, some economists argue that alternative metrics better capture Latvia's true income and suggests inequality at world-high Sub-Saharan African levels.[33] Self-perceptions of status, particularly marked with high inequality, create neurosis and stress among its people.[34]

Mental health has suffered under conditions of economic insecurity. Reported mental disorders increased with the 2008 crisis. Mental health disorders were at 274.8 per 100,000 in 2003. They dropped to 229.2 by 2007 when easy credit and property prices peaked. After the crash they were up to 335.6 by 2011. The high stress brought on by austerity not only broke people's mental health but then provided much less infrastructure for treating the victims.

Suicide rates have also been high. In 2011 Latvia had the third highest suicide rate in the twenty-eight member European Union. Men are killing themselves at roughly 400 percent over the rate women are, largely a consequence of men not having a place in the deindustrialized economy of this post-Soviet state. Yet, suicide rates are down from the punishing levels of the mid-1990s when factories shut down en masse. The situation is still bad, however. The number of suicides dramatically rose with austerity after 2008 in the fashion of the U.S. Great Depression "Black October" in 1929, when many Americans committed suicide.[35] Moreover, Latvians have also committed suicide once they have reached their emigration destinations. In fact, in 2009, 60 percent of Latvian deaths in the United Kingdom were from suicide.[36]

Poverty has risen since the crisis and its accompanying austerity budgets. At the trough of the crisis, Latvia's poor were living on less than 215 euros a month (and one must bear in mind that food and fuel are more expensive in Latvia than in the United States). Moreover, 5 percent of its population was living on less than 65 euros a month in a kind of gardening and gathering existence outside the modern economy of the European Union.[37]

By 2011 a massively high 40.1 percent of Latvia's population was at risk of poverty.[38] Meanwhile those deemed in "severe material deprivation" were nearly one-third of the population at 31 percent in 2011, which was 300 percent above the figure for Greece. These numbers reflect the high unemployment and much vaunted internal devaluation wage reductions that EU policymakers breathlessly described as a "success."

Social infrastructure was savagely hit. Austerity's defenders argued that Latvia had too much redundancy in its educational and health systems.[39] This was partly true, but it also provided cover for gutting social budgets. On the one hand, neoliberal policies during the past twenty-two years have driven a demographic exodus and a curtailing of birthrates that contributed to shrinking the country's population by roughly one-third. Deploying cuts to deal with "redundancies" risks sounding a bit too much like Joseph Stalin's maxim "No people, no problem."[40] While fewer people may indeed suggest to some the need for reductions in social infrastructure, others might counsel it means the need for more. For example, state kindergartens are in exceedingly short supply. If one takes the position that pursuing balanced budgets is the end in itself, the former interpretation on the need for social infrastructure may be persuasive. However, if promoting sustainable population levels is the desired goal, then one might come down on the latter opinion that better social infrastructure is needed. Even on purely economic grounds the investment in social infrastructure makes sense if only to produce the next generation of taxpayers.

In short, austerity in Latvia may have repaired the country's macroeconomic balance sheet, but the social costs have been exorbitant—so high, in fact, that the viability of this nation is now open to question. Are the working and middle classes under neoliberalism being asked to sacrifice the economic and social gains made over the past century in favor of precarity in order to "save" capitalism or, to use an old military metaphor from a lost war, "to destroy the village in order to save it"? Capitalism has reached a stage where it must sacrifice society to save the economy, yet without the ability to reproduce society, one wonders how the economy will be preserved.

Germany is pinning its hopes on salvaging the euro project and capitalism generally by exporting the Latvian model. But has it worked in Latvia? Has it delivered economic recovery in the highly specific conditions of its own country? It's too early to tell. What is possible to say, however, is that even if austerity works in Latvia the price paid might be seen in too few people to sustain the country into the future. Writ large onto Europe, the continent's survivability is also in question. A wholesale reorganization of EU rules facilitating national development—to liberate its member states from usurious ties to European banks currently delivering its people into penury—would appear to be the only salvation, yet the inability of Syriza in Greece to take that first step in the summer of 2015 suggests no clear way forward.

Thatcher remarked that there was no such thing as society and then pursuant to that statement undertook policies assuring that her assertion would reflect reality. The vision of a privatized economy taking little heed of social concerns came to find its greatest resonance in the post-Soviet Baltic states. Latvia's experiment in austerity returned this small nation to visibility on the international stage as much of the world looked to reconcile neoliberal economic policies of recent decades with the economic crisis those policies produced. The solution selected to defend that order was austerity. Rather than appearing out of nowhere, neoliberalism and austerity took root in the soil of a changing global political economy in which several seemingly discrete interests came into alignment. Represented on one hand was the usual complement of new post-Soviet leaders "always ready" with their rote recitation of economic catechisms emanating from the American Midwest freshwater school of economics.[41] Also on hand were oligarchs from the East who in reality formed a mosaic of seemingly disparate factions for a kind of contemporary Molotov/Ribbentrop Pact. Western bankers, neoliberal economists and policymakers, along with former Chekists and Komsomol members now turned oligarchs, congealed into a de facto alliance. In short, neoliberalism did not produce enlightened, fair market economies but, instead, kleptocracies with increasing inequality.

Abba Eban remarked, "nations always do the right thing after exhausting all other options." After the economic crisis of 2008 laid bare the contradictions of neoliberalism, many supposed there would be a policy correction in capitalism toward more society-sustaining economies. The implementation of austerity despite the failures of neoliberalism leads one to question Eban's assertion. In the main, those earlier bad choices were doubled down on after 2008, and among the casualties is Europe's Social Model, which formed the basis for the relatively humane societies constructed in Europe's social democracies following World War II. With the fall of the Soviet bloc, history seems to be resetting itself—not to a liberalism that "evolved" into free societies but back to the economic and social patterns of the massive inequality that existed prior to 1917.

Meanwhile Germany—the new Romans—have placed Greece on the cross to pay for the sins of a liberalized capitalist system. Has neoliberalism met its end? From the vantage point of 2015, solutions are not visible. The rollback of wages and social benefits in the 1980s in response to the crises (economic, political, and social of 1968 through the 1970s) could not be squared with the need to consume the goods our economies produce. Supply-side economics dictated that capital liberated by wage/benefit repression would be channeled into investment, thus creating the new "supply" of goods. Said investment never occurred in the world's richest countries on the scale predicted. Instead, capital found its way into speculative financial instruments and real estate. Yet productive capacity remained. Globalization's addition of hundreds of millions of laborers into the global system did create more supply of goods, but access to this very reserve army of labor (factor accumulation) worked to slow productivity. Removing upward wage pressures undermined incentives to accelerate labor-saving technologies. How to consume the glut of new production from global expansion to the market? The answer in the 1970s and 1980s was a cycle of government debt followed by its withdrawal when debts became large. But lowering government debt restored the demand problem. This was cured by the extension of personal credit, which could not go on indefinitely because debts ultimately must be either paid or defaulted on.

Offshore centers like Latvia played key roles in repairing the economic crisis of the 1970s. They provided the financial and transit infrastructure essential for the spatial fix of expanded geographic access to natural resources. Latvia's role as savior of capitalism appeared to be reprised with the "success" of its internal devaluation/austerity cure following the 2008 economic crisis, but if the Latvian "cure" is applied to the global economic crisis, then in effect it would mean the end of capitalism. Internal devaluation and austerity can restore to modest economic growth a poor country with richer neighbors bordering it, but the potential for economic growth is limited both by the lack of demand in the economy to consume imported goods and also by the generation of domestic economic activity. Latvia and Greece—for which Latvia is often held up as an example to emulate—are the proverbial apples and oranges. Latvia entered the 2008 crisis with only a 9 percent government debt to GDP ratio (this ultra-low level because it inherited zero debt from the Soviet period). Its credit crisis was almost entirely in the private sector. By contrast, Greece's large public debt resulted from the above-described dynamic of making recourse to public debts in order to address the economic crises beginning in the 1970s. Greece never managed to push public debts back down, and it couldn't, given their large size.

Capitalism for the past five hundred years has expanded through the twin drivers of spatial fixes and technological innovation. Spatial fixes have run their course, given the environmental constraints of the planet. Thus, both technological innovations *and a means to distribute their benefits* are necessary for continued economic sustainability and growth. Yet the very ability to produce these innovations is undermined by the trend toward austerity. The Latvian example of austerity is one marked by equally high levels of inequality and precarity. The model has more in common structurally with serfdom than with the dynamism once possessed by capitalism. Latvia is indeed leading the way to a New Europe, but to a Europe that represents patterns of inequality and economic structures that are in fact archaic. Referencing Europe's Dickensian past, Latvia may prove to be a "ghost of Christmas future," a warning for what lies ahead unless Europe changes course.

Notes

1   Brian Blackstone, Matthew Karnitschnig, and Robert Thomson, "Europe's Banker Talks Tough; Draghi Says Continent's Social Model Is 'Gone,' Won't Backtrack on Austerity," *Wall Street Journal*, February 24, 2012, at http://www.wsj.com/articles/SB10001424052970203960804577241221244896782/.

2   John Gray, *False Dawn: The Delusions of Global Capitalism* (New York: W. W. Norton, 1998).

3   Francis Fukuyama, "The End of History?" *The National Interest* 16 (1989): 3–18.

4   Karl Polanyi, *The Great Transformation* (Boston: Beacon Press, 1985).

5   Mark Blyth, *Austerity: The History of a Dangerous Idea* (Oxford: Oxford University Press, 2013); Thomas Piketty, *Capital in the Twenty-First Century* (Cambridge, MA: Belknap Press, 2014).

6   Guy Standing, "The Precariat: From Denizens to Citizens?" *Polity* 44 (2012): 588–608.

7 A. Juskka, Jeffrey Sommers, and Charles Woolfson, eds., *The Contradictions of Austerity: The Socio-Economic Costs of the Neoliberal Baltic Model* (London: Routledge, 2014).

8 Adam Smith, *An Inquiry into the Nature and Causes of the Wealth of Nations* (Hazelton: Pennsylvania State University Electronic Classic Series, 2005).

9 Incidentally, this was roughly when North and South Korea were still at developmental parity.

10 D. Karcev, "Plan Andropov-Putin," *Expert* 1 (Nov. 2012), accessible at expert.ru/russian_reporter/2012/43/plan-andropovaputina/.

11 Oil and gas were already exported in large quantities under Soviet rule, but the collapse of the USSR permitted the export of more metals. Less domestic use of oil made up for some of the declining Russian oil production in the 1990s.

12 David Harvey, *The New Imperialism* (Oxford: Oxford University Press, 2005).

13 Tom Parfitt, "Gleb Pavlovsky: Putin's World Outlook," *New Left Review* 88 (2014): 55–66.

14 Karen Dawisha, *Putin's Kleptocracy: Who Owns Russia?* Kindle eBook (New York: Simon and Schuster, 2014), 285–295.

15 "Who Is Leonid Wolf and What Is behind Government Action?" *Kyiv Post*, July 1, 1991, at kyivpost.com/content/ukraine/who-is-leonid-wolf-and-what-is-behind-government-a-356.html.

16 Joaquin Almunia, "B-1049 D(08)30 to Latvia's Prime Minister and Finance Minister," January, 21 2009.

17 Anatol Lieven, *The Baltic Revolution* (New Haven: Yale University Press, 1993).

18 Aaron Eglitis, "Swiss-Style Latvian Banking Hub Thrives on Ex-Soviet Cash," *Bloomberg*, August 29, 2012, at http://www.bloomberg.com/news/articles/2012-08-29/swiss-style-latvian-banking-hub-thrives-on-ex-soviet-cash-flood/.

19 A. Hirschman, *Exit, Voice, and Loyalty: Responses to Decline in Firms, Organizations, and States* (Cambridge, MA: Harvard University Press, 1970).

20 Paul Krugman, *End This Depression Now!* (New York: W. W. Norton, 2012), 101–110.

21 Leo Panitch and Sam Gindin, *The Making of Global Capital: The Political Economy of American Empire* (London: Verso Books, 2012).

22 Gary Peach, "IMF Chief Praises Latvia for Handling Crisis," *Businessweek*, June 5, 2012.

23 Chrystia Freeland, "The Euro Zone, Slow-Motion Crashes and Latvia," *Reuters*, June 5, 2012, at http://in.reuters.com/article/2012/06/07/column-freeland-idINL1E8H7ARR20120607/.

24 Lato Lapsa, "Algas samazinājums Rimšēvičam draud ar personiskās maksātspējas problēmām," *Pietiek*, November 14, 2010, at http://www.pietiek.com/raksti/algas_samazinajums_rimsevicam_draud_ar_personiskas_maksatspejas_problemam/.

25 Michael Hudson, "Stockholm Syndrome in the Baltics: Latvia's Neoliberal War against Labor and Industry," in *The Contradictions of Austerity*, ed. Jeffrey Sommers and Charles Wolfson (London: Routledge, 2014).

26 Indeed, while I was at the Japanese embassy in Latvia in June 2006 I met the head of the real estate division of the largest Swedish bank in Latvia. Asked why

they continued making real estate loans when it was clear a property bubble was in place, she responded by suggesting I was naïve in assuming that the ability to service loans was the chief consideration for making them. Instead, she informed me, it was simply a matter of getting bonuses in the present for making loans. Long-term loan performance simply was not a consideration.

27 Mihails Hazans, "Recent Trends and Economic Impact of Emigration from Latvia," presentation at OECD/MFA Conference, Riga, December 17, 2012, OECD Publishing (2013), 65–110, available at doi: 10.1787/9789264204928-en/.

28 Central Statistical Bureau of Latvia, "People," (2014), accessible at data.csb.gov.lv/.

29 Central Statistical Bureau of Latvia, "Current International Migrants—Gender and Age" (2014), accessible at data.csb.gov.lv/.

30 Central Statistical Bureau of Latvia, "Population," (2014), accessible at data.csb.gov.lv/.

31 Eurostat, "Demographics," (2014), accessible at epp.eurostat.ec.europa.eu/.

32 United States Central Intelligence Agency, "Latvia," *World Factbook* (2014), accessible at https://www.cia.gov/library/publications/the-world-factbook/geos/lg.html.

33 Vyacheslav Dombrovsky, Konstantin A. Kholodilin, and Boriss Siliverstovs, "Using Personal Car Register for Measuring Economic Inequality in Countries with a Large Share of Shadow Economy: Evidence for Latvia," *The Review of Income and Wealth* 60, no. 4 (2014): 948–966.

34 S. Loughnan et al., "Economic Equality Is Linked to Biased Self-Perception," *Psychological Science* 22, no. 10 (2011): 1254–1258.

35 Disease Prevention and Control Center Latvia, *Mental Health Report 2011*, accessible at spkc.gov.lv/.

36 Center of Health Economics Latvia, *Mental Health Report 2008*, accessible at vec.gov.lv/.

37 Kristina Rizga, "The Invisible Side of Latvia's 'Success' Story: Life with God's mercy and the Goodness of Others," *Re:Baltica*, October 17, 2012, accessible at rebaltica.lv/en/.

38 Eurostat, "At Risk of Poverty or Social Exclusion in the EU27," December 3, 2012, accessible at ec.europa.eu/eurostat/.

39 Anders Aslund and Mark Weisbrot, "Latvia's Recession and Recovery: Are There Lessons for the Eurozone?" Center for Economic Policy Research Online video clip, April 11, 2012, accessible at https://www.youtube.com/watch?v=g6reqmmzWIE/.

40 It has been argued that this Stalin quote is apocryphal.

41 The quote is the motto of the Communist Young Pioneers.

Part II

Media/Art

5

Austerity Media

PATRICE PETRO

Scholars across a range of disciplines have discussed and debated the impact of austerity measures on contemporary politics and culture. What I call "austerity media" comprises a central and popular but under recognized aspect of this contemporary economic condition. As Diane Negra and Yvonne Tasker point out in their recent collection of essays on gender, media, and recessionary culture, "While fields ranging from economics to sociology to equality studies have much to contribute in analyzing the recession's social character, media studies offers a unique disciplinary pathway for interpreting recession culture given its focus on the analysis of collective symbolic environments that hold enormous sway in shaping public views."[1] Austerity media texts reveal that we have too much information, but no ability to process it; too much stuff, and nowhere to store it; too much feeling, and no way to express it. Moreover, this state of affairs is pathologized and gendered as female or feminine, despite the reality of the real hoarders in our midst (the banking industry and corporations) and the very real poverty among men and women and families after 2008.

There are four main areas of focus for the following analysis. First, I begin by offering definitions of "austerity" and "austerity media" in both reality and fictional television programming. Second, I turn to representations of women and housing in austerity media texts, with a focus on two very similar serialized reality shows on hoarding: A&E's *Hoarders* and TLC's *Hoarding: Buried Alive*. I compare these hoarding shows with Todd

Haynes's ambitious 2011 HBO miniseries *Mildred Pierce*, starring Kate Winslet, which recalls the 1945 Hollywood classic starring Joan Crawford but also attempts a more faithful adaptation of the James M. Cain novel published in 1941, on which the 1945 film was loosely based. Third, I revise and update Mary Ann Doane's classic 1984 essay "The 'Woman's Film': Possession and Address" in the context of austerity media and austerity measures. Here, my aim is not simply to show the ways in which media today is neither simply "possessed" nor "addressed" to women but, rather, how "possessions" and "addresses"—things and stuff, real estate transactions and concepts of home—have recast notions of space and the uncanny, medical discourses and ways of seeing, and economies of subjectivity. Finally, I conclude by speculating on the contemporary status of what Doane identified decades ago as "the medical gaze." What we see in both hoarding shows and recent fictions about housing crises are pathologies surrounding accumulation: information-processing deficits; dysfunctional beliefs about, and exaggerated attachments to, possessions; and difficulties with separation and organization. As a result of the crisis in the housing market and the resurgence of homelessness (a homelessness at once existential and material, generated by the unequal distribution of wealth), what we are witnessing is a collapse of distinctions between subject and object but also of distinctions between mental illness, depression, hoarding, and excessive accumulation.

Austerity and Austerity Narratives

So, to begin, I offer a definition of austerity. As economist Mark Blyth explains in his recent book *Austerity: The History of a Dangerous Idea*, "Austerity is a form of voluntary deflation in which the economy adjusts through the reduction of wages, prices, and public spending to restore competitiveness." Over the past five years and more, proponents of austerity policies in Europe and the United States have succeeded in characterizing government spending as being reckless wastefulness that has worsened the countries' respective economies. They have argued that we have all lived beyond our means and now need to "tighten our belts." According to Blyth, this view conveniently forgets where the debt originated from: it is not from an orgy of government spending but, rather, the direct result of bailing out, recapitalizing, and adding liquidity to the broken banking system. He explains:

> As the Occupy movement highlighted in 2011, the wealth and income distributions of societies rocked by the financial crisis have become, over the past thirty years, extremely skewed. The bursting of the

credit bubble has made this all too clear. In the United States, for example, the top 1 percent of the U.S. income distribution now has a quarter of the country's income. Or, to put it more dramatically, the richest 400 Americans own more assets than the bottom 150 million, while 46 million Americans, some 15 percent of the population, live in a family of four earning less than $22,314 per annum.

Blyth argues that the global economic crisis began with banks and was solely their responsibility, but it quickly became a sovereign problem inasmuch as the sovereign states that hosted the banks saw a very dire and real risk of upheaval and violent rebellion if these banks were allowed to fail. As a result, instead of making banks pay for the crisis they created, private citizens were made to foot the bill. This is how a sovereign problem became a civilian problem; states decreased wages and spending, siding with the banks to avoid social upheaval. As Blyth puts it, "Austerity is not just the price of saving the banks. It is the price that the banks want someone else to pay."[2]

So what do austerity practices and policies have to do with media? "Austerity media" seems almost an oxymoron; commercial media tends *toward* consumption, while austerity is all about cutting back on consumption and debt. As Laurie Ouellette and James Hay have argued in their book *Better Living through Reality TV*, in our current era of privatization and self-responsibility, television is now more intensely aligned with the rationalities of deregulation and welfare reform. As a result television, especially in the United States, is not required to do much more than maximize profit. Reality television in particular, they argue, advances "a reasoning about governing by teaching individuals to take responsibility for a range of lurking risks, from bankruptcy to weather emergencies. Whether or not society has become riskier—and many would dispute this assumption—we are now offered a whole barrage of technical resources for managing our own personal, physical, household, and 'homeland' security."[3] While these shows ostensibly aim to empower their viewers to achieve domestic proficiency, they also intervene in social and psychological hurdles "from poor self-esteem to 'compulsive shopping,' a recurring diagnosis across the intervention format that exists in perpetual tension with reality TV's commercialism." Ouellette and Hay cite an episode of *Clean House* (an earlier reality home makeover and interior design television show originally broadcast in 2003 and now no longer on the air) as an example. The hosts "aimed at helping a single mother who turned to shopping to 'fill a void in her life was encouraged to recognize her 'problem' and learn a rational and controlled approach to consumption at the same time she was acquiring new products to transform her overcrowded and chaotic home into a functioning environment for herself and her child."[4]

To be sure, there is an array of reality television programming that addresses both austere and excessive consumption. *American Pickers* on the History Channel, *Extreme Cheapskates* and *Extreme Couponing* on TLC, and *Storage Wars* on A&E are a few such examples. This last series, which began airing in 2010, follows professional buyers at public auctions who take advantage of purchasing storage lockers that have been repossessed by the storage company, when their renters miss payments for more than three months. These shows obviously reflect larger shifts in US culture. As psychologists Gail Steketee and Randy Frost explain:

> There are twice as many shopping centers in the United States as there are high schools. . . . More than a hundred professional journals are devoted to the science of marketing and selling consumer goods. The success of this marketing has been remarkable. Increasing numbers of rental self-storage units cater to an apparently insatiable appetite for stuff. Forty years ago, facilities for storing unused personal possessions were virtually non-existent. Now, nearly two billion square feet of space can be rented for storage in more than forty-five thousand facilities, and most of that space is already full. . . . Alongside this growing appetite for rented storage space, the average house size has increased by 60 percent since 1970—although this trend may be changing since the real estate crash of 2008. Many of these oversized homes, often referred to as "McMansions" also come with their own storage sheds.

"Perhaps," they conclude, "we are becoming a nation of hoarders."[5]

Indeed it is fascinating to trace how reality television focused on housing and real estate has changed since the 2008 financial crisis. Prior to 2008, shows like *Flip This House* (which aired on A&E from 2005 to 2009) and *Flipping Out* (which aired on Bravo beginning in 2007) celebrated the ease and easy money of renovating homes for huge profits. In the wake of the housing collapse, however, both shows had to readjust to new audiences and new market realities. *Flip This House* began emphasizing the difficulties with, and near impossibility of, making a profit from the practice of quick renovation. *Flipping Out* shifted its focus from flipping real estate for profit to home decorating and the host's own consulting business. Other home improvement shows have followed in the wake of this shift, with a similar focus on austerity measures: *Love It or List It*, for instance, a Canadian home design show that began airing on HGTV in 2008, features a home-owning couple who have to decide between keeping their newly renovated current home ("Love It") or buying a new home and selling their current one ("List It"). Costs and comparables—not easy money through renovation—are the new key variables, as homeowners adjust to the new realities of a stagnant housing market.

Reality television programs exhibit the hallmarks of all austerity narratives—they are cheaply produced (and hence, industrially austere), they interact with the crises of nonfictional economies (and hence both offer and validate narratives of austere living), and they promote an ethos of individuality and self-help (and hence are ideologically aligned with austerity policies). Even popular fictional narratives are shaped by ideological, industrial, and aesthetic austerity forms. To cite only two examples among the many on television today, both *Hung* (HBO 2009–2011) and *Breaking Bad* (AMC 2008–2013) feature struggling high school teachers who need to find new sources of employment in order to secure their families' financial futures—the former through prostitution, the latter through the illicit drug trade. Both shows recognize the impossibility of living on a teacher's salary.

In the final season of *Breaking Bad*, the logic of austerity shifts from work, from keeping one's job or becoming one's own boss, to keeping control of one's savings; in other words, it becomes a question of retirement. The teacher-turned-drug-dealer protagonist's quest to accumulate money in massive amounts follows an affective shift in the relation to money: the show emphasizes the physicality of money, the difficulty of storing and concealing it in large amounts, but reflects very little on what the money is actually used for, that is, buying things. Money, for Walter White, is not the object of hope but the object of fear and the threat of its loss.

Hung, while equally a story about the downward mobility of a middle-class teacher, is also a story of the city hardest hit by the recession. Set in Detroit, the series follows an unhappy high school history teacher and athletic coach named Ray who is short of money. He is also the father of twin teenagers who are currently living with their remarried mother. After a fire destroys the childhood home he still owns and lives in, Ray is left without options. With the help of a friend, he decides to turn his extremely large penis into an opportunity to make money. The episodes center on Ray's attempts to maintain a normal life while starting his business as a prostitute. Together with his female pimp (the daughter of a professor), he begins a new prostitution business, catering to middle-class housewives, called "Happiness Consultants." In *Hung*, the male protagonist needs to take stock of his assets and recalibrate his identity in the wake of the financial crisis; his run as a prostitute nearly comes to an end when a younger man offers competition to his fledgling business and then absolutely comes to an end when the series was canceled in 2011 after just three seasons.

A similar recalibration of identity and skills marks the narrative of *Mildred Pierce*, the story of a recently divorced single mother who must find a way to provide for her family during the Great Depression. Like *Hoarders* and other reality television shows, this is also an austerity narrative: it deals in housing crises and real estate deals (and hence offers narratives of austere living) and promotes an ethos of individuality and self-help (and hence is ideologically aligned with austerity policies). So now let us turn to *Mildred Pierce* and *Hoarders*, to see how even fictional representations partake of austerity measures (industrially, narratively, and ideologically) after 2008.

Mildred Pierce and Hoarding

Of his decision to remake the Hollywood classic *Mildred Pierce* (1945), Todd Haynes explains:

> Jon Raymond [his co-writer] had been telling me to read Cain's novel. And he had never seen the film, so we came at it from two different sides. When I was reading it in the summer of 2008, Bear Stearns had collapsed and everything on the financial horizon was trembling, and I'm reading this novel about the Depression and a woman thrust into being a single mother, trying to find a job and work out how she will make ends meet and maintain her middle-class life. It was so full of themes that I didn't remember from the film—it turns out they weren't there.

Haynes insists that his *Mildred Pierce* is best understood, not as a remake of its 1945 classical Hollywood predecessor (where themes of financial crisis are largely absent) but in relation to contemporary media representations of middle-class identity: of fears of downward mobility, of women's work and maternal desires, and of economic collapse and the accumulation of things. "The novel felt intensely relevant," Haynes explained. "I love how it links potential pathologies in maternal desire with potential excesses in middle-class yearning." Haynes depicts Mildred's relationships much as Cain's novel does; her relationships with a series of feckless and unreliable men and her self-absorbed older daughter, Veda, are played out, as Haynes puts it, primarily as transactions "through money, through finance, through class."[6]

Haynes further recounts first seeing the 1945 film *Mildred Pierce* in the 1980s in a feminist theory class at Brown, which he took with Mary Ann Doane. There he read Pam Cook's 1978 essay "Duplicity in *Mildred Pierce*," which traces the tensions between generic conventions of a male-inflected film noir and a female-inflected melodramatic tradition. "I love how melodrama is a denigrated term—a lower-class citizen to other genres," Haynes recounts in an interview in *The Guardian*. "And yet that's what life is, man. We don't live in westerns, noirs, murder mysteries and shit. We live in families and we have relationships that come and go; we suffer under social constraints and we have to make tough choices. And that's really what these stories are about."[7] In another interview connected with the release of the miniseries, Haynes says, "Stories about women in houses are the real stories of our lives. They really tell what all of us experience in one way or another because they're stories of family and love and basic relationships and disappointments."[8]

Women in houses, of course, are central to reality television, from *Hoarders* to *Hoarding: Buried Alive* to *Extreme Couponing*, but they are also central to Haynes's work. His film *Superstar* (1987) uses Barbie dolls to tell the story of Karen Carpenter's losing battle with anorexia. In *Safe* (1995) he recounts the life of an unremarkable homemaker who is nevertheless remarkable in her level of wealth (she literally has nothing to do with her life), who develops multiple chemical sensitivities triggered by everyday household and industrial products. *Far from Heaven* (2002) is Haynes's homage to Douglas Sirk's 1950s melodramas about the artificiality and repressions of suburban life.

Haynes's *Mildred Pierce* is also a revision of what some have called "the mother of all mother movies," casting a softer and more sympathetic Kate Winslet as Mildred and a more complex and sympathetic Evan Rachel Wood as her daughter Veda. Haynes's *Mildred Pierce*, in returning to the Cain novel, extends the story of Mildred's rise and fall as a businesswoman, her transgression of traditional gender norms, and her unfailing, nearly obsessive maternal sacrifices on behalf of Veda, expanding the temporal frame to the ten years of the Great Depression. In the process, this story of "women in houses" is equally a story about real estate booms and busts. Mildred builds her chicken and pie restaurant empire, first in Glendale (on the remains of the model home for Pierce Homes, her husband's bankrupt business), then in Beverly Hills, and finally in Laguna (in another abandoned home, located on a beachfront that is inhospitable to swimming). In the novel, as well as in the miniseries, the notion of "home" has been turned inside out: homes are not dwellings for people or families or children but places of real estate expansion and new businesses—in Mildred's case, the business of selling "home cooking" to a rapidly expanding Southern Californian clientele.

At least one critic has argued that the miniseries is a faithful, almost literal adaptation of the 1941 novel.[9] Given that this is an ambitious, serialized, and cinematic rendering of the novel, the notion that the miniseries has nothing to do with the 1945 film is highly debatable. (Pam Cook has argued as much in a recent essay in *Screen*, and I will have more to say about her essay and this issue later on.) It is nevertheless useful to compare *Mildred Pierce* the miniseries to reality television shows like *Hoarders* and *Hoarding: Buried Alive*, which aired simultaneously, since in all these examples, the home is at once a thing, a domain, and a meaning; a property, a dwelling, and an aspiration. It is also the site of horror, a place where the characters experience a breakdown in perception as a result of trauma. In hoarding shows and in *Mildred Pierce*, middle-class life is under duress, and the compulsive behaviors that emerge as a result (intense motherly love in one case, an overaccumulation of possessions in the other) betray an unsentimental, almost material, approach to the loss of real or illusory control in a world in which most are powerless.

To be sure, *Mildred Pierce* the miniseries is all about an earlier time of economic depression, an era before Wal-Mart, big box stores, internet shopping, eBay, and Pinterest—all of which lend themselves to hoarding behaviors. Mildred may not be a hoarder, but hers is a story about houses, real estate, and excessive consumption, much like the underlying narratives of hoarding shows. Indeed, in the hoarding shows, the hoarders experience their things as an extension of themselves (when items are removed from the home, the hoarders describe the experience as "like losing a limb" or part of themselves). Haynes's Mildred Pierce experiences a similar collapse of boundaries; Veda is "part of her," and the five-part series traces Mildred's difficultly in actually seeing and separating from her only surviving daughter. Both the hoarding shows and *Mildred Pierce* are tales of family and trauma and loss. The miniseries—like the reality television shows—emphasize what the central female characters cannot or fail to see; their gaze is pathologized and their behavior obsessive, revealing a lack of boundaries and distinctions.

The popularity of hoarding shows accounts for the fact that there are two very similar shows on two different networks: *Hoarders* debuted in 2009 as the most watched series premier in A&E history among adults aged 18–49 and tied for the most ever watched shows among adults in the 25–54 demographic. *Hoarding: Buried Alive*, a more sensational knock-off of *Hoarders* (with a male voice-over narrator and use of horror conventions in its credit sequence), premiered on TLC in 2010 and is now in its seventh season (the original *Hoarders* was recently canceled in 2013, after a six-season run). Hoarding, however, is not a uniquely contemporary phenomenon. As historians have pointed out, depictions of hoarding and hoarders can be found in literary texts such as Dante's *Divine Comedy*, Charles Dickens's *Bleak House* and the writings of Naturalists such as Frank Norris, who were greatly concerned with post-Darwinian notions of selfhood, including themes surrounding early forms of modern psychology. Representations of hoarding have appeared as well as in the popular press and on film (the famous Collyer Brothers who died among their junk in their Harlem brownstone in the 1950s, not to mention William Randolph Hearst, the inspiration behind Orson Welles's story of excessive accumulation in his 1941 film *Citizen Kane*).

Yet hoarding, as a symptom of hyper-consumption, is nevertheless something of a distinctively modern illness and material practice, a pathology of a particular time and place. Political theorist Jane Bennett makes this point in a recent essay on "Powers of the Hoard," where she theorizes that hoarding is a pathology of capitalist accumulation, and hoarders are subjects with "an exceptional awareness of the extent to which all bodies can intertwine, infuse, ally, undermine, and compete with those in its vicinity."[10] In a related argument, cultural and queer theorist Scott Herring takes up the proliferation of hoarding television shows in order to offer a theory of "material deviance," bringing together material cultural studies with queer theory in an effort to discern nonnormative identities (exemplified by the hoarder) within hoarding practices framed as instances of material perversion that do not conform to normative standards of object conduct.[11]

Scholarly analysis of hoarding has a larger history as well. Early twentieth-century psychologists including William James and Eric Fromm discussed the problem of hoarding as a pathology of ownership and acquisitiveness. By the 1980s hoarding appeared in the *Diagnostic and Statistical Manual of Mental Disorders* (DSM)—the handbook of American psychiatry—as a form of obsessive-compulsive disorder (OCD). Over the course of the 1990s, this view of hoarding was challenged and revised, and just this past year, with the release of the newest *Diagnostic and Statistical Manual*, hoarding is now listed as its own disorder, distinct from OCD and in need of specific treatment by psychologists and the newly founded businesses of professional organizing and trash removal. For researchers today, the excessive acquisitiveness exhibited by hoarders is a kind of ritualized compulsion, and the distress hoarders exhibit when possessions are moved or thrown away is rooted in a similar kind of obsession with order associated with obsessive-compulsive disorder. And yet the pleasures of hoarding are distinct from the anxieties of OCD. Interestingly for our purposes, hoarders only experience anxiety when their hoard is brought into public view (whether discovered by family members or neighbors or exposed via the public shaming of hoarding shows). More importantly, although hoarding behaviors occur more often among men than women and increase with age, reality TV nonetheless focuses primarily on middle-aged women as hoarders rather than older men (or the banks, who are the real hoarders in our midst), returning us to questions about the relationships among home, accumulation, and dispossession, and the linkage of all three to a kind of modern, gendered pathology.[12]

In one especially compelling episode of *Hoarders* from season five in 2012, we learn about two different hoarders with a similar disorder. Carrie from Washington state is a survivor of rape and abuse and has an adult daughter who despairs of her mother's living conditions (Carrie lives among trash, feces, and bottles of her own urine); James, a former member of the military living in California, hoards sporting equipment and rusted out tools and has appeared in court to fight code violations from the city. Both are victims of trauma, and both identify intensely with their hoards. Carrie believes she is worthless, not much different from the trash, excrement, and detritus in which she lives; James also identifies with his things, insisting there must be a use for old, used-up items, much like he sees himself.

The key issue here is one of "not seeing" and of merging with the hoard. Hoarding television shows take pains to explore different types of hoarders: organized versus disorganized hoarders, for instance, or animal hoarders, who believe they are saving pets that no one else wants, even though they lack the means to house and feed them. There are hoarders of excrement and urine, hoarders of rusted and dilapidated materials, and hoarders who hoard to keep people out, fill a void, or to cover over a loss. Some hoarders consider themselves environmentalists, letting nothing go to waste, while others collect "things" as barriers against the world, where the hoard becomes the outward manifestation of interior states—much like melodrama itself, which projects inner states onto music and mise-en-scène, as symptoms to be read by the viewer because they cannot be accessed by the characters themselves.

All types of hoarders have one thing in common: they cannot see the trash, cannot smell the excrement, and seem unfazed by the lack of mobility in their hoarded homes, where their so-called goat trails—small paths that help them navigate the excessive clutter—always lead to the television set. While hoarders are often accused by family and friends of caring more for things than for people, they themselves claim not to occupy a position of agency. They speak of finding themselves called to amass the stuff and frequently offer rich and impassioned descriptions of how the "things just took over." The hoarded objects are not tools, not even things, but part of the self; the hoarders prefer the slow decay of stuff to the more precarious decay in humans and human relationships. The hoarder's body and the hoard are fused. In this fusion, one might be tempted to ascribe a kind of rebellion against conventional notions of domesticity, a rejection of the homemaker ideal and a protest against the woman's role of maintaining the home as both memory and storage space. But there is an almost obsessive association of the female hoarder with separation anxiety or a deviation of some norm of mental stability or health, which demands a more complex reading. In order to accomplish this, I turn now to Mary Ann Doane's 1984 essay, "The 'Woman's Film': Possession and Address."

In her essay Doane argues that in the woman's film of the 1940s "dramas of seeing become invested with horror within the context of the home." "The paradigmatic woman's space—the home—is yoked to dread, and a crisis of vision."[13] Doane emphasizes that her ambitious essay actually has a rather limited aim: to trace certain obsessions associated with the female protagonist in these films who deviate from some norm of mental stability or health, "resulting in the recurrent investigation of psychical mechanisms frequently linked with the 'feminine condition'—masochism, hysteria, neurosis, paranoia."[14] The specific obsessions that Doane explores include the deployment of space and the activation of the uncanny, the de-specularization of looking and the medical gaze, and the economies of female subjectivity. Most important is her insistence on the way in which scopophillic energy is deflected in the woman's film into other directions, away from the female body. Unlike the film noir, the woman's film does not configure its female protagonist as mysterious or enigmatic; instead, potential knowledge about the woman is transferred from the law to medicine. Doane maintains, "the very process of seeing is now invested with fear, anxiety, horror, precisely because it is object-less, free-floating." Such instability, she argues, does not remain unrecognized by the texts themselves but is instead recuperated as the sign of illness or psychosis. As a result the erotic gaze becomes the medical gaze, and the female body is not so much located as spectacle but as an element in the discourse of medicine, "a manuscript to be read for the symptoms which betray her story, her identity."[15]

TV hoarding shows transfer knowledge about hoarding from law to medicine. The stories may begin with the threat that authorities will repossess or condemn the hoarded home, but ultimately these shows are more interested in deploying a medical gaze and an arsenal of self-help strategies for the hoarder's recovery, which very often fails. If hoarding shows are austerity narratives of a particular kind—they are cheaply produced, and thus industrially austere, they deal in stories of trauma and depression and loss, and thus are narratively austere, they emphasize the virtues of self-help and recovery, and thus are ideologically austere—they also offer a subtle commentary on the larger idea of adapting to austerity conditions, revealing in the process how the status of things and the ingenuity of their imagined repurposing indicate newly revised borders of gender and class.

The same is true of *Mildred Pierce* the miniseries, which explores an earlier era of economic depression through the story of one woman's upward mobility and business success and failure, coupled with a critique of her men's lack of drive or ambition and her daughter's unbounded consumer desires. Although set in Los Angeles, Hayne's *Mildred Pierce* was filmed in New York, given financial and economic incentives offered for filming there. Hence it, too, is an austerity narrative from an industrial point of view; one place aims to pass for another, the East Coast for the West, which perhaps goes unnoticed by viewers unfamiliar with Southern Californian locations and vegetation. There are, for instance, no grassy broad beaches in California.

From the very start the miniseries evokes conventionalized and gendered social spaces, only to then unravel and collapse them. In the opening scene of Part One, Mildred is in the kitchen making pies while her husband Bert is outside mowing the lawn on a hot afternoon. We first see only Mildred's hands preparing luscious lemon meringue pies, which we soon learn she sells for pocket money. Mildred's pies and cakes are highly charged objects: neither bread nor fruit, the pies are an extravagance, a luxury item for paying customers in this time of economic depression. Her labors in the kitchen are matched by images of Bert working outside, viewed through the kitchen window. When Bert comes inside, and Mildred criticizes his work ethic, and then his affair with Mrs. Biederhof, she tells him to get out and to never come back. While they argue, the camera pans over the framed prints in the couple's home: first a photo of Bert, followed by the architectural plans and photos for the now-failed Pierce Homes business; then a photo of Bert and Mildred on their wedding day; then a photo of Ray, their younger daughter, and finally a photo of Veda. In short order, this family "photo album" represents the normative ideal—business, marriage, children—each of which is now in crisis. In the first minutes of the film, we learn that Bert's business is defunct and he is unemployed; then he and Mildred separate and their marriage collapses. By the end of Part Two, Ray, their younger daughter, is dead after suffering a brief but acute virus contracted while Mildred was in Santa Barbara with Monte (rather than at home with her children, as if maternal absence were somehow responsible for her daughter's death). Much like the hoarding shows, trauma permeates *Mildred Pierce*.

After Bert stomps out of the house, Mildred begins a new journey, recalibrating her identity and her skills in an economy inhospitable to most people but especially to "grass widows" without a formal working history. The end of Part One reveals that Veda has been listening all along to everything that has gone on in the household. As Mildred begs her friend Lucy not to tell the children—and especially Veda—about her new job as a waitress, for which she is extremely ashamed, she exclaims: "You don't understand her. She has something in her that I thought I had, and now find I haven't." What Veda has, and what Mildred thinks she lacks, is pride or, rather, what her friend Lucy has diagnosed as an overriding sense of entitlement. In Haynes's version, Veda does indeed possess special talents (she is an operatic prodigy who sings at the Los Angeles Philharmonic, and in this she is very different from the Veda of the 1945 film, whose career amounts to singing "The Oceana Roll" in a dingy dive). In the miniseries, as in the novel, Veda eventually succeeds beyond her own and her mother's wildest ambitions for her, when she becomes a well-known concert and radio star as a coloratura soprano. She eventually leaves provincial Southern California for a career in New York, taking her mother's husband Monte along with her.

Unlike the 1945 film Haynes's adaptation has no flashbacks, no voice-over, and there is no murder mystery; the miniseries follows the novel in its explicit treatment of money and sex and the passions that link and surround them both. Unlike the 1945 film, for example, Veda does not shoot Monte in a fit of jealous rage but, instead, has an explicitly sexual affair with him (an affair that is ambiguous and even implausible in the 1945 film). In Haynes's version, it is Mildred who discovers Veda in bed with Monte, and it is Mildred who flies into a blind, murderous rage at the revelation of this betrayal. In the 1945 film, Mildred's story is book-ended by noir conventions and the police investigation of Monte's murder. In the miniseries, the conventions of melodrama prevail; inward states are projected outward, as mother and daughter merge with each other and their environment. Haynes created color palettes for every scene in the miniseries and was careful and particular in his choices. As one critic remarks, "the pale greens and dusty corals evoke the colors of depression glassware; Mildred's friends, played by Mare Winningham and Melissa Leo have the unadorned, care-etched faces of the women in Dorothea Lange's FSA photographs."[16] In several scenes, Mildred and Veda not only resemble one another but appear trapped in their home(s), viewed behind staircases and windows and home furnishings that produce dread, anxiety, and even horror. Finally, and again unlike the 1945 film, where Mildred first sets up Wally Fay for the murder, then confesses to it herself when her ex-husband Bert becomes the prime suspect, the film noir frame is absent from Haynes's version. In the earlier film the police trick Mildred into revealing the truth about the murder; mother and daughter are forcibly separated by the law, and Bert and Mildred are reconciled. "The moment of self-knowledge, which stabilizes the film's moral universe and provides closure," writes Pam Cook, "is absent from the novel and the miniseries. . . . Mildred remains a victim of forces she does not understand."[17]

In her essay Cook takes further issue with the notion that Haynes's version of *Mildred Pierce* has little to do with the classic Hollywood film, which he first viewed as a student in the 1980s. Although she recognizes that the miniseries follows the novel more closely than the 1945 film, she argues that a closer look reveals more than a faithful adaptation in homage to the literary source:

The nihilism of the noir aesthetic, in which stylized low-key, high-contrast lighting is used to show uncomprehending characters trapped in a hostile environment, is not directly referenced, but the miniseries is dominated by frames within frames and views through windows and doorways that curtail vision. This denaturalizes space: rather than give the illusion of transparency, as with naturalism, it produces a sense that characters are constricted by their surroundings. By implication, viewers are also limited in what they are able to see and understand, as with film noir.[18]

Cook continues:

Haynes's aesthetic excludes viewers from the scene, placing them at a distance so that they struggle to understand what they see. . . . Just as Mildred finds herself on the outside, even when she thinks she is on the inside, viewers are on the outside looking in. Mildred is excluded by her class, gender and inability to understand the privileged world to which she aspires. Similarly, viewers are positioned as watchers, obsessively scrutinizing from a distance.[19]

This difference in self-knowledge is perhaps best underscored by comparing the scenes of Mildred on the pier in the 1945 classic and the 2011 miniseries. Cook examines these two scenes to show how the 1945 film is still "remembered" in the 2011 miniseries. I would like to extend her reading to show the difference between these scenes in the two versions and two renditions of the Mildred character. In the 1945 film Mildred is indeed fully and finally aware of her daughter's transgressions, whereas this self-knowledge is completely withheld from Mildred in the miniseries.

The 1945 film, in noir fashion, opens with the scene of the beach house and Monte being shot; he murmurs the name "Mildred" as he collapses to the floor and dies. A car speeds away from the scene, and we find ourselves at the pier, with a tearful Mildred (Joan Crawford), dressed in her iconic fur hat and coat, contemplating suicide. A policeman stops her from "taking a swim," but the character we gain from this scene is a strong if daunted woman, whom we later learn is well aware of her daughter's crimes, which she nevertheless attempts to cover up. In the miniseries, this scene on the pier is recalled, well into the story rather than the beginning. In Part Four, Mildred and Veda have separated after Mildred throws Veda out upon learning that she blackmailed her young lover for money via a trumped-up pregnancy and annulled marriage. With months of no word from Veda, Mildred becomes more and more despondent. Bert tells Mildred about Veda's success as a singer on the radio, and at Mildred's newest Laguna restaurant she and Bert listen to Veda's radio performance. As they stare at the radio and Veda begins to sing, Mildred recognizes that, no matter how close Veda may seem (her voice envelops the scene), she is nonetheless very far away. Mildred walks to the pier, overcome with emotion. Looking out over the water, she does not contemplate suicide but instead gathers her resolve to do whatever it takes to win Veda back. As Cook emphasizes, Mildred does not gain knowledge about Veda, or self-knowledge about herself, her motivations or obsessions; she remains "a victim of forces she does not understand."

In this way *Mildred Pierce* the miniseries is very much connected to other post-2008 austerity narratives in which dramas of seeing collapse subject/object divisions and become invested with horror within the context of the home. These narratives are concerned with possessions and addresses, accumulation and things, business booms and busts, and separation anxieties. They also explore a collapse of perception. Haynes's Mildred is horrified by her daughter's actions as much as by her own inability to understand them, which is similar to the staging of domestic horror in the hoarding shows.

In austerity contexts everyday objects and relationships are the objects of passion—for property and things as well as emotional investment. As Jean Baudrillard has written:

> The everyday passion for private property is often stronger than all the others, and sometimes even reigns supreme, all other passions being absent. . . . Apart from the uses to which we put them at any particular moment, objects in this sense have another aspect which is intimately bound up with the subject: no longer simply material bodies offering a certain resistance, they become mental precincts over which I hold sway, they become things of which I am the meaning, they become my property and my passion.[20]

All other passions being absent, property relations and an overriding lack of agency are gendered as feminine/female in an array of austerity media texts (as hoarding, obsessive compulsive disorder, and maternal pathology). Women in houses merge with their things, their children, and their passions, now opened up for public view and public therapy. Haynes may have never imagined that his miniseries had anything to do with hoarding or houses or obsessive consumption. His *Mildred Pierce* is nonetheless very much a part of the time in which it was made—a time when people are trapped in their houses, and where any movement forward is revealed as circular and repetitive (from the goat trails leading hoarders to their televisions or from Mildred's rise and fall in a Glendale subdivision). These are stories of capitalist accumulation, which are also and simultaneously stories about the pathologies wrought by austerity and economic despair.

Notes

1 Diane Negra and Yvonne Tasker, eds., *Gendering the Recession: Media and Culture in an Age of Austerity* (Durham: Duke University Press, 2014), 1.

2 Mark Blyth, *Austerity: The History of a Dangerous Idea* (Oxford: Oxford University Press, 2013), 2, 13, 7.

3 Laurie Ouellette and James Hay, *Better Living through Reality TV: Television and Post-welfare Citizenship* (Hoboken: Wiley-Blackwell, 2008), 7.

4 Ibid., 93.

5 Randy Frost and Gail Steketee, *Stuff: Compulsive Hoarding and the Meaning of Things* (New York: Houghton Mifflin Harcout, 2010), 263–264.

6 Haynes quoted from Dennis Lim, "'Mildred Pierce': A Mother's House of Love and Hurt," *New York Times*, March 18, 2011, at http://www.nytimes.com/2011/03/20/arts/television/kate-winslet-in-todd-hayness-mildred-pierce-on-hbo.html.

7 Haynes quoted from Malcolm MacKenzie, "Todd Haynes's Kitchen Confidential," *The Guardian*, June 20, 2011, at http://www.theguardian.com/tv-and-radio/2011/jun/20/todd-haynes-mildred-pierce.

8 Lim, "'Mildred Pierce': A Mother's House of Love and Hurt."

9 Sarah Churchwell, "Re-reading *Mildred Pierce* by James M. Cain," *The Guardian*, June 24, 2011, at http://www.theguardian.com/books/2011/jun/24/mildred-pierce-sarah-churchwell-rereading.

10 Jane Bennett, "Powers of the Hoard: Further Notes on Material Agency," in *Animal, Vegetable, Mineral: Ethics and Objects,* ed. Jeffrey Jerome Cohen (Brooklyn: Punctum Books, 2012), 256. Bennett writes, much like Herring, that hoarders are not bearers "of mental illness but . . . differently-abled bodies that might have special sensory access to the call of things. . . . If the hoarder is a human body positioned at one end of a continuum between human and nonhuman bodies (owner, connoisseur, collector, archivist, packrat, 'chronically disorganized,' hoarder), then because the hoarder's body forms unusually resilient, intense, and intimate bonds with nonhuman bodies, she may have broader access to thing-power, access from the inside out, so to speak" (see ibid., 244–245). Where Bennett focuses on a hoarder's extreme perception as a special gift or ability rather than a deficiency, Herring sees in hoarding examples of those whose material lives do not conform to normative standards.

11 Scott Herring, *Material Deviance in Modern Culture* (Chicago: University of Chicago Press, 2014).

12 One professional organizer explains, "The stereotypical hoarder is the overweight, elderly woman, unkempt, dressed in layers of clothes, sitting in front of the TV all day long." See Matt Paxton and Phaedra Hise, *The Secret Lives of Hoarders: True Stories of Tackling Extreme Clutter* (New York: Perigee, 2011), 15–16.

13 Mary Ann Doane, "The 'Woman's Film': Possession and Address," in *Re-vision: Essays in Feminist Film Criticism,* ed. Mary Ann Doane, Patricia Mellencamp, and Linda Williams (Lanham: University Publications of America, 1984), 286.

14 Ibid., 285.

15 Ibid., 286, 290.

16 J. Hoberman, "Raising Cain in Todd Haynes's *Mildred Pierce*," *The Village Voice*, March 23, 2011, at http://www.villagevoice.com/film/raising-cain-in-todd-hayness-mildred-pierce-6430323.

17 Pam Cook, "Beyond Adaptation: Mirrors, Memory and Melodrama in Todd Haynes' *Mildred Pierce*," *Screen* 54, no. 3 (2013): 381.

18 Ibid., 384.

19 Ibid., 386.

20 Jean Baudrillard, *The System of Objects* (New York: Verso, 2005), 91.

6

Imagining Beyond Capital

Representation and Reality in Science Fiction Film

SHERRYL VINT

In *Seeds of Time*, Fredric Jameson proclaims, "It seems to be easier for us today to imagine the thoroughgoing deterioration of the earth and of nature than the breakdown of late capitalism; perhaps that is due to some weakness in our imaginations."[1] The overwhelmingly dystopian tenor of recent science fiction film reflects this failure of the imagination—from the exuberant slaughter of masses of zombies (that is, those no longer relevant to the economy), in films such as *World War Z* (Marc Forster, 2013), to the vision of access to health care as the horizon of utopian expectations in *Elysium* (Neill Blomkamp, 2013). Such films seem to reinforce Jameson's truism that we can't imagine a world after capitalism.

Yet even as films imagining the end of the world seem to capitulate to this logic, they simultaneously express a desire for life beyond capitalism, generally in images rather than narratives. Many of these films resolve the contradictions they stage in unrealistic, Hollywood-style, wish-fulfillment happy endings. Despite the disappointments of their banal narratives, such films provide the seeds of change at the visual level in their affecting representations of the vicissitudes of global neoliberalism triumph and the desires they stage for a world beyond its strictures. Science fiction film foregrounds the gap between reality and representation, the difference between the imagined world of the mise-en-scène and the social world of the viewer. Through their fantastic settings, science fiction films become a privileged site for interrogating the troubled relationship between representation and reality under capitalism. Thus the blurring of ideological fantasy and reality under neoliberalism is made visible by such science fiction films, which thereby give us a new perceptual tool for grasping—and changing—the givens of neoliberal capital.

Science fiction has often been imagined as a privileged site for utopian thinking, and many writers have used the genre to imagine worlds beyond capitalism. Even in its dystopian form, Jameson argues, it can provide us with cognitive maps to help us grasp and navigate the dystopian present of global capital.[2] Yet the genre is as strongly implicated in histories of colonialism and in the imperial imagination. The technology it celebrates has inevitably become bound up with visions of a better future through corporate brands, and Peter Sloterdijk recently nominated the Crystal Palace—that first in a series of techno-topian simulacral worlds that run from this 1851 exhibit through the 1939 World's Fair to Disney's Epcot Center and beyond—as exemplar of the capitalist world. Self-contained worlds like the Crystal Palace or a space station, Sloterdijk contends, operate via a biopolitical logic in which the entire world is a "great comfort structure" within while those banished outside this self-referential world of privilege no longer register as part of the world at all. This image of the Crystal Palace as capitalist world highlights the troubled relationship between representation and reality created by capitalism, particularly in its speculative instruments of fictitious capital such as derivatives, which consume future value in the present.[3]

Although they do not provide real solutions to the problems of capitalist exploitation, a number of science fiction films make visible a logic of surplus value extraction that capitalism seeks to obscure. *In Time* (Andrew Niccol, 2011), for example, literalizes that workers must give up their vital energies by making the unit of currency time—if one does not work enough hours to sustain life until the next shift, the person simply expires. In *Daybreakers* (Spierig brothers, 2009), a virus transforms most of the population into vampires, but they simply continue to live lives of consumerist accumulation, using products such as vehicle navigation by cameras instead of windows allowing them to avoid the sun. In *Branded* (Bradshaw and Deleryn, 2012), corporate brands are personified as entities that literally feed off their loyal adherents, growing *kaiju*-sized and fighting for market share along the lines of Godzilla battling Mothra. Such films offer compelling images of our real conditions, and even if they offer only gratifying fantasies in their conclusions, they nonetheless articulate more than the escapist illusion "that the outside world is the straightforward continuation of that presented on the screen," as Adorno and Horkheimer would have it.[4]

Hollywood "perpetually cheats its consumers of what it perpetually promises," as the Frankfurt school contends, its pleasures often promoting "resignation to what it ought to help to forget."[5] Yet Hollywood is not alone in seducing us into accepting an ideological image of the world as if it were reality, as Mark Fisher makes clear in his book *Capitalist Realism*. Capitalist realism is the cynical belief that there is no outside or beyond capital, an ideological fantasy that unconsciously structures our experience of social reality. Capitalist realism is "a pervasive *atmosphere*, conditioning not only the production of culture but also the regulation of work and education, and acting as a kind of invisible barrier constraining thought and action." Thus the unrealistic conclusions to the problems of capitalism staged by some science fiction films can become a way of showing us the similarly unrealistic "pervasive atmosphere" of capitalist realism, encouraging us to penetrate this barrier and consider alternative possibilities for thought and action.[6]

Upside Down (Solanis, 2012) exemplifies the quality of science fiction film visually to capture the realities of global capital in ways that realism cannot. The film is set in a solar system structured by "double gravity" such that each planet has both an upper- and an underworld that face one another across a gap of shared sky. Double gravity, we are told, is an "unchangeable" law of the universe, one of whose effects is that "inverse matter" brought from the other gravity spontaneously combusts. On this particular world, "down-below" is a space of poverty and harsh struggle for subsistence while the world above is a glimmering urban paradise. Capitalizing on the energy of siphoned inverse matter, TransWorld Corporation (an entity whose skyscraper tower has floors across the sky that link the two realms) takes cheap oil from down-below for its own use and sells back overpriced electricity to those below, capturing not only the transfer of wealth from the Global South to the Global North but also the flows of capital via commodities—such as privatized water—that often belong to the economically colonized nations in the first place. The film's stunning visuals make manifest a gap between global elites and global subalterns, mirroring David Harvey's description of the inequities produced by the global banking system as a scenario in which "the banking community . . . retired into the penthouse of capitalism where they manufactured oodles of money by trading and leveraging among themselves without any mind whatsoever for what the working people living in the basement were doing."[7]

The film makes visible and critiques the dynamics of capital's flow in globalized neoliberalism. The narrative of the film, however, does not live up to the promise of its visual design. Solanis uses his richly imagined world to tell a rather banal love story about an orphan boy from below, Adam (Jim Sturgess), who falls in love with a girl from above, Eden (Kirsten Dunst).

This shift of her name from the expected Adam and Eve to Adam and Eden suggests not only that they are the couple of the new future but also that she embodies a geographical heritage Adam has been denied, the paradisiacal space of retreat for a global elite is similarly visualized in the orbital colonies of privilege in *Elysium*. Adam and Eden meet as adults through a series of events that involve Adam being willing to give up intellectual property (IP) in his inventions for the sake of access to the technological resources above. The details of their love story and the machinations they undergo to meet despite coming from worlds of inverse gravity provide the context for a number of compelling spectacles that demonstrate the vast gap of wealth and privilege between the dark and shabby world-below and the bright and polished world-above. More important, however, such visual details also compel us to see the logic that connects these mirror-opposite worlds in which deprivation and excess mutually produce one another. In one scene children down-below scavenge scraps of discarded "inverse matter" from the world-above because their spontaneous combustion makes this trash from above a key source of heat in the world-below. In another scene Eden, in a luxurious club above, decadently sips a cocktail made with traces of down-below ingredients that require it be drunk from an inverted cocktail glass to prevent this anti-gravity concoction from floating to the ceiling. Deep deprivation and conspicuous excess both draw on such moments of contact between the worlds.

Until its final ten minutes the film seems poised to end in tragedy: Adam has been caught accessing forbidden spaces above and is banished down-below; Eden is in despair. "Up there, they always win, down here, we always lose," Adam announces. A friend from above, laid off from his TransWorld job due to age and thus disinclined to support the status quo, saves them at the last minute by discovering an innovation for Adam's dual-world technology that will enable migrations between the worlds. Amplifying the unrealistic utopianism of this eleventh hour salvation that unites our segregated lovers, we also discover that Eden is pregnant, *and* having twins, *and* her pregnancy enables her to move between worlds without technology. Thus, after ninety-some minutes of a film that represents the gap between worlds of privilege and poverty as so vast as to be a matter of physics, the film seems to concede that it is intolerable to live with the idea that such a gulf is inevitable and irrevocable and provides a vision of a transformed world beyond these inequities in its final moments. "Our love would forever alter the course of history," Adam tells us in his final voice-over, "but that's another story." The camera pulls back, and we see a transformed image of the dual worlds, which are now true mirror images rather than mirrored contrasts—the same architecture, green spaces and wealth both above and below.

The refusal to say how or why their love changed everything eviscerates the film's political potential, but there is a seed of hope in its powerful visual evocation of the equities of global capital. Capitalist realism is a fantasy that encourages us to believe that capitalism is as natural and unchangeable as gravity; we see in this film a change in such "unchangeable" laws of physics and thus a hint that it is perhaps only in a genre beyond realism that we can visualize our possibilities for thought and action outside the ideological fantasies that capital encourages us to take as "reality." In order "to combat the world that . . . imperialism imagines and replace it with a more habitable one," Randy Martin argues, "we need to map [affective investments in the space imagined by empire] as a way of getting to those other worlds that may lie within reach but that we have yet to grasp. Dreaming the imperial unconscious, we may awaken elsewhere."[8] *Upside Down* is an attempt to awaken elsewhere. It shows us that our values and social arrangements are morally upside down, making visible and contesting what Sloterdijk calls capitalism's "modus operandi of universal apartheid [that] involves making poverty invisible in zones of affluence on the one hand, and the segregation of the affluent [from] the no-hope zones on the other."[9] Yet in its failure to work through the difficult transition from such segregation to a more habitable world, the film offers us another dream, not a full awakening into another kind of politics.

Repo Men (Miguel Sapochnik, 2010), a film about a future health-care system based on debt-financed artificial organs that can be violently repossessed upon failure to pay, seems—at least initially—even less promising than *Upside Down*. In its refusal to take itself seriously, however, I suggest it gives us back reasons to believe in a world outside the visions of capitalist realism—a reading that emerges particularly if we contrast *Repo Men* with a more earnest and serious film on the same topic of commodity organs, *Inhale* (Baltasar Kormákur, 2010). In the latter, district attorney Paul Stanton (Dermot Mulroney) goes to Mexico looking for a Dr. Navarro who, Stanton has been told, can procure a lung for Stanton's dying daughter sooner than would be possible via the United Network for Organ Sharing (UNOS). A liberal melodrama, *Inhale* evokes all the emotional dilemmas of Paul's situation: the conflict between "law" and "justice," indexed by intercut scenes of a case he is prosecuting in which a Latino man is jailed for shooting someone who molested the man's son; the loss of a perfect match from UNOS shipped to another recipient and the irony that the organ dies in transit; the danger Paul faces given the seemingly ubiquitous criminality in Mexico; the relationship Paul cultivates with a group of street kids named Los Olvidados (perhaps a reference to the Luis Buñuel film *The Young and the Damned* [1950]) that compels him to put a human face on what he is otherwise imagining as an anonymous country of "unused" organs. The film frames its narrative with opening and closing intertitles that give statistical information about the demand for transplant organs and from Organ Watch about trends in international organ trafficking.

Inhale's narrative culminates when corrupt local officials orchestrate the death of one of Los Olvidados to get a matched lung for Paul's daughter on schedule. Paul witnesses the "accident" and is outraged, chasing down the ambulance that transports the child to a location where, instead of treating him for survivable injuries, they begin to harvest his lung. Paul confronts the surgeon mid-procedure and his outrage is thrown back in his face: "you knew exactly what you were doing when you crossed the border," he is told, and then he is offered the choice of the surgeon saving the boy by reattaching the lung or saving Paul's daughter by continuing the procedure. A cut to the daughter's funeral confirms that Paul made the conventionally moral choice, an ending we expect in melodramatic cinema but, judged by people's material choices, one that rings just as false as does the ending of *Upside Down. Inhale* is all the more sinister because of its pretense to be a kind of realism rather than a fantasy world of science fiction. Belying the reality of organ markets and those lives ground under by a culture in which body parts are the only commodity they might bring to market, the film makes this economic and political crisis a matter of individual morality and personal choice.[10]

Repo Men, in contrast, is played with such excess that it is difficult to imagine theme factored into its production despite overt connections to neoliberal economics and commodified body parts. "My job is simple," protagonist Remy (Jude Law) tells us in his opening monologue, "you can't pay for your car, the bank takes it back; can't pay for your house, the bank takes it back; can't pay for your liver, that's where I come in." The film's first sequence is a visceral demonstration of Remy's work repossessing "artiforgs," that is, artificial organs sold on 20 percent interest payment plans to desperate people. After a ninety-day grace period, such overdue organs are ripped from the defaulter's bodies in legalized murder, making visible the otherwise metaphorical violence of an insurance industry that unevenly distributes chances at life and death. Their employer, the Union, encourages clients to leverage their futures to insurmountable debt with the rationale "you owe it to your family, you owe it to yourself," equating the value of life with the value of debt accumulated to continue life. In a brief glimpse of an interview recruiting a new repo man, we hear the manager assure him, "you're not *taking* a life. You're keeping the Union viable so that we can continue to give life." The intellectual prestidigitation of turning the taking of some lives into the cultivation of life overall suggests something of the fantasy-infused reality under the logic of neoliberalism.

Remy has a crisis of conscience after a near-death experience when he awakens to find himself among those he has called the "schmucks," clients of the Union. He now has an artificial heart and, like them, must work to pay for the privilege of continuing to live. He can no longer perform his job without seeing it as killing, falls behind in his payments, and is eventually pursued by his former colleagues as he hides out with rebels, writing the narrative he reads in the voice-over. This is not a novel or a memoir, he insists, but "a cautionary tale" that refuses the mantra "a job is just a job" that had sustained him and his best friend Jake (Forest Whitaker) in their work. Now antagonists on different sides of the economic war, Remy and Jake confront each other and fight into unconsciousness, from which Remy awakens first and escapes. The final third of the film is an excess of action-film jouissance as Remy and his rebel girlfriend, Beth (Alice Braga), decide that, since there is no way to escape the system, they will confront it head-on and destroy it. In lovingly choreographed scenes of escapist action cinema, complete with swelling scores, Remy and Beth seem impervious to bullets as they infiltrate the Union system where a single computer, locked behind a pink door at headquarters, monitors all accounts. They will go there, "wipe the system, no more accounts, nobody overdue." Once inside they fight their way to the pink door in a battle reminiscent of the famous hallway fight in Chan-wook Park's *Oldboy* (2003), with Remy single-handedly defeating more than a dozen antagonists. In one stunningly unrealistic scene, he is pinned to the floor and, it seems, will be kicked to death, only to have Beth throw him a saw she just happens to have in her bag, so he can rise and kill them all as he spins in a circle, blade out. Realism has clearly been left behind, but such scenes are not uncharacteristic in action cinema, even in films set in realist rather than science fiction worlds.

Once behind the pink door, they gain access to the system, using its scanner to "repo themselves" in scenes that combine the aesthetics of action-movie sex scenes with literal penetration by the scanner as they scan still-attached organs to mark them as repossessed. Near the end of this process, Jake joins them, decides to switch sides, and all three then deposit grenades rather than organs into the waiting trays, blowing up the system and escaping to island paradise. *Repo Men* thus seems to end in the most naïve and escapist way possible, even more unrealistic than *Upside Down* in this individualistic rather than world-transforming conclusion. As we watch the beach of their island paradise, however, the image on our screens momentarily glitches. We are pulled from this fantasy and into the diegetic reality just moments after the fight with Jake. Remy did not wake up—as our screens had led us to believe—but is permanently brain damaged and hooked up to the latest artiforg, the M.5 Neural Net for which Jake is now indentured to pay because he loves his friend, whatever their ethical disagreements. "He's happy right now?" Jake anxiously enquires, and technicians assure him that Remy is happy, "so long as someone keeps paying for the system."

The film ends on this cynical note, with us watching Remy's happy—but clearly fake—ending. In this dreamworld Jake reads Remy's manuscript, *The Repossession Mambo*, but the final words heard by the audience are not this critique but rather voice-over PR for the M.5 Neural Net, which we've glimpsed peripherally throughout the film: "With the M.5 Neural Net, yesterday's dreams are today's reality. Imagine your loved ones living out the rest of their natural lives in a world where they are always happy, always content, always taken care of," that is, precisely the opposite of a world of for-profit health care, neoliberal erasure of the welfare state, and global markets in transplant organs. In contrast to Remy's happy-ending fantasy world within the M.5 Neural Net, the film's science fiction "reality" of repossessing artiforgs now seems less fantastical and more diagnostic of real conditions under neoliberal capital. From one point of view, then, *Repo Men* is bad escapist cinema, even more unrealistic, perhaps, than *Upside Down*, or certainly less interested in giving a gloss of even emotional realism to its narrative. From another, the film is no more unrealistic than the more heartfelt *Inhale*, a film that, for all its critique of organ markets, seems simultaneously to participate in the capitalist realist delusion that there is no alternative. If only people knew the costs of their transplant organs—or their privatized water, or their cheaply manufactured goods, or their agricultural imports—*Inhale* seems to suggest, most would make the inclusive and equitable choice.

Forced to confront that capitalism posits a zero sum game between one's own economic and physical health versus abstract ideals of equality, good people will choose equality, *Inhale* tells us. The system need not change: people just need to behave morally, as Paul does when he chooses to let his daughter die, even though he is told that the street child from whom the lung would have been harvested would in any case most likely be dead from violence within the year. This rationale for allowing the transplant is the logic of capitalist realism, a logic that encourages us to believe there is no other choice but to take capital's bad with its good, and it is the logic that has created an international market for transplant organs. The more socially just ending of *Inhale*, then, can be seen as no less unrealistic than the pulp-action conclusion of *Repo Men*: the latter's action-fueled conclusion does not reflect contemporary global realities, of course, but neither does Paul's choice to save a homeless Mexican child rather than purchase a lung from a globalized body market, as statistics from Organ Watch provided by the film itself confirm. There is a crucial difference, however: *Repo Men* not only knows that its resolution of these economic issues is unrealistic, it forces us to recognize the complicity of our pleasure in imagining that things will all work out for the best. In its glitching final images, *Repo Men* reminds us that cinema is not life, while *Inhale* offers us the more dangerous fantasy that life's moral dilemmas can be solved as easily as films can conclude.

Emotionally investing in the ideological "reality" of the visions provided by science fiction film, then, can help us resist the equally fantastic formulations of capitalist realism that convince us there is no alternative. Such films might help us to see that, although capitalism tries to convince us that it is merely a fantasy to imagine the world otherwise, such other visions might yet be materialized. Hal Haberman and Jeremy Passmore's *Special* (2006) uses science fiction imagery to draw our attention to this dialectic between the world that capital gives us and the world as it might be. The film's protagonist, Les (Michael Rappaport), believes that a new pharmaceutical has given him super powers, and much of the film is his subjective point of view that makes these powers "real"—in the way they are real within the diegesis of other superhero films. Scenes filmed from the point of view of other characters, however, suggest that these powers are merely the delusion of a mind broken both by the drugs and by the daily vicissitudes of a life that continually reminds Les he is powerless and meaningless, struggling to survive within a system in which he is largely invisible. For example, in one scene where he is showing his powers to his stoned friends, we see Les run through a wall, disappearing, and then returning to run out of the wall again. He returns with a bloody nose and comments that the powers take a "physical toll" on him. In a later scene, we see him try to demonstrate the same power at a police station where he offers his assistance in fighting crime, and here the disenchanted desk sergeant's viewpoint becomes our own as we see Les simply crash head on into the wall, briefly collapsing, then getting up again and behaving as if the demonstration went flawlessly. The film never lets us believe that Les really has superpowers, but at the same time it keeps us mainly within his point of view, the visuals behaving as if his powers are real and the tone encouraging us to be sympathetic with the earnestness of his desire to do good and make a difference.

The film's satire draws attention to a medical system that exists for profit rather than for treatment. Les uses the branded icon for the proposed drug as his superhero emblem, and the bad press he receives due to his vigilante activities makes the IP owners, Jonas (Paul Blackthorne) and Ted Exiler (Ian Bohen) pursue him. To Les these "suits" are icons of evil who want to steal away the powers he is using for good, and he believes them to be using the drug to create an army of compliant soldiers. Financial gain being their real motivation, they want to cover up Les's adverse reaction because they fear that knowledge of it would scare away the investors who have finally offered to buy their startup. The drug does not give Les actual super-powers but merely a sense of increased self-confidence that makes him feel super-powered compared to how helpless he felt before. Designing his costume and reflecting in his voice-over journal on the importance of the superhero emblem, Les comments, "I want my costume to tell people that they shouldn't give up no matter how down they sometimes feel because anything is possible." The drug was intended only to help people perform better at work (that is, to improve the economy), yet, as Les points out, "the suits" cannot direct where this increased self-confidence might flow, how he might use it to undo capital rather than augment profits as intended.

By visually mingling realism and science fiction in cuts within scenes that show the same actions from two points of view—such as when Les shows his clinical trial doctor that he can float, which we see in the first shot, while the doctor only sees him lying on the floor (our second such)—the film blurs reality and representation in ways that both mirror Les's con-fused consciousness and also gesture beyond mere delusion. From another point of view, Les's superpowers *are* real in the sense that he truly does completely transform his life and begins to exhibit more agency while under the influence of the drug. Things that previously seemed impossible for him now prove not to be—merely by shifting his perception, not his actual ability—and although this is largely played to comic effect there is a more serious point at work here as well. As Les tells us in his opening voice-over, describing a recurring dream, "I realized I could fly . . . that's not quite right: I realized there was no reason I couldn't fly." Inspired by the belief that he has superpowers, Les quits his soul-destroying job as a parking attendant, gains the courage to speak to the girl he has admired from afar, and finally shows the strength to continue to stand up to the Exiler brothers, despite the severe injuries he has sustained in their con-frontation. In the end Les has detoxed and realizes he does not have chemi-cally produced superpowers. As we watch him walk home, his voice-over seems dejected and defeated: "most people are not unique or important," he laments, "we don't have any magical power . . . no evil forces to defeat."

His lament is interrupted when Jonas Exiler hits him with a car. This is a final confrontation through which the film shows us that it takes a superhu-man effort to break away from our habituated perception and that there is no alternative to capitalism while it simultaneously insists that such super-human effort is within our grasp. Les is beaten and damaged by his conflict with the Exiler brothers at the end of the film, the price he has paid to face them with mere human strength is high, but nonetheless he is still victori-ous. Refusing to stay down, he rises again, prompting Jonas to reverse and hit him with the car again; but yet again, Les rises. "You can't make me stop" he says several times as he struggles to stand. Losing heart at the violence it takes to defeat a tenacious opponent, Ben Exiler flees while Jonas grips the wheel and tries to run Les down a third time. Jonas, too, loses his nerve, however, and eventually releases the steering wheel as Les turns and continues his walk home. The last shot of the film focuses in on his smiling face, injured but not broken. Les persists in his vision of a better world in which he can help people—rather than passively observe but feel helpless against the injustices he witnesses. This conclusion moves the story firmly out of a science fictional frame, but Les retains the power of thinking how the world might be otherwise that science fiction gave him. The blurring of reality and fantasy in the film and in Les's experience allows him—and us—to see through the fantasy of capitalist realism. There is an alternative, and believing that there is not is as delusional as believing he had super powers.

If *Special* can be read as a kind of science fictionalization of reality, the final kind of science fiction film I want to consider—pseudo-documentaries that show us reality as if it were dystopian science fiction—suggest even more forcefully the power of science fiction to help us perceive things capitalist realism otherwise obscures. Both Peter Watkins's *Punishment Park* (1971) and Lizzie Borden's *Born in Flames* (1983) convincingly announce themselves as documentaries, making clear the intense relationship between ideological fantasy and material reality that structures our experience within and beyond science fiction film. These films ask us to consider the ongoing role of the ideological imagination in structuring our perception of possibilities for action but make clear how easy it is to depict reality as a kind of science fiction. *Punishment Park* is set in an imaginary near-future America in which the McCarran Internal Security Act (1950)—a real piece of McCarthy-era legislation—is used to set up concentration camps to detain those accused of subversive activities. The film is presented as if it were a documentary filmed by the BBC about these Punishment Parks, located in the southern California desert. Two sites of action are intercut: first, at pseudo-trials detainees, mostly youth and people of color, critique American economic hierarchies and systemic racism and are silenced by law-and-order review panel members; in another, a group of detainees who have been sentenced to the Park are pursued by law enforcement, an exercise that doubles as a punishment for the prisoners and a training exercise for the officers. Ostensibly the agreement is that, if the prisoners can cross the Park and reach a designated safe zone, they are free; in reality, the police use any pretext to increase the violence of their engagement and kill everyone, even those who have reached the safe zone. The entwined scenes end with the "journalist" finally intervening as the police beat the last survivors, while in the courtroom the defendants are offered a choice of twenty years imprisonment or the Park, most choosing the latter. In many of its screenings, *Punishment Park* was mistaken for a real documentary.[11] It gave so accurate an insight into the class, race, and generational politics of a contemporary United States that it was considered too controversial by its distributors, was panned in many reviews, and disappeared from circulation for more than two decades.

Punishment Park makes all too visible how thin was the dividing line between a dystopian vision of science fiction and a documentary of 1970s America, split by generational and ideological conflict evident in events such as the trial of the Chicago Seven and the gagging of Bobby Seale, the Kent State National Guard shootings of protesting students, and the public controversies over events in Vietnam such as the My Lai massacre. Using a well-established science fiction technique of literalizing metaphor, the film makes dreadfully clear how easily we might read the contemporary United States as a kind of science fiction. The film opens with an overview of the McCarron Act and makes no reference to a temporal or other setting that would create a gap between this real piece of legislation and the fictional mise-en-scène we then enter. The actors, espousing their own critiques of American imperialism, curtailment of civil liberties, and systemic racism, improvised many of the scenes in the film. In scenes of the hearings, defendants hurl accusations against those sitting on the judgment panels, while those in authority ignore or actively silence these critiques. Official charges are read, but the proceedings imply a guilty verdict is a given, and that the purpose of these panels is to criminalize dissent of any kind, especially critiques of the U.S. invasion of Vietnam. Meanwhile, in scenes of the convicted group about to traverse the Park, debates ensue about the legitimacy of using violence against a clearly violent police force and about the likelihood that the process going forward will be "fair"—that is, according to the rules they have been told. As the police response becomes more aggressive, even those counseling restraint become militant: "the only legitimate thing that I can think to do is to use my body or my freedom or . . . my life to back up what I say," says one despairing detainee as he prepares to sacrifice himself rather than capitulate. Another announces, "I am loyal to the people of this country" but not to "the government because the government is against the people." Ending on a dire note, where even the "objective" journalist feels compelled to intervene, the film aims to prompt us to action in the material world.

Lizzie Borden's ambitious *Born in Flames* is initially framed as a news story about the ten-year anniversary of the socialist revolution, but it includes segments of what seems to be contemporary (to the film's diegesis) police surveillance of the subversive Women's Army and private moments of women discussing their place in this postrevolutionary world.

Intervening into a 1980s working-class movement that saw gender as a secondary concern and a second-wave feminism insufficiently attentive to lesbians and women of color, the film shows the need for an intersectionalist analysis of how gender, race, and class exclusions overlap. The main narrative is about the death of the Women's Army founder, Adelaide Norris, while in police custody, and how her fate radicalizes all women to resist party discipline and finish the incomplete revolution. Ending on the cusp of more social change with Phoenix Radio's call "black women, be ready; white women, get ready; red women, stay ready," *Born in Flames* connects its fictional world to the real one even more overtly than does *Punishment Park*, especially in scenes where the Woman's Army is defending women from violent assault by men on the streets and where we can see that the working class movement has been fragmented by patriarchal sexism and systemic racism.

A woman of color, Adelaide finds her own activism, prompted by losing her construction job, the result of a "work fair system" in which working-class men seek to regain the ground "lost" by the extension of employment to women, a movement that echoes the "family wage" rhetoric of Reagan's America contemporary to the film's release. Another woman asks a foreman to stop all work until everyone can be put back on the job together, but the unfinished sexual revolution means that working-class solidarity is easily exploited by capital and the layoffs continue. Meanwhile the feminist editorial collective of the *Socialist Review*, all white women (including a performance by a young Kathryn Bigelow), fragments gender solidarity as well when they condemn the Women's Army's resistance to party policy as "removing the only structure we have for progress." Only the radicalized women of color—who militarize through partnership with the women who are part of the Algerian independence movement—can provide the necessary impetus to finish the revolution. Adelaide's suspicious death while in police custody unites all women beyond racial lines, including the journalist editors of the *Socialist Review* who had previously held themselves aloof from the radicalism of the Women's Army. *Born in Flames* offers a vision in which those who are observers are compelled to become participants in public events, much as in *Punishment Park*. The film's revolutionary conclusion in which news of injustice prompts collective action perhaps now seems naïvely unrealistic in a world suffused by capitalist realism, while *Punishment Park*'s dystopian conclusion perhaps seems frighteningly possible. But both films operate by a logic in which observers within the diegesis must become agents, which implies that viewers of these pseudo-documentaries are similarly enjoined to take action in order to prevent our reality from becoming the science-fictionalized reality of these films.

I want to turn in conclusion to briefly considering the recent documentary *Detropia* (Heidi Ewing and Rachel Grady) and consider what it might mean to read a documentary as a kind of science fiction. What insight might this offer us into the reality of contemporary capitalism beyond the fantasies of capitalist realism? I take license to read the film in this way not only from its title but also from the world-through-alien-eyes images of performance artists Steve Coy and Dorato Coy, featured in the film. As the Coys point out, the abandonment of Detroit by forces of global capital has created both crisis and opportunity: they do not have to submit themselves to the debt entailed by living in more expensive places, so they and others have more freedom to experiment with alternative ways of living and forming community in this exiled space outside the Crystal Palace of capital. The film does not romanticize the tremendous suffering faced by Detroit residents, and I do not intend to do so either in positing the unscripted quality of life in Detroit as a seed of hope. Much of *Detropia* is like watching a dystopian near-future science fiction film, such as the dismal meeting of the Union Auto Workers Union in which they are bluntly told the company has no interest in a "livable wage" and cares only about the cuts that are necessary to "keep Detroit viable," language reminiscent of the sales pitches in *Repo Men*. In a scene where manual laborers destroy abandoned infrastructure to harvest the metals, the laborers chat about the purpose of their work and decide it is to ship raw material to China "so that they can make more shit and sell it back to us," another real-world moment that feels like part of a dystopian science fiction future.

What Mark Fisher calls "science fiction capital"—the use of glossy utopian images of a future of shiny new products as a kind of currency to get people materially to invest in the future of capital—has historically been attached to Detroit through its auto industry. The filmmakers intercut the ruins of contemporary Detroit with a 1970s Cadillac commercial that deploys such science fiction capital, in which the company and its automobiles are celebrated as centers of the "highways of tomorrow." The contrast in the documentary between these images and contemporary Detroit has the effect of making the city itself feel something like the burnt-out ruins of a formerly utopian science fiction franchise. Yet, like the citizens of Detroit, the film refuses to let the city be relegated to the dystopian. The Coys are part of the Urban Innovation Exchange (UIX), an aligned group of people and projects fostering things such as cooperative work, apprenticeships, urban farming, and more.[12] Such projects—and the science fictional reading of *Detropia* as another world where anything is possible— foster a vision of what David Harvey has called "co-revolutionary theory," a theory of society that understands that social change must be thought through at all levels from "grand revolutionary strategies to the redesign of urbanization and city life."[13] Harvey argues in *The Enigma of Capital* that new ways of living—such as those explored in the science-fictionalized space of Detroit—could create "daily life as the free exploration of new kinds of social relations and living arrangements, mental conceptions that focus on self-realization in service to others, and technological and organizational innovations oriented to the pursuit of the common good rather than to supporting militarized power and corporate greed."[14] The experiments and collectives highlighted as spaces of hope in *Detropia*, the spaces for new possibilities that open up when capital and all its strictures leave, are suggestive of precisely such new social and living arrangements. It may not be *after* capitalism, but reading *Detropia* as a kind of science fiction that allows us to imagine a future beyond the dystopic is possible in the spaces abandoned by capital. It allows us to see through a capitalist realism that would tell us that there is no alternative but to dismantle the city. In its visions of new ways of thinking and living, new collectives and opportunities, the science-fictionalization of daily life in Detroit accomplished by the Coys' artwork, the film reminds us that life continues beyond the Crystal Palace inhabited by those still privileged by this system.

Notes

1 Fredric Jameson, *Seeds of Time* (New York: Columbia University Press, 1994), xii.

2 Fredric Jameson, *Postmodernism, or, The Cultural Logic of Late Capitalism* (Durham: Duke University Press, 1991), 44.

3 Sloterdijk writes, "As any glance at the relevant documents shows, the empirical and the fantastic were inextricably intertwined in the early Age of Discovery. By means of its rapid effective new media—whether chapbooks, travel accounts, novels and utopias or broadsheets, globes and world maps—thoughts of the genuine New World and its imaginary variants produced a post-metaphysical wish regime which believed that its fulfillments were perhaps not within reach, but at least in the not-too-distant future. This set in motion a form of self-fulfilling wishful thinking that learned to steer a course, both in fantasy and in reality, towards distant worlds and their fortunes in happiness, as if their supposed appearance at some distant point already held the promise of their imminent appropriation." Peter Sloterdijk, *In the World Interior of Capital*, trans. Weiland Hoban (New York: Polity, 2013), 80.

4 Theodor Adorno and Max Horkheimer, *The Dialectic of Enlightenment*, trans. John Cumming (New York: Continuum, 2002), 126.

5 Ibid., 139, 142.

6 Mark Fisher, *Capitalist Realism: Is There No Alternative?* (London: Zero Books, 2009).

7 David Harvey, *The Enigma of Capital, and the Crises of Capitalism* (Oxford: Oxford University Press, 2010), 30.

8 Randy Martin, *An Empire of Indifference: American War and the Financial Logic of Risk Management* (Durham: Duke University Press, 2007), 147.

9   Sloterdijk, *In the World Interior of Capital*, 194.

10 See Nancy Scheper-Hughes, "Bodies for Sale: Whole or in Parts," in *Commodifying Bodies*, ed. Nancy Scheper-Hughes and Loïc Wacquant (New York: Sage, 2002), 1–8; Aslihan Sanal, *New Organs within Us: Transplants and the Moral Economy* (Durham: Duke University Press, 2011).

11 See overview by Joseph A. Gomez included in the liner notes with the Project X DVD edition of the film released in 2005. Joseph A. Gomez, "Punishment Park [liner notes]," *Punishment Park*, dir. Peter Watkins (1971, New Yorker Video/ Project X Distribution, 2005), DVD.

12 See http://www.uixdetroit.com/about/about.aspx, accessed April 2, 2014.

13 Harvey, *The Enigma of Capital, and the Crises of Capitalism*, 138.

14 Ibid., 231.

7

Mistaken Places

Unemployment, Avant-Gardism, and the Auto-da-Fé

MARCUS BULLOCK

They also serve who only stand and wait.

—John Milton

It is hard to imagine a realm of knowledge based on measurement and calculation whose predictions are less dependable than those of economics. The discipline distinguishes itself most brilliantly in accounts of what should have been done to avoid catastrophes after they happen. Nonetheless, it would be foolish not to acknowledge its real and indispensable insights. For example, certain things are generally understood to cause changes in unemployment, and certain things are known to be caused by changes in unemployment. This places unemployment among the necessities of social management. In consequence, even voices that have a strong interest in maintaining the generous face of capitalism sometimes allow a slight lack of human sympathy to color their language on this topic when they represent the exclusion of people from work as a natural phenomenon. An article in *The Economist* bringing joyful news about the American economy at the start of 2015 under the title "A Happy New Year" remarks, "unemployment has fallen to 5.8 percent. On current trends it could drop close to 5 percent within a year, less than many estimates of the natural rate of unemployment."[1] And indeed, that trend did continue, and the normal response came about in the form of the inevitable next decision, that is, when and how much to slow or halt this trend by raising interest rates.

This conception of a "natural value" for unemployment and the consequences of deviating from it play directly into policy decisions that sustain unemployment despite recognizing it as an evil. In a 2014 article entitled "Opportunistic Overheating," *The Economist* offered a commentary illustrating the normal framework of decisions regarding people without jobs: "When officials at the Federal Reserve meet next week, they will wrestle with a problem most other central banks would love to have: what to do if unemployment gets too low?"[2] Even though it is recognized by all as a social evil, unemployment serves an economic purpose, and the unemployed, in their imposed idleness, produce a kind of indirect value enjoyed by everyone else. The stability they provide, keeping the economic machine at its optimal operating temperature, will falter if their numbers fall too low.

Too low? one might ask, were one naïve enough not to understand what nature dictates. Does unemployment not afflict families and individuals with real suffering? How can we worry about not having enough of it? The metaphors are, as always, telling. The "opportunistic" febrile state we fear casts the unemployed in the role of an antibody to disease, like that which grows deficient in the etiology of AIDS. But the utter irrationality of social attitudes toward unemployed persons becomes apparent through the rationality of their economic function, which requires that their existence radiate a degree of anxiety through the various levels of their employed compatriots. The stability of aggregate business activity—in the form of sustainable growth—depends on an elaborate balance between the availability of money on the one hand and the availability of goods and services on the other. The direct measurable effect of unemployment in that equation depends on the extent to which consumer demand is tempered by the number of people who are not receiving a paycheck and the effect on wage rates of that "reserve army" of the unemployed, which figured so large in Marxist theory in the nineteenth century. These effects operate through market forces as the "hidden hand" that regulates monetary values. Such effects are in principle susceptible to calculation within the limits of their complexity, and their outcomes are susceptible enough to prediction on the basis of history to justify their application as economic policy. Nonetheless, the metaphor of the "reserve army" suggests something rather different from the metaphor of an antibody required to fend off a fever.

If the figure of 5 percent—or any other number that arises in the course of the business cycle—operates as the necessary casualty rate suffered by the workforce, why do those sacrificed in the struggle feel so stigmatized?

Why do we not respect those whom the struggle leaves without jobs in the way, by tradition, we honor those who sacrifice themselves in the nation's struggles with foreign enemies? In the grand perspective of the Federal Reserve, the unemployed appear as a measurable force held back according to the requirements of policy to sustain the community's economic health and security. Yet in no other sense does this body of people resemble an army. While a financial reserve or a reserve in the inventory of a commodity, including that of labor, can operate through the hidden hand of the market, there is an important element in the function of the unemployed as a sacrifice that requires their visibility not as soldiers at the ready but as casualties. And yet, these are not honorable casualties. On the contrary, a person without a job is considered a person who has failed. A sacrifice has indeed been exacted of them, but it is the movement of money itself that inflicted these losses. The effect of throwing people out of work or keeping them in that state resembles an act of terrorism more than a strategic military measure. While this sequestered population on the margin of society does function as a "natural" market force in its role as a necessary excess of supply that holds the level of wages in check, it also operates in the realm of what economists like to call "sentiment." That is another way of saying the visible presence of unemployed people acts directly on the feelings and the fears of those who are thereby made to feel grateful that they still have jobs.

Has anyone experienced losing his or her job as a sacrifice made in service to one's country? That would be strange. At an individual level, it would be more likely to feel as though one had not earned the right to keep one's place among those who do serve by their labor; one receives one's dismissal as a punishment that others, more deserving, had avoided. An intimation of that experience—and the anxiety radiating from it—enters the social order as a factor in the working of the larger benefit. The attachment of the employed majority to the system that sustains them and the economic behavior the system requires of them depend on the meaning of the line between working and not working. The form of sacrifice that expels a person from the status of employment creates an additional value for employment. In leaving that realm, one enters what will feel all too much like a zone of the dead. While it is a realm from which one may return, the blow of expulsion from the workforce means being driven out of the army of virtue and into a place with little light. The human catastrophe depends, to a great extent, on the faith in the state of remaining in the army of virtue that the act of leaving it expresses.

To be sacrificed in this way functions to produce an effect all too similar to the auto-da-fé in times of religious crisis. The auto-da-fé—an act of faith—in that older tradition represented the division between the world of adherence to an order of value and the alternative realm by which those values were defined when someone was cast out. To understand this side of a capitalist social order requires looking at it from a perspective quite complementary to the model by which it sees itself as a system of monetary management. We can find that perspective in an early fragmentary piece by Walter Benjamin in which he frames a wide-angle view of capitalism by constructing it according to the model of a negative religion. Even though he does not discuss unemployment as such in explicit terms, his view of labor as a religious value does support the account offered here of unemployment as a sacrifice and an act of faith.

Those who fall in the nation's wars are honored because security depends on inculcating a desire among the citizenry to enter the struggle and bear the risks. Those on whom idleness descends like a punishment serve in the opposite function. Their presence inspires a kind of terror. The worth of a job to those who still possess one acquires an additional value beyond that of its monetary compensation. It acquires a symbolic function, a kind of aura, that marks out the worker as a full participant in society. The struggle to redeem the lives of the unemployed would have to be played out at the line between these two realms of representation and misrepresentation. After all, they may well not be "idle" in any real sense, but their contribution to the well-being of their families and communities no longer figures as real production. It has no measure as money and disappears from view and from calculation. Social engagement takes many forms and embodies many forms of real value beyond that of paid labor.

In its simplest terms the terror operates because, in parallel with the purely monetary evaluation of work, the social order remains cruelly parsimonious with any other means to earn respect. To reduce that loss of respect requires that we reduce the role of monetary earnings in their symbolic function. We should admit a corresponding rise in the value of activity outside the realm of paid labor.

Those who set macroeconomic policy have no reason to imagine anything about the conditions they impose. They will prosper in good times and bad times without significant change as the business cycle rolls by beneath them. The calculations that arrive at specific numbers on which such institutions as the Federal Reserve decide are bets made on the basis of how the business cycle has turned its roulette wheel in the past. For everybody else, the issue of where one places one's faith depends on the effect of that pervasive terror, which radiates always from the image of unemployment as it rises and comes closer, and as it recedes a little but never disappears. Does the terror enhance one's faith in the system, or does the system reveal itself as a repugnant imposition on human substance?

The argument that follows here does not aspire to dispute with the various schools and masters who recommend when and how such policy bets are laid. It seeks to extend the horizon of our awareness to include just what the losses entail in realms outside the measure of money. Money operates, as far as it produces calculable results, by causing people to act in ways to acquire more of it and to avoid losing it. The simplest model of the business cycle in its measure of an aggregate economic activity, however, expects people to make decisions that might very likely put them out of business by misallocating resources according to the measure of the economy as a whole. That is to say, activity increases to the point where unemployment drops, pressure of demand rises, and the resulting inefficiencies express themselves in "overheating." If one thinks of the economy as a system comparable to a living body, then that very "creativity" by which it grows also produces a fever that weakens it and causes it to diminish again. We are all too familiar with other destructive aspects of this capitalist mode of creation—cities that are hollowed out by devastation because the money that built them moves elsewhere, and a planet pockmarked by ruined landscapes and threatened by another form of overheating—but the subtleties of desire that afflict human identity within this incoherent tumble of forces will elude our focused attention as long as we think in the language that represents money as a force of nature.

If we try to model history as a system of causes and effects, then indeed nothing really fits together as it should. Like the retroactive predictions of economists, the larger designs of history compete with one another with their different rationalizations, which seek to place the present as a natural outcome of the past. And yet the impulses in play that bring about each decision in human life, as well as the aggregate of such decisions that we understand as the movement of history, do not just follow the model of the economic "hidden hand" adjusting monetary exchange. This perception promoted a much discussed remark in Benjamin's final commentary on capitalist politics, "On the Concept of History," written in 1940. He criticizes the rationalizing historical narratives that represent the past as a journey through scenes that necessarily brought about the condition of the present by arguing that "no state of affairs having causal significance is for that very reason historical."[3] And by alienating history from these narrated inventions of its necessity, the alternative materialist historiography he envisages can force events to show their hand as decisions of a quite different character.

The unique strength of capitalism throughout its long and varied historical expression has lain in its ability to integrate ever more intricate relationships or interdependencies between systems of production and consumption. One can argue, as a general principle, that it is not itself a "system" in the sense of a calculable process of coordinated forces, nor in the sense of a living body that sustains itself in a condition of "health" by a set of endogenic compensations. Nonetheless, as long as one feels the destructive side of capitalist creativity as private insecurity in one's individual existence and also as necessitated by the causalities of free monetary movement, then one does remain in thrall to that terror. But anything that acts to expose how far this image of the economy as an integral system is indeed fallacious also acts to expose the purely arbitrary elements in the ideology that supports the social relations of a market economy but are not integral to the management of money. What Benjamin identifies as the religious structure of capitalist labor, and the aspect of this structure we have identified as the terroristic working of unemployment as auto-da-fé, extend into another dimension beyond that of the monetary economy. The term "capitalism" itself functions largely as a veil over this distinction. The historical formation we know as capitalism with all its characteristic institutions and social controls can certainly be distinguished from other possibilities of society and culture that would still incorporate free exchange of goods and the free allocation of resources. More specifically, the action by terror can be counted among the inefficiencies of our economic system insofar as the pervasiveness of insecurity counts as an economic disvalue. The arbitrary stigma of unemployment taints employment with its threat and reduces the value of a job that always hangs under that threat.

Such additional measures of value should guide the appropriate response to the anxieties that supposedly threaten when levels of unemployment fall "too low." If that measure falls any lower than the natural level of 5 percent, and the millions of people encircled within it start finding work, then the system, *The Economist* article warns, will "overheat." That metaphor might bring more rhetorical force than aptness to the discussion. If a motor tended to "overheat" and grow dangerous unless restricted to performance that injured one person in twenty, one would think seriously about a recall. It would be naïve, of course, to think of zero as the ideal for which adept political management might strive. Stability in any market requires a certain level of "inventory," and insofar as labor functions as a commodity that applies in the same way. Yet "inventory" signifies one thing when coal piles up somewhere in "idle" heaps and means another when human beings stand around in lines waiting for an opportunity to work. The issue in play does not need to question whether supply and demand need to be kept in balance. The question concerns how quite separate symbolic values are drawn into a monetary equation.

If we set *The Economist* aside and go to another corner of the news media, we can gain a different kind of information about this phenomenon of unemployment. *Al Jazeera* carried an online opinion piece by Sarah Kendzior on October 7, 2013, under the heading "The Men Who Set Themselves on Fire: Due to Joblessness and a Bleak Economy, Self-Immolations in Industrialized Societies Are Rising Rapidly." Individuals, we discover, feel a different heat from the metaphorical temperature of an economy. Kendzior reports on a phenomenon that seems to have attracted little attention, though it offers a deeper insight into what losing a job means. She begins by responding to an event that happened three days earlier, on October 4, 2013, when a man poured gasoline over himself on the National Mall in Washington, DC, and burned himself to death. This did cause something of a stir simply for the horror of such a scene in this most privileged locality—yet still, it was not much more than a stir: "As I write this, no one knows who the man was or why he did it. But his act is not unique. He joins a long list of men who have self-immolated since the global financial collapse and subsequent austerity. Around the world, men are setting themselves on fire because they cannot find work." That is a startling assertion indeed, but she bases it on reports from countries around the world:

> These events are occurring in the world's richest and poorest nations, in its allegedly stable democracies and in its most ruthless dictatorships. The men who do this are young and old, of all races and religions, united only by their joblessness and their despair. In the UK, an unemployed 48-year-old man set himself on fire outside a job centre after not receiving a needed payment. In Morocco, a group of young law students, belonging to a group called "Unemployed Graduates," set themselves on fire after not finding work. In Spain, a man burnt himself alive because he did not have enough money for food. In Greece, a 55-year-old man set himself on fire after screaming that he was in debt. In Bulgaria, several unemployed men self-immolated after condemning graft and corruption. In France, over a dozen people—both French nationals and immigrants, from different occupations and social classes—set themselves on fire because they could not find jobs. . . . Unemployed men have self-immolated in Germany, Iraq, Jordan, China, Algeria, Tunisia, Egypt and elsewhere. Many cases receive little media attention. The week before the man burned himself alive on the National Mall, a man in a business suit tried to set himself on fire in Houston, Texas, after telling passersby that he could not find a job. The case did not make the national news.[4]

It is interesting to note that, even though the article mentions Greece, the number of incidents remains small there despite the intensity of the current crisis.[5] We can find one reason for this in the way Greece has identified the crisis as a national rather than a private tragedy. The dramatically visible role of international bankers and foreign nations has changed the symbolism of joblessness among Greeks to signify a fate visited on the community as a whole—thereby carrying with it a possible sense of national solidarity. The deepest suffering of unemployment depends on the hiddenness of its causes in the abstractness of economic relations. The impossibility of holding it below the level apparently dictated by an iron law of economics operates as a tragic flaw in economic life precisely because it isolates individuals, which it does because it has this character of fate or nature, acting through the "hidden hand" of monetary shifts. These move under the influence of impersonal forces. The "Happy New Year" article explains to anyone who does not already understand that falling unemployment causes "upward pressure on wages and prices."[6]

Different people ring this alarm bell at different times and with different solutions when this abstract force begins to take hold, but everyone accepts that overheating will disrupt the stable circulation of money and eventually throw people out of work once more. No one seems to have a plan to improve this highly inefficient and dangerous design in the economic machine. Even economists who approach the question of unemployment with the best will in the world merely calculate a different balance among factors like currency values, commodity prices, taxes, interest rates, and tariffs. A different set of calculations might shift the "sustainable" level of unemployment down a notch or two, but the phenomenon still persists and follows cycles beyond prediction and control.

The alternative to this precarious balancing of markets and prices applies raw power rather than the flow of money as an alternative to the management of "heat" in the economy. The reconstruction of society to permit no idleness abolishes the human content of work. In place of social labor, as Ernst Jünger pointed out just before Hitler astonished the world with this very solution, the state introduces a new model of work, that of "total mobilization."[7] Along with the social burden of unemployment, the totally mobilized state eliminates the entire realm of community relations. This problem does not express itself merely in the material domain, where things are produced to serve the interests of the state and not the community, but in the communal realm itself: human relations and values are no longer embodied in work. Perhaps Martin Heidegger provides the most grotesquely instructive philosophical failure to grasp the human stake at risk here. On February 22, 1934, he delivered a lecture to six hundred men whose labor had just been mobilized by the new policies of the National Socialist regime. Heidegger, as the recently appointed *Rektor* of Freiburg University, invited them to convene in the main lecture hall in order to congratulate them on their return to the possession of language, being, and knowledge. The only right to speak they had regained, however, restored nothing of what they had lost. Once Heidegger's speech was ended, he led all six hundred as a single voice in the chant "Heil Hitler."

It would appear from this particular history that in unemployment we might be faced with a curse from which we cannot free ourselves except by a yet more vicious curse. We seem to owe Stalin an insight into the character of this ill fate. Even though there appears to be no certainty as to whether the famous line is really his, we can reformulate the position attributed to him on military and political catastrophe by acknowledging that while the unemployment of a million people is a statistic, the unemployment of one person is a tragedy. But this misses the point of that simpler and yet deep question of human value to which we have already alluded. Why is it such a tragedy? After all, it lies in the nature of paid work that we usually hanker for its interruption. We consider it the symptom of a disease, workaholism, not to welcome the end of a shift, the beginning of the weekend, the arrival of a holiday. Of course the factor of material privation plays a part in the hardship of losing a job, but people do not self-immolate just because they find themselves short of cash. The difference between a paycheck and an unemployment benefit check often doesn't always run so very high in dollars or euros. The real difference is paid out in the intangible social value of respect.

The unemployed find themselves shut out and endangered by a split that runs through the word "tragedy" itself. The meaning of the tragic as explored in literary expression and sustained in tradition adds a dimension to suffering that ennobles it by conveying a transcendent value. Such a tragedy invites us to share in an experience for the sake of this value and creates its appeal in aestheticized emotions. The individual tragedy of a person isolated in the silence of unemployment offers no such invitation. That suffering embodies no high value. We incline to turn away when confronted by people who stand and wait for an end to this emptied-out time and respond not in human but in abstract terms, returning to solutions in numbers.

The 95 percent who benefit from full employment do recognize that there is something owing the 5 percent for whom that fullness still remains empty. The system transfers a small amount of wealth in the form of unemployment benefits from the majority to the minority. And yet the systemic exclusion remains intact, and that is what motivates the horrors to which Kendzior draws our attention. Nonetheless, not even she attempts to articulate the larger social harmony that should, according to all human reason, unite these two groups. The solution she offers returns once more to the concept of masses and statistics. She brings up the extraordinarily high levels of youth unemployment in countries like Greece and Spain, which signify, she says, "a social and political crisis."[8] They do indeed. But the crisis of a system and the crisis in an individual life need to be understood differently, not least because the system can by its nature never exclude a component of crisis.

As the standard concept of "overheating" establishes, the economy that hums along and shelters those who are working depends for its sustainable working temperature on those who are not. They are part of the system. They are as integral to the prosperity of the whole as the radiator and coolant are to the mechanical devices from which we take that metaphor. Yet they do not feel included in the integrity of the whole. No economist with normal sensitivity would disagree in principle with Kendzior when she writes, "Unemployment is not only the loss of a job. It is the loss of dignity. It is the loss of the present and, over time, the ability to imagine a future. It is hopelessness and shame, an open struggle everyone witnesses but pretends not to see. It is a social and political crisis we tell a man to solve, and blame him when he cannot."[9] Kendzior's rhetoric certainly emphasizes the effect of this crisis in terms of individual misery, but it also leaves the responsibility for a solution precisely where an economist would necessarily agree it belongs. The answer to unemployment is employment, and better management will bring this about—but only up to a natural limit.

The comments in the *Al Jazeera* article are clearly true and well meant, yet we should note that they not only fall back into the kind of well-meaning advice we find in the pages of *The Economist* about managing and reducing levels of unemployment, but they also lie alarmingly close to what we find in Martin Heidegger's lecture to the formerly unemployed in 1934. Setting aside the Heideggerian jargon his speech, too, offers the relief of "hopelessness and shame," the "putting aside of inner hopelessness and despair," and promises that the man restored to work "will win back his self-respect and a proud bearing, and will show firmness and decision in meeting his comrades."[10] It is not enough to say "Well, yes, these are just the kind of easy platitudes with which anyone might praise the virtues of work." That might be true, but then we need to ask why would people listen to such talk, and why would they believe it? We might put it another way: what do any of these texts actually tell us about the condition of unemployment? Not only what would Heidegger, the pompous Nazi apologist, know about it, but how does anyone who is not immersed in the experience itself contain that experience in language?

Now, of course, one could pose that question about any distinctive experience. Language always operates at a certain level of abstraction and generalization, but in this case one suspects that the phenomenon of self-immolation reveals a relationship between speech and speechlessness of a radically different cast. Does something in all this discussion in the public arena about unemployment still remain unsaid? The only thing that cannot be said is what it is like not to speak. Perhaps that is the key to what we need to ask here.

My own remarks that follow are not motivated by curiosity or speculation about such experience but, rather, by all too vivid memories. I do not speak *for* myself in what follows insofar as there is no theoretical substance to be derived from one unique recollection, but I do speak *from* myself insofar as I can say where a theoretical claim successfully corresponds to my own case. And I will say that, while I survived a prolonged period of unemployment, I was astonished at how hard it was and, indeed, at how the shock has persisted long afterward, even into years of employment with tenure. I had considered myself unusually well equipped to cope with that situation. I had seen the effect on my family as a child growing up and thought I had learned how to adjust; I was very adept at making the most of limited resources; I felt no personal share in the system of judgments that burden an unemployed person and held on to an otherwise intact life. Nonetheless, it was so unpleasant that I have seldom mentioned it in any context since. Unpleasant enough, moreover, to render the stories related in Kendzior's account less impenetrable than one would like. As an unemployed person, one does indeed feel extinguished, posthumous.

The only theoretical view I have found that frames the shock in a form that I recognize occurs in that short piece written in 1921 by Benjamin, unpublished in his lifetime, entitled "Capitalism as Religion." Although he does not raise the matter of unemployment directly, Benjamin's argument addresses the artificially created division between employment and unemployment by what he calls the "cultic" function of work. Labor under the economic conditions he takes as his particular definition of capitalism narrows all the significance of work to this cultic or symbolic function. Admitting no other source of meaning, capitalism completely separates all activity from its human content. The title of Benjamin's text, "Capitalism as Religion," can mislead the reader who takes it too simply and too literally. The quality an economic system takes on as a religion subverts all the usual characteristics that define either capitalism or religion. Benjamin's attack on the cultic force emanating from the practices of work, on the other hand, strikes precisely at the heart of the problem afflicting an unemployed person.

At one's first encounter with this text, Benjamin's presenting Freud, Nietzsche, and Marx as subordinated within the realm of capitalist thinking stands out as particularly bold—perhaps implausibly so. After all, one's first thought exalts these three figures beyond restrictions within markets and among commodities. And yet, against the backdrop of the events listed by Kendzior, the descriptions of human experience in their three theories begin to look like mere shadow play. Certainly, the perspective of an unemployed person will frame something much more concrete and direct than any such theoretical speculation. One might "know" according to the assertions of a theory that one has been caught by the backhand of an unfair set of circumstances, but no such knowledge can rescue one from the loss of value that losing one's job inflicts. The resources of individual language simply cannot resist that collective cultic force.

Benjamin offers no historical analysis of capitalism as a system of production or exchange. The time of writing (1921) fell substantially before he embraced the politics of social revolution that would figure so largely in his later positions. Changes in systems of ownership would therefore not, in his view, change that form of work. On the contrary, the cultic economy would prove the decisive element that conditions all such historical changes: "the capitalism that refuses to change course becomes socialism."[11] Nonetheless, the revolutionary socialism he invokes in 1940, in the context of "On the Concept of History" from which we quoted his remark about causality and history, clearly envisages a quite different order of change and a quite different conception of the theoretical understanding of history. His Messianic view of history in 1940 engages the unique perspective of a radicalism in politics that breaks entirely with all systems and institutions.

What Benjamin in 1921 identifies as characteristic of capitalism also makes it unique among religions, namely, that it is not a system of belief. He makes the point repeatedly that capitalism has no dogma. It does not express its religious character by outlining concepts and ideas to which it demands allegiance but manifests itself in an unbounded demand for symbolic activity, the fulfillment of the work cult: "in the first place, capitalism is a purely cultic religion, perhaps the most extreme that ever existed. In capitalism, things have meaning only in relation to the cult." It follows from the logic of this description that unemployment, as exile from the realm of an all-encompassing symbolic activity, would precipitate a spiritual catastrophe. The component of belief on which other religions base their appeal endows worship with the power to "allay . . . anxieties, torments, and disturbances" beyond the days set aside for devotion. Since "capitalism has no specific body of dogma, no theology," only the sustained effort of work provides religious support. Workdays occupy precisely the opposite place that they would in a world with a theology. Although the pragmatics of work impose periodic breaks, the meaning of Sunday as a Sabbath vanishes. It merely serves the purpose of sustaining labor by the function of a break. It is the activity of actual performance in the material realm that supplies the sole source of meaning, which Benjamin terms "the concretization of the cult." Since every day renews the cult, no other kind of time intervenes; in consequence, "There are no 'weekdays.'"[12]

What sets capitalism as Benjamin sees it alongside religion is a division of life between the saved and the damned, albeit one in which ultimately there is no salvation equivalent to that created by reconciliation with God. What Freud, Nietzsche, and Marx have in common is their shared rejection of a divine reconciliation. Therefore at this stage of his thinking, Benjamin does not regard their critique of inauthentic relations as an opposition to capitalism but as a sectarian expression within it. Each theory defines a world of the lost—whether lost because of erotic repression, or because of an enfeebled will to power, or as the dying class on the wrong side of history. And yet all three of these claims to prophetic authority ring hollow in the face of capitalist reality. Each claim devises a rhetoric to repudiate alienation from an imagined vital body, but what does that offer to those who are caught up in the concrete expression of exile from their homeland when the sudden earthquake of unemployment breaks away the ground under their feet?

The repetitions of work within the cult offer no security. As long as unemployment consigns one segment of the population to a rejected underworld, then its inevitable persistence condemns everyone to live under a threat of damnation. Without a transcendent version of reconciliation offered in the usual tradition of religion, there is no theoretical place of safety. Anyone can lose a job, just as anyone can lose his or her money. And while only those who have experienced unemployment directly will know exactly what kind of pain it brings, those who contemplate that fate from outside get no pleasure equivalent to that which theology promises those in heaven who look down into hell. Those who remain among the employed know enough, as with any pain from which one is not absolutely preserved, to fear what fate might yet bring. And this insuperable threat of unemployment vitiates the economic solution to a "crisis." The passing of a crisis offers a remediation in time but never in perpetuity.

Neither *Al Jazeera* nor *The Economist* offers an answer to this terror. They do not even recognize the question, Why does this inexplicable power to desolate hold such sway? Although Benjamin offers a unique and penetrating way to identify these cruel effects, his attack on capitalism does not offer a worldly solution either. The political positions that he takes in his essay "Critique of Violence" (also written in 1921) indicate unequivocally that the religious problem of capitalism would require a religious solution. The notions of "divine violence" or "pure violence" for which he argues in that essay depend on a mystery; they do not offer a concrete alternative to the concretization of the cult. In the essay on nature and representation he wrote from 1919 to 1922, "Goethe's Elective Affinities," he insists that, "In fact, there is true reconciliation only with God."[13] Redemption of alienated human relations can proceed only through the divine, so he argues, but the divine radicalizes alienation only between its adherents and those it excludes. Nothing is less human than God.

Even so, Benjamin's analysis of the way human experience has been fragmented by this religious component of economic ideology does identify an absurdity that runs through both Kendzior's voice of protest and the ongoing commentary on the world economy in *The Economist*. That voice of liberal capitalism has no more interest than she does in denying the values of dignity, hope, and progress toward a better future for all. The concern with "overheating" in the end constitutes little more than a rhetorical difference. Any form of destabilization ends up increasing the number of people without work, and no policy can eliminate either the continuing misery of unemployment at some level or the fear that it will rise and blight more lives at any time. The absurdity lies in the division between those who work for pay and those who do not.

One is not transfigured in oneself according to where one is placed in the flow of money. This is a mystical transformation—as grotesque as the transformation that excludes Gregor Samsa in Kafka's story "Metamorphosis" from his place in the world. Kafka's story uses the model of waking up as a vermin to convey the inconceivably cruel and unnatural break between the life of a man who works and his condition where he cannot. Paradoxically, the entirely correct and justified description of what unemployment takes away from a human life in the *Al Jazeera* article treats this as a natural consequence. Making the connection so direct gives the appearance of a simple causality, and yet, clearly, we have to think of a complex process of mediation here. The *Al Jazeera* article does not concern itself with that mediation, with how the economy cools its overheated condition by freezing out those who fall from its embrace, whether they resort to the ultimate symbol of self-immolation or not.

The greatest mistake made on the conservative side of this debate lies in the idea that the forces of the market are forces of nature. They have nothing to do with natural laws, but nonetheless this bizarre machine on which we depend, the economy, can't be controlled beyond certain limits. The means of expression in tragic self-immolation, however, does tell us something about what can be controlled. Self-destruction offers a desperate substitute for control, as Kendzior has seen correctly in these acts: "When you are unemployed, your past is dismissed as unworthy. Your future is denied. Self-immolation is making yourself, in the moment, matter."[14] One has turned oneself, one might say, into a symbol—like the flag whose burning constitutes a convention of political speech. And yet the meaning in this case depends on the reality in which one's body is nothing like a flag. The flames that consume a person speak an entirely different language. That explains why such an act seems to fall outside the discourse of the news, and why, sometimes, it produces seismic forces at another level.

The language of symbol and sacrifice truly does matter when it creates a form of speech where before there was none. Kendzior reminds her readers of the impact achieved by Mohamed Bouazizi, the young unemployed Tunisian whose self-immolation sparked an explosion of embittered feeling out of which the Arab Spring emerged. The effect of a crisis in that one life, nonetheless, spoke in a manner beyond the crisis of numbers. Self-immolation adds nothing to the debate about what can be done about levels of unemployment. It reveals the *effects* of unemployment. By pursuing the horror of exclusion to the personal crisis point of self-destruction in this public spectacle, self-immolation illuminates and inspires the possibility of a retrieved solidarity. One person speaks for all and, in this sacrifice, creates a form of freedom out of a genuinely tragic horror.

The symbol does not restore the fiscal conditions and capital inflow required to change the economy; it affirms a hiatus in the succession of authority. The self-annihilation of one person in that act takes possession of a fraction of public space. We do not know how many privately enacted suicides or other more veiled acts of self-destruction draw on this poisoned root in the life of a national economy. In the intensity of a public expression, however, something passes by an almost invisible means from the life that is lost into the lives of those who understand it. This inversion of the auto-da-fé exposes the counter-natural character of the religious oppression at work. Where this act takes possession of public space, the power of a ruling order to inflict the disvalues of unemployment briefly undergoes an eclipse. A horizon of solidarity lights up beyond the experience of individual powerlessness in isolation. In this regard, self-immolation by the unemployed takes its place alongside other kinds of political demonstration, such as those in which Buddhist monks—most notably Thich Quang Duc in 1963—immolated themselves in protest against the South Vietnamese government of Ngô Đình Diệm. Yet protest against a government signifies the solution of disbanding and replacing it or, perhaps, merely altering a policy in its management of social relations. Protest against the expulsion of an unemployed person from the body of working life needs to be understood in its own language, in the ferocity of an almost unimaginable passion.

The protest of self-immolation articulates first of all a claim on a fragment of public space. In a form that no longer fears any challenge, it briefly occupies a piece of ground for the person otherwise cast out among the lost and landless. In that brief moment of return, the life that vanishes in flame and smoke becomes an absolute of speech. As Benjamin himself pointed out in his essay "The Storyteller," the moment of death frames a life with an ineluctable retroactive eloquence: "suddenly, in his expressions and looks the unforgettable emerges and imparts to everything that concerned him that authority which even the poorest wretch in dying possesses for the living around him."[15] But is this the only moment in which a person can speak about the fragmenting of social space perpetrated by unemployment? And is death the only medium of expression? It is true that, in such moments, something does pass from the dying to the living, and yet something passes out of the world into silence too. If this constitutes an absolute of speech, that very quality contains it and restricts it.

The question of what we mean by calling this act speech—or what the drama of self-destruction might penetrate into the formation of those values that precipitate such pain—brings us back to Benjamin's refusal to accept Marx, Nietzsche, and Freud as independent voices speaking outside the capitalist cult. But if these theories belong, as Benjamin insists they do, "to the hegemony of the priests of this cult," then why do they not figure as its dogma or its theology? From Benjamin's point of view, they exemplify the neutralization of all language in the capitalist project of secularization, that is to say, the incorporation of all expression within the negative religion or cult that has annihilated any language that might transcend it. Their particular ideological inventions offer no resistance to the expansive power encircling them—Quite the reverse: what they achieve in each case amounts to an elimination of anything that could stand outside the capitalist system and resist it. "God's transcendence is at an end. But he is not dead; he has been incorporated into human existence."[16] What remains for expression is neither the "divine language" nor the "pure language" that Benjamin posits as the sole antagonist to the cult, but the ultimate sacrifice in self-immolation that holds up a mirror to the social order that destroys an ill-fated minority of its workers by exacting from them the sacrifice of unemployment.

A difficulty in understanding Benjamin's point here arises with a minor slackness in the English translation. Benjamin concludes the paragraph in which that statement regarding the death of God appears with "Der Kultus wird von einer ungereiften Gottheit zelebriert, jede Vorstellung, jeder Gedanke an sie verletzt das Geheimnis ihrer Reife."[17] The English version reads, "The cult is celebrated before an unmatured deity; every idea, every conception of it offends against the secret of this immaturity."[18]

Two things stand out. The German word *Reife* (ripeness or maturity) with which the passage concludes stands in negation of *ungereift* (unripened or immature) and the word *von* suggests "by" as the most likely meaning. "Before" would be the meaning of *vor*, which does not appear here. Since the "deity" (or possibly godhead) celebrated here has been assimilated to the human image of itself, all ideas represented by these various priests are in fact self-reflexive. They constitute the immature deity, and the cult is not celebrated "before" a deity who exists independently of them, but by them. Their ideas, therefore, insofar as they concur in what Benjamin regards as a cult of human activity, whether Freudian, Marxian, or Nietzschean, all offend against a secret of maturity, which is to say that of the now hidden or lost transcendent God.

This presents us with a problem that Benjamin remains very far from having solved, though he does identify it with great vividness. Where do we actually find a vital opposite to capitalism that would restore an integral coherence to the fragmented state of social relations? Lines of fragmentation crisscross a capitalistic social order, running in our own society between the 1 percent and the 99 percent in the dimension of wealth and power, as it does between the 95 percent and the 5 percent in "full employment," as noted above, and many other breaks and fractures in class, race, and gender and any other competitive interest between conflicting identities. Benjamin's own insistence that "true reconciliation exists only with God" might, at best, lure us with a dream beyond death but offers no help within history. The image of God constitutes one of the most terrifying splits that divide the human community against itself. Insofar as an ideology contains a "project" (to mobilize a term from Heidegger), it identifies itself in a struggle to realize society in a new form, unified under its own sway. If it actually aspires to remove all contradictions, it has to imagine itself under the magical number of 100 percent. Its outer limit, therefore, runs along the police line since all who remain separated out by heresy fall into the role of criminals or vermin. That was exactly the implication of Benjamin's political theory in the essay "Critique of Violence" (1921). In its historical and political ramifications, nothing could be less transcendent than that line of distinction between the human and the divine. Division between a dogmatic identity of the saved and the true and the image of the rejected and the guilty against which it defines itself by opposition tends ever downward into violence. It also provides us with a model for the exclusion that inspires the self-inflicted violence of immolation.

The essay "Capitalism as Religion" remained the outline for a project that Benjamin never realized, because not long after he had sketched out its ideas he changed course and embraced the idea of a socialist revolution as a real historical alternative after all. For this reason it has been easy to overlook the importance of the critical position he took in this earlier period. The philosophical and theoretical consequences of Benjamin's demoting the towering intellectual figures of his age to the rank of priests in the cult of capitalism necessitate that critical distance from them all. Benjamin feels compelled to take up a radical opposition to any mode of worldly representation that lures its adherents away from the divine with an alternative to reconciliation with a transcendent God. In fact, Benjamin goes beyond critical distance. The purpose and method of criticism becomes the complete destruction of its object. The idea of political destruction he develops in "Critique of Violence" in 1921 reappears in a further evolved theory of literary and philosophical criticism in the Goethe essay. Benjamin writes that this destructive criticism turns its "sublime violence of the true" against any form of merely worldly representation.[19] Any major secular text might seek to express an image of the world, as do the inventions of Marx, Nietzsche, and Freud (according to "Capitalism as Religion"), and Benjamin resists this from the point of view of what he terms "the expressionless." The work of criticism itself then elaborates its own text in a form that resembles the self-immolation of discourse. Instead of arriving at an interpretation or an aesthetic evaluation of the work, this criticism undertaken in the sign of "the expressionless" mirrors the radicalism of a divine rejection of the worldly object. Benjamin writes, "Only the expressionless completes the work by shattering it into a thing of shards, into a fragment of the true world, into the torso of a symbol."[20]

The critical process that invokes the symbol in order to undermine its expressiveness obeys the same dialectical rule as the effect of protest in self-immolation. The symbolic power of that bodily sacrifice still echoes the peculiar dialectics of religious symbolism, which manifest a material event at the outer limits of representation. One cannot represent the divine in any sense of "the true" except in the significance of marking a line of division—that which Benjamin represents between alienation and reconciliation with God. His reconciliation shortly after this period with Marxist political commitment testifies to the philosophical problems in even this structure of representation as a religious principle. But self-immolation as a protest against the alienated condition of the unemployed, outcast from the symbolic value of work, derives its drama from that implicit citation of the auto-da-fé. It cannot "express" anything about political or economic policy beyond this tragic force in setting itself out as the final scene of expulsion, marking out the stage of this tragic drama as the last fragment of space to which the victim lays claim.

To apply concepts from the realm of art criticism as exemplified by Benjamin's writings in no way implies what might be understood as an "aestheticization" of human suffering. On the contrary, Benjamin's critical practice in the 1920s and 1930s draws the artistic avant-garde much closer to the direct manifestation of political protest and away from the classical tradition of aesthetic objects. His destructive critique of the traditional idealized artistic creation questions the entirety of that ideal, revealing, instead, a destructive side of capitalist creation. Moreover, this shift in the modern meaning of art should not be reduced to the direct political expression of a "content." Benjamin's subsequent alignment with Marxist political praxis does not define what is most radical about his position. Not only is his position far removed from the aesthetics of social realism propagated as part of that political praxis but the element of a propagandistic function for art at any level falls away with the function of traditional expressiveness.

The spatial model of exclusion would best define the current of connection between avant-garde art and the language of self-immolation as protest. Avant-garde artists do not create objects that embody an aesthetic harmony expressing an essence of our world in its imaginary integrity. The notion of the world as an ideal has vanished from symbolic function. We do not expect to feel the presence of an ideal truth when we contemplate a formally modern work of art. Avant-garde works eschew the means of classical genres to evoke aesthetic emotions. Although they may acquire a separate allure in harmonious form, attractiveness must be counted a peripheral quality and one with which such production can if need be dispense. Moreover, while they may incorporate some ideological expression or even aspire to a propagandistic effect, this too lies outside the realm in which their innovations present their real political challenge. The innovative character itself does not generate that challenge.

After more than a hundred years, we no longer need to explain our contemporary experience with avant-garde works as the "shock of the new." The shock effect continues in the by now venerable struggle to occupy contested spaces. This struggle connects them with direct political manifestation—they assert a claim to appear in a place and in a manner that carries the power to give offense simply by being there. The avant-garde artist nearly always stands in some kind of tension with the police for having his work appear somewhere it should not. The spirit of the avant-garde renews its political responsibility in that tension. The discovery of freeway bridges by artists Lane Hall and Lisa Moline as a space for messages in colored lights, in a project known as the Overpass Light Brigade in Milwaukee, Wisconsin, gives a sense in which that tradition will always discover a new enterprise—a shock to some, a delight to others.[21]

Yet part of the artistic presence depends on a fugitive effect. Those lights will not stay up for long; their time is borrowed, their place tenuous, and darkness soon supervenes. A truly avant-garde work is likely to be pushed aside and soon vanish. That is the essence of what it "says" as a work of art—that it appears in a form that restricts what it says. An avant-garde work must necessarily incorporate an element of silence in the realm of "ideas" and an equivalent absence of the very aesthetic quality that earned the traditional work of art its permanent claim on a privileged site of display. Whether in a gallery, in a public place, or projected onto a screen, the avant-garde work in some sense has to remain out of place. That is how such works express what is otherwise inexpressible. They fulfill the military implication of the term "avant-garde" by invading a privileged space to manifest their protest against the web of language that nothing else interrupts. Like self-immolation, they too articulate a kind of voicelessness.

This mode of self-assertion carries over into the world of popular entertainment too, precisely the realm where celebrity and money rule in their crassest form. That very crassness turns out to provide a medium into which the language of destruction in the avant-garde has found its most direct access. One can see at a glance how surrealistic and dadaistic sensibilities have passed into the realm of popular performances, but some manifest a more explicit and more extreme enactment of that avant-garde relation of site to speech. Pete Townshend of The Who reported in an interview with Barry Miles carried by the *International Times* of February 1967 that while studying at the Ealing School of Art he had attended a lecture by Gustav Metzger, instigator of the Auto-Destructive Art Movement in the late 1950s.[22] In direct application of Metzger's ideas, he added the spectacle of smashing his guitar to his stage act and, later, blowing up his sound equipment to conclude a performance.

The idea of incorporating its own destruction into a work of art in the manner explored by Metzger certainly indicates the course of the shock wave that passes between the effect of a self-immolation and a protest against the aesthetics of authority. Metzger has a long history of combining political activism and artistic experiment. Based in London as a stateless person since his escape from Germany as a child in 1939, he has emerged (or rather, reemerged) in the past few years as a remarkable figure exercising far-reaching influence in Britain and Europe. In 2009 a major retrospective show, "Decades," at the Serpentine Gallery in London testified to his significance for a new generation of artists. A typical article in the mainstream press—"Gustav Metzger: The Liquid Crystal Revolutionary," by Jonathan Jones printed in *The Guardian* on September 28, 2009—overplays that connection to a familiar past in popular entertainment by drawing attention to his involvement in light shows for prominent rock groups in the 1960s, but even there, his larger though more obscure significance comes through. "Decades" consists primarily of installations that stage destruction in order to express political protest. Jones warns his readers to expect a display of works that "seethe with passionate denunciations of nuclear weapons, climate change, and capitalism."[23]

The article can't resist describing Metzger as "an 83 year old troublemaker," though he has to the best of his ability only been making trouble for real troublemakers. In 1960 he joined with Bertrand Russell as a founding member and coiner of the name taken by the antinuclear group "The Committee of 100" and was imprisoned for participation in its program of civil disobedience in 1961. In September 1966 he organized an international Destruction in Art Symposium for which he was also arrested.[24] In 1974 he wrote a manifesto for an "Artists' Strike," calling for a three-year global cessation of all artistic activity from 1977 to 1980. During that period he did in fact produce nothing, though he does comment in the Jones interview that "auto-destructive art doesn't exist except in the mind." But the sense of inescapable contradictions in the artist's position always reappears. "A poster calling for an end to flights to international art biennales will be one of the uneasier works for the cognoscenti to view," Jones notes, because "over the last 15 years, this veteran activist has been shown at one biennale after another."[25]

The decisive event in that long career undoubtedly came in 1959 when Metzger issued his "Auto-destructive Art Manifesto" and began devising a number of techniques for the creation of works of art that would then undergo their own destruction. One of the most dramatic of these was a process of painting on sheets of nylon with hydrochloric acid. The acid caused the material to tear, shrivel, and then vanish into a few tatters. The inherently transient nature of these works meant they could not be put on display as artistic objects, although they could be re-created as performed events. The "Auto-destructive Art Manifesto" opens by claiming a place for these events in the contemporary public arena: "Auto-destructive art is primarily a form of public art for industrial societies."[26] And in this function as event, these demonstrations fulfill the most important consideration expressed by Benjamin for a politically radical work, namely, that "free floating contemplation is not appropriate to them."[27] Indeed, they fulfill that requirement far more completely than those Dada collages that Benjamin in his time considered "useless . . . as objects of contemplative immersion," but which are now gathered in venerated collections, radiant with the aura of a modern classic.[28] What all these avant-garde tendencies have in common, as long as they retain their quality of event, is that they negate a space set aside for that contemplative aesthetic enactment of human isolation. The function of a traditional aesthetics in bourgeois history provides an equivalent to the transcendent value in the older modalities of tragedy by creating an ideal position for the isolated subject. And like the values of sacrifice embodied in tragedy, these contemplative experiences redeem our loneliness at the cost of sinking us yet more deeply into it. That is precisely what Benjamin rejects in his essay "The Storyteller" (1936) in the way he represents the reader of a novel, who is "isolated, more so than any other reader."[29] In the Surrealism essay he decries this form of aesthetics as "that most terrible drug—ourselves—which we take in solitude."[30]

Unemployment is precisely the negative form of that solitude. Aesthetic emotions offer relief in the form of an internal emigration that the frame around the artistic object permits by separating it from a general framework of incorporation into a world of work: unemployment encloses us in the indeterminate state of icy immobility outside of time. Perhaps we can illustrate this best by returning to Kafka—to a passage in Kafka's *The Castle* that portrays unemployment as a kind of negative ecstasy.

The circumstances in the opening scenes of Kafka's novel have caused the protagonist, K., to embark on a struggle against the Castle bureaucracy to compel it to hire him as a land surveyor. He is never able to articulate why he is willing to sacrifice everything in this self-negating passion. He only knows that all other values grow void until this one desire has been fulfilled. But Kafka grants us an insight into how all things have been transfigured, all meaning thrown into reverse, where he shows us what remains of K.'s consciousness when it is emptied of his plans and ploys for battle. This occurs only once in the novel. K. has attempted to waylay an official in his horse-sleigh on his return to the Castle from a village inn. Kafka captures the chill night of a mind shut out of all touch with the obscure order of things as K. watches a groom back the horse and sleigh out of the inn courtyard into a shed whose doors then slide closed. Everything withdraws from him and he is left completely alone:

> And now as all the electric lights went out too—for whom should they remain on?—and only up above the slit on the wooden gallery still remained bright, holding one's wandering gaze for a little, it seemed to K. as if at last those people had broken off all relations with him, and as if now in reality he were freer than he had ever been, and at liberty to wait here in this place, usually forbidden to him, as long as he desired, and had won a freedom such as hardly anybody else had ever succeeded in winning, and as if nobody could dare to touch him or drive him away, or even speak to him; but—this conviction was at least equally strong—as if at the same time there was nothing more senseless, nothing more hopeless, than this freedom, this waiting, this inviolability.[31]

It seems strange at first glance to read this condition as a "freedom"—but not if one considers it in a German context. The background concept against which Ernst Jünger developed the idea of total mobilization divides freedom into two precise opposites. In Jünger's view it was the bourgeois component of French and English traditions that developed the idea of freedom as a matter of human rights, but the German felt no inner relationship to that idea: "Therefore wherever anyone in Germany began to speak in those terms, it was easy to see that this was just a matter of mistranslations."[32] The German concept expects fulfillment of life in dedication to authority as a freedom *to* carry out that commitment. The alternative foreign meaning signifies freedom *from* something, an ability to refuse it, to keep it at bay, to be (in Kafka's word here) "inviolable" in relation to it. The impulse that holds K. in thrall permits him to see only the world of formal authority as the place where activity begins in a coherent form. Until he is taken into employment, he remains as free as the dead. The realm beyond work has no limits and no shape. That is why one can call his reflection on his condition beyond those bounds a negative ecstasy. It carries him out into an expanded consciousness of the world, but one that comes over him as a loss, an absolute exclusion from what he desires. The only escape from this chill of exclusion lies in the contradictory ambition to impose his will on the Castle and somehow force it to permit him entry into its service. One cannot imagine him rebelling against its authority in the violent repudiation of self-immolation. He only feels the iciness, the smallness of an immobility where he stands, not the possibility of demonstrating against the violation he has already experienced.

For this reason, the meaning K. discovers does not correspond to the constriction of the present in what amounts to Kendzior's rationalization of what leads to self-immolation. She writes, "your past is dismissed as unworthy. Your future is denied." Yet this does not fully capture the motivation of an extreme act that requires such an intense form of conviction in order to carry it through. This intensity includes the rejection of the future with a ferocity that outbids its denial and connects it with the embrace of destruction in avant-garde art. The artists' strike organized by Metzger suggests a sense of revulsion toward all production corresponding in its own way to that conveyed by the self-destruction of a person enduring this miserable position within the labor market. Nor indeed was Metzger's suspicion of all production, including artistic production, without precedent in theories of the avant-garde. We find it expressed quite distinctly in Benjamin's essay on Surrealism where he asks whether, for the artist under these new conditions, "mightn't the interruption of his 'artistic career' perhaps be an essential part of his new function?"[33]

This, too, falls short of stating what that function is. A "function" suggests a part to play in the general system, perhaps a kind of release or hygiene required by the social machine, the way the cooling effect of 5 percent unemployment is required by the economic machine. But the function of silence as a rejection brings us back to the unknowable knowledge of what defines the experience of a person who cannot speak. How does that knowledge pass from one person to another? Is there, we need to ask, a medium for that particular message? The phrase "the aesthetics of revulsion" comes up frequently in Metzger's discussions of his purpose in auto-destructive art and how he imagines its function in a society for which the place of art in general grows ever more questionable. In his forthright account of avant-garde art and politics, *The Assault on Culture*, Stewart

Home necessarily misrepresents the spirit in which Metzger refrains from explaining himself. Home writes that "Metzger developed his 'aesthetic of revulsion' (auto-destructive art) as a therapy against the irrationality of the capitalist system and its war machine. In many ways it represents a form of institutionalised waste with fewer anti-social consequences than those generally employed by capitalist states."[34]

But this makes sense in the wrong sense. The function lies closer, in the term used by the Jonathan Jones article for *The Guardian*, to the aesthetics of troublemaking. This motivation steps outside the limits of discourse the way self-immolation steps outside the realm defined by employment and unemployment. The moment an interpreter like Home represents that rejection as a theory, he begins to render it as a negotiating position; this begins once again to approach the realm of politics as management. In the talk given in London at the Architectural Association in 1965, so Home reports, Metzger emphasized that auto-destructive art was "not limited to theor(ies) of art and the production of art works. It includes social action. Auto-destructive art is committed to a left-wing revolutionary position in politics, and to struggles against future wars."[35] The performance of such action does not, however, speak in the voice of an alternative policy. It has much more to do with extracting some part of the artistic sphere from total absorption into the system of waste and of violence in a gesture that also rejects the language of negotiation.

Many years later, Alison Jones initiated an interview, conducted in connection with an exhibition of holocaust photographs that Metzger had organized in August 1998, by asking him if he had changed his thinking about the aesthetics of revulsion. Clearly that question was important to him. Metzger returns to precisely the problem that occurs over and over again when he responds to interpretations of his work that see it in a representational modality that simply creates visual metaphors to portray the self-destructive activities of our society. That would be a supererogatory function of art, close to the forms of expressivity that Benjamin subjects to critique through the position of "the expressionless" that shatters all forms of illusion in representation. Because Metzger's aesthetic intentions do not enter into an informative language of such expression, his demonstrations do not give us a clearer picture of the dangers to which we expose ourselves in our tragically dysfunctional political relations. Metzger is not entering into a debate about war. He is not contemplating diplomatic policy in the sense that economists enter into debates with one another in the politics of unemployment. One could say that his art is useless for such a debate, just as Benjamin voices the hope in the introduction to his essay "The Work of Art in the Age of Its Technological Reproducibility" that his new concepts are "completely useless for the purposes of fascism."[36]

The aesthetics of revulsion do not and should not—Metzger responds to Alison Jones's question—transfigure the emotion of revulsion before representations of violence into a perverse state of pleasure in "looking at horror, looking at the revolting, looking at the extremely dangerous." The effect of his installations and his presentation of auto-destructive media in public places involves something subtly but essentially different. They create their own state of exteriority, because "as you said earlier they are repellent, they block off the approach of the spectator." This exteriority signals a radical change in the ambitions of art in a world that cannot be redeemed by representing it in an aesthetically idealizing mode. The truth of art, the reality that it embodies, has come about because the world we inhabit has revealed itself as categorically beyond the reach of representation: "Art needs to be sensitive to this and to some extent because it never will be able to achieve the complexity of reality—never, never, never—even the greatest artists couldn't confront, couldn't embrace and contain what is actually happening world-wide, globally."[37]

This experience of exteriority is yet more radical for the contemporary artist than anything even Kafka could confront. For Kafka the language of expulsion and revulsion is perpetually kept in motion by the desire for a return. The moment that desire vanishes, as it does when the unemployed subject surrenders any grasp on a future of returning to the cultic world of work, then even that language is stilled. Kafka balances in the tormenting irony of seeing the world he portrays as repulsive and yet as still luring his protagonist ever onward in the desire to find a place there. It is sunk in filth, pervaded by cold, or stifling in airless heat, and ruled by brutality and stupidity, and yet none of this weakens the desire that still holds his protagonists in thrall, their desire to return to work and fold themselves into that community.

For this reason K.'s negative ecstasy differs entirely from the loss of the "Ekstasen" whose restoration Heidegger promises through labor in service to the National Socialist state. These are the three ecstasies of past, future, and present time that Heidegger developed in *Being and Time*, the modalities in which an existence extends beyond itself and embarks on projects, decisions, and engages with history. K.'s existence has been dispatched outside of time, posthumous (though he is not dead), waiting as though for release from waiting, and yet incapable of imagining what it is that might yet come. The totalitarian state offers the complete manifestation of what in Heidegger's view would amount to a positive, desired form of the "violation" from which K. is held harmless. The "freedom" to enter the domain that Heidegger promises absorbs the individual totally, without any restriction or surplus, in the field of work so defined:

> The compatriot who gets work will find that he is not cast off and left to fend for himself, but that he belongs to the people, and that

every service and every achievement has its own value and leads on to other tasks and achievements . . . No. To us "work" is the title of every regulated act and undertaking that is performed with responsibility toward the individual, the group, and the State, and so becomes of service to the people. Work is found wherever, and only wherever, men's free power of decisions sets itself to perform a task under the governance of a resolve. Work is therefore something spiritual in its own right, for it is founded upon freely acting knowledge of the circumstances, and regulated understanding of the work—that is to say, upon its own knowledge. The production of the miner is not fundamentally less spiritual than the action of the scholar.[38]

But we know that every decision K. makes is wrong. His past life has not been dismissed as unworthy, nor has the chance to take it up again for the future been denied. While Benjamin identifies the absurdity of our submission to the authority of capitalism in his critique of work, Heidegger conjures his hapless audience to act like Kafka's K., "under the governance of a resolve." He stands there as an instance of a mind that has submitted to mindlessness. He speaks in violation of his listeners insofar as he commits them to the impositions of the Nazi state, in violation of the colleagues in whose expulsion he has collaborated to deny them their work, and in self-violation insofar as he entered on all these projects by his own resolve. The miner's work is indeed not less spiritual than the life of the scholar because as Heidegger speaks here, nothing could be.

One hesitates, of course, to say anything in favor of self-immolation. And yet one hesitates to say anything in condemnation of those who go to this extreme. One hesitates, indeed, to speak at all in the face of such an annihilation. Whatever one says in the language of division will always be wrong. A secret connection links up all the forms of life that are silenced by the divisions imposed by cultic relations of any kind, certainly including the redemption in theology offered by Benjamin and the violence it entails. In an interview with Kerry Brougher, chief curator of the Hirshhorn Museum, on April 25, 2014, Metzger reflects from the position of his current recognition on all his ideas and statements and concludes that the most important was the statement he made to the press at the time he received his prison sentence in 1961. His primary commitment then, and ever since then, was to "absolute non-violence."[39] To this I can add a piece of information from conversations with Metzger long ago that, to my knowledge, does not exist in the historical record. Following his experience of police power in street demonstrations during the civil disobedience campaign by the Committee of One Hundred, Metzger proposed a change of tactics to Bertrand Russell. He was ready to lead the nuclear disarmament movement in a new tactics of self-immolation. One has to say that, fortunately, this idea came to nothing. Russell was appalled, and no one can blame him for that. Would it have been any more effective than those protests against unemployment? Probably not. Britain still has nuclear weapons, about which no one is really surprised. The world is as it is. Yet the long story of Gustav Metzger's quixotic resistance has a place among the values of peace, even though war never comes to an end. He has preserved a space, a stage, on which acts of absolute nonviolence oppose themselves to the world as it is. One could call this quixotic to a degree that would embarrass Don Quixote himself. But it would be a tragic loss if none of it had happened.

Notes

1 "America's Economy: A Happy New Year," *The Economist*, January 3, 2015, 21.

2 "Opportunistic Overheating," *The Economist*, December 13, 2014, 75.

3 Walter Benjamin, "On the Concept of History," in *Selected Writings, Vol. 4: 1938–1940*, ed. Howard Eiland and Michael W. Jennings (Cambridge, MA: Harvard University Press, 2003), 397.

4 Sarah Kendzior, "The Men Who Set Themselves on Fire: Due to Joblessness and a Bleak Economy, Self-Immolations in Industrialized Societies Are Rising Rapidly," *Al Jazeera*, October 7, 2013, at http://www.aljazeera.com/indepth/opinion/2013/10/men-who-set-themselves-fire-20131075515834438.html.

5 Further information on distribution of these events is available at http://newamericamedia.org/2013/05/the-tragedy-of-self-immolation---no-one-cares.php/, and at http://www.bbc.com/news/world-europe-22439961/.

6 "America's Economy: A Happy New Year," 21.

7 Ernst Jünger developed this idea in an essay first published in 1930, "Die totale Mobilmachung" (Total mobilization), and a book entitled *Der Arbeiter* (The worker), which appeared in 1934. In these writings, the process of labor has little if anything to do with the production of goods and services but everything to do with producing a new post-human figure.

8 Kendzior, "The Men Who Set Themselves on Fire."

9 Ibid.

10 Martin Heidegger, "Follow the Führer!" in *Martin Heidegger: Philosophical and Political Writings*, ed. Manfred Stassen (New York: Continuum Press, 2003), 12.

11 Walter Benjamin, *Selected Writings, Vol. 1: 1913–1926*, ed. Marcus Bullock and Michael Jennings (Cambridge, MA: Harvard University Press, 1996), 289.

12 Ibid., 288.

13 Ibid., 342.

14 Kendzior, "The Men Who Set Themselves on Fire."

15 Walter Benjamin, *Selected Writings, Vol. 2: 1927–1934*, ed. Howard Eiland and Michael W. Jennings (Cambridge, MA: Harvard University Press, 2002), 151.

16 Walter Benjamin, "Capitalism as Religion," in *Selected Writings, Vol. 1*, 289.

17 Walter Benjamin, "Kapitalismus als Religion" in *Gesammelte Schriften Bd VI*,

Hrsg. Rolf Tiedemann and Hermann Schweppenhäuser (Frankfurt am Main: Suhrkamp, 1991), 101.

18 Benjamin, "Capitalism as Religion," 289.

19 Walter Benjamin, "Goethe's Elective Affinities," in *Selected Writings, Vol.1*, 1:340.

20 Ibid.

21 See http://en.wikipedia.org/wiki/Overpass_Light_Brigade/ for information on this interesting enterprise.

22 Barry Miles, "Miles Interviews Pete Townshend," *International Times*, February 13, 1967. The interview frames The Who in this radical role with this introductory synopsis: "WHO? Pete Townshend, that's Who. Lead guitarist, song-writer, destructivist for this off-number-oned-pop group. He walks, he talks, he smashes. The WHO is the most popular among many auto-destructive groups on the scene at the moment. They are in the forefront of the smoke-bomb generation and are raping [*sic*; reaping] the boredom and expectation of the pop music world. WHO speaks."

23 Jonathan Jones, "Gustav Metzger: The Liquid Crystal Revolutionary," *The Guardian*, September 28, 2009, at http://www.theguardian.com/artanddesign/2009/sep/28/gustav-metzger-auto-destructive/.

24 This was quite a substantial event, including artists from many different countries, that, through its connection with the Indica Gallery in London, established a further degree of contact between the world of popular entertainment and the avant-garde. Yoko Ono was a major participant, and the political movements were represented by, among others, the PROVO from Holland, and some breakaway elements from the Situationist International from Paris. Guy Debord himself declined Metzger's invitation in a letter that testifies to the delicate rivalries in play, saying: "Art has already been destroyed for a long time. This sort of contemplation is fortunately obsolete. Today, to organize the communal spectacle of the debris and copies of the debris—Enrico Baj, for example—is no longer to destroy but to paste back together. It is to be the academic art of the era of the contemplation of art. The situationists estimate that their own manner of surpassing art is the only good one: we will only suppress art practically by realizing it. Obviously, we do not want to participate in any manner in a 'symposium' in which the creativity and revolutionary position of all of the participants are not evident to us." Text of a letter originally sent in English, published in *Guy Debord, Correspondance, Vol. 3, 1965–1968*, footnotes by Alice Debord, translated from the French by NOT BORED! August 2005, at http://www.notbored.org/debord-12August1966.html.

25 Jones, "Gustav Metzger: The Liquid Crystal Revolutionary."

26 Gustav Metzger, "Auto-destructive Art Manifesto" (1959), accessible at http://www.391.org/manifestos/1959-auto-destructive-art-manifesto-gustav-metzger.html.

27 Walter Benjamin, "The Work of Art in the Age of Its Technological Reproducibilty," in *Selected Writings, Vol. 4*, 258.

28 Walter Benjamin, "The Author as Producer," in *Selected Writings, Vol. 3: 1935–1938* (Cambridge, MA: Harvard University Press, 2006), 266.

29 Benjamin, *Selected Writings, Vol. 3*, 156.

30 Walter Benjamin, "Surrealism," in *Selected Writings, Vol. 2*, 2:216.

31 Franz Kafka, *The Castle*, trans. Willa and Edwin Muir (New York: Schocken Books, 1974), 139.

32 Ernst Jünger, *Sämtliche Werke 8: Der Arbeiter* (Stuttgart: Klett-Cotta, 1981), 18, my translation. In this context he elaborates that "the amount of freedom that any power has at its disposal is determined entirely in proportion to the amount of attachment on which it can call" (19), or more explicitly still: "This expresses the identity of freedom and obedience" (155). It is significant that neither Jünger himself through his long life nor his literary executors permitted an English translation of this particular book to be published.

33 Benjamin, *Selected Writings, Vol. 2*, 217.

34 Stewart Home, *The Assault on Culture: Utopian Currents from Lettrisme to Class War* (New York: Aporia Press/Unpopular Books, 1988), 62.

35 Ibid.

36 Walter Benjamin, *Selected Writings, Vol. 4*, 252.

37 Alison Jones, "Introduction to the Historic Photographs of Gustav Metzger," and "Interview with Gustav Metzger," University College London Forum for Holocaust Studies, August 14, 1998, at http://www.ucl.ac.uk/forum-for-holocaust-studies/metzger.html.

38 Heidegger, "Follow the Führer!" 12.

39 *Art Talk: Gustav Metzger and the Art of Destruction*, streamed live on April 25, 2014, at 12:30 P.M., from the Hirshhorn Museum and Sculpture Garden, accessible at https://www.youtube.com/watch?v=KyUMi-NE9os/.

8

Liquid, Crystal, Vaporous

The Natural States of Capitalism

ESTHER LESLIE

Liquid crystals represent a phase of matter that has always existed. They exist in us, in our nerves, in living cells, and elsewhere, but they were found only in 1888 and thoroughly probed from then on.[1] Named "liquid crystal" in the first years of the twentieth century, the form appears to be something that emerges into light and history alongside industrial capitalism. Liquid crystal is even more present in our world today, in a variety of devices that have made themselves indispensable to modern life, such that we might as well name this epoch "the liquid crystal epoch." This epoch may end, like any epoch, though the invention of new technologies to replace liquid crystals, such as Organic Light Emitting Diodes (OLEDs), have not fundamentally altered the form and manner of the screens that constitute one of the main ways in which we daily encounter liquid crystals. After liquid crystal capitalism perhaps something more airy will emerge, organized by the Cloud, by invisible yet pervasive technologies, vaporous ones—though this would not be for the first time, because such a thought was already contained in the first conceptualization of this industrial capitalist epoch, when Marx and Engels wrote of sublimation, the leap from one phase of matter (the crystal, or solid) to another phase of matter (gas) without passing through liquid. Marx and Engels's phrase on sublimation notes, famously: "all that is solid melts into air." The crystal form of solids is forced through temperature change into its gaseous form, without becoming liquid. But for now we inhabit, mostly, liquid crystal worlds, ones defined by screens—by computer systems whose communicative interfaces are a result of liquid crystal activity, by televisions on which liquid crystals dance colorfully, by advertising screens that populate the cities and shape our dreams in super-sizes and saturated colors, and on those little handheld devices whose messages punctuate our existence.

Capitalism is generally seen as a period in which massive technological and industrial developments occur, or to put it more structurally than that, capitalism is, through a complex looping, the economic and social system that arises in relation to technological and industrial developments. Some commentators short-circuit the relationship between the economic and political forms of capitalism and the technological forms that are flung up within its context. When demonstrations racked the streets of the United States in December 2014, protesting the killings of black men by U.S. police, pundits on Fox News and elsewhere repeated again and again, "These kids, they don't know what they are doing. They are protesting against capitalism, but capitalism gave them the iPhone, the very thing they plan their demonstrations on." The implication is that the protestors are hypocritical, caught in a loop, criticizing the things that make their criticism possible. It is an argument equivalent to the circular one stating that protest is undeserved in any society that allows such protest. There is no way to criticize the smartphone, except for ones that eschew it altogether, and this sets the critic socially apart, so that their criticism fails to be social.

The identification of capitalism and technological form goes both ways. Protesting over the grand jury decision to acquit the policeman responsible for the choking of Eric Garner, a "die-in" was staged in the Apple Store on Fifth Avenue, New York City. Widely reported were the words of a protestor: "'The CEO of Apple knows we shut his store down—that means capitalist America is going to take us seriously," he said. "We are going to shake up your business and we want to hit you where it hurts."[2] The dissenters target the stores of glossy, liquid crystal technologies of communication as a synecdoche of contemporary capitalism, which mobilizes those communicative devices to marshal the self as consumer and as object of surveillance. Technology, so the argument goes, embeds capitalism in our lives, and it embeds our lives in the needs of capital and the state while making massive profits for the few. But the identification is wielded against the protestors. The defenders of the status quo target the activists' mediated selves as emblematic of the corrupt nature of protest. "They buy smart phones, they wear sneakers, they are implicated and yet they are not satisfied with the world that gives them all this." Moreover, that the protestors recognize its power, the power of sleek capitalist technology, is a signal of the unbeatable superiority of capital and its technologies, with the free market's elves beavering away to invent and refine products, and in analogy to the Darwinian natural world, the strongest, fittest, shiniest survive. Communism could never, apparently, have invented the smartphone. Kevin D. Williamson, correspondent for the conservative *National Review* voices the overlap of technology and capitalism in an appraisal of Steve Jobs, just after his death:

> Mr. Jobs's contribution to the world is Apple and its products, along with Pixar and his other enterprises, his 338 patented inventions—his work—not some Steve Jobs Memorial Foundation for Giving Stuff to Poor People in Exotic Lands and Making Me Feel Good About Myself. Because he already did that: He gave them better computers, better telephones, better music players, etc. In a lot of cases, he gave them better jobs, too. Did he do it because he was a nice guy, or because he was greedy, or because he was a maniacally single-minded competitor who got up every morning possessed by an unspeakable rage to strangle his rivals? The beauty of capitalism—the beauty of the iPhone world as opposed to the world of politics—is that that question does not matter one little bit. Whatever drove Jobs, it drove him to create superior products, better stuff at better prices. Profits are not deductions from the sum of the public good, but the real measure of the social value a firm creates. Those who talk about the horror of putting profits over people make no sense at all. The phrase is without intellectual content. Perhaps you do not think that Apple, or Goldman Sachs, or a professional sports enterprise, or an Internet pornographer actually creates much social value; but markets are very democratic—everybody gets to decide for himself what he values.[3]

Giving or selling, these motives are irrelevant. Profits are value, indeed, but an economic one, though here the value is interpreted as social, as the just surplus of desire and success, not as the margin of surplus value that Marxists harp on. However, this sociality is, contradictorily, a matter for individuals, the many selves who make the choice to buy Apple or whatever gleaming bauble draws their eyes. Williamson goes on to make the pervasive identification of anticapitalist protestor at Occupy and technology: "And to the kids camped out down on Wall Street: Look at the phone in your hand. Look at the rat-infested subway. Visit the Apple Store on Fifth Avenue, then visit a housing project in the South Bronx. Which world do you want to live in?"[4]

Steve Jobs—and capitalism—created an "iPhone world," which is beautiful. Any sane person would rather exist in the super-illuminated Apple store than in what purports to be a home but is by implication dark, dull, and dirty. Something else, unnamed by Williamson, created the ugly rat-infested world and the world of poverty housing. Somehow we can choose which one to inhabit—like we can choose, as individuals, our "social" values. Or we wait until the iPhone world subsumes the other world, the one that is somehow connected to socialism and the state and all that is fettering. The conservative's thinking is banal and perhaps not worth engaging with, but it is influential. It is influential because this moment of capitalism is mediated by a certain set of digitally based technologies—ones that act in specific ways to relay backward and forward between all the sites of resistance and repression. The links between capitalism and technology exist of course, but not in what is simply asserted as a context—capitalistic free markets—matched by a spirit of invention that finds opportunities to exploit the market. The dialectic is more intricate, and plenty of inventions will fall by the wayside or be channeled into specific modes, in order to inhabit the only space allotted to the invention within the logic of the market. And so, the smartphone that could be a tool of connection and communication develops also—and perhaps increasingly exclusively— into a tool of what calls itself now not advertising but "relevant messaging." These technologies are corralled to give us tightly bound circuits of gendered subjectivity, commerce, and nature, such as this: "Pantene partnered with the Weather Channel at Walgreens to deliver relevant messaging along her path to purchase based on localized weather conditions. We created geo-targeted mobile ad units with a coupon to drive her in-store where she would see a display featuring products to fix her immediate hair concerns. This program drove base and total category sales making Walgreens one happy customer."[5] This is a world in which massive corporations are customers too, and customers are objects that must be driven, be cajoled, and must endlessly meet their natural environment as a problem to be surmounted. "Weather is the enemy of beautiful hair," as the advertisement for the Pantene/Weather Channel tie-up puts it, and the smartphone allows the woman to make the effort that she is required to make, visibly, or else be judged as negligent. The Pantene/Weather Channel campaign garnered plaudits, such as the 2014 awards Digiday best mobile brand experience and Digiday finalist most integrated retail experience. In this way and others, capitalism and technology form intense partnerships through the power given them by liquid crystals. Being able to check the weather in your area and be immediately recommended a Pantene product available at Walgreen with a voucher discount led, certainly, to increased sales and, apparently, to increased "self-confidence," "optimism," and "sunny dispositions." Through new technologies such as smartphones and tablets capitalism can reach right into our emotions, defy nature, shape our whole being, and in that circuit, replicate the authority of capitalism itself.

What is it about these new technologies that makes them—not exclusively, but also—amenable to capitalism and to its circuits of self-propagation and replication? Is the genius of the new technology as it is mobilized by capitalism (and also by anticapitalists) that it has become so intimate? It is ubiquitous. It is inescapable. It is pervasive, and most important, it is close to us, always there, close, and always there, everywhere. Daily we touch these screens with their diversions and advertisements. We jab them and stroke them and swipe them and poke them. We gaze at them more than we gaze at our lovers. This engagement is affective. It is physical—not detached and immaterial, as might have previously been argued of digital culture. There is something uncanny about the unity that our bodies form with these objects, our fingers resting on the glass making capacitive or resistive contact, or interrupting surface waves or infrared beams, completing electrical circuits, in order to trigger events.

According to a Marxist analysis, the various contours of a society are marked out by the material conditions pertaining at the time. Those material conditions relate to the emergence not simply of new technologies and forms of industrial organization but also the discovery of new "materials," which make new forms of technology and new techniques possible. We live—and those who found and probed liquid crystal lived—in a liquid crystal epoch. How or in what ways do societies get the phases of matter they deserve, and in what ways do forms of physical matter play into the technologies and techniques of a particular time? In a liquid crystal epoch it seems that everything might be conceptualized in relation to the liquid and the crystalline, the fluid and the frozen. The state of liquid crystallinity joins our world of concepts and initiates immense social change, as it eventually makes possible a world built of screens, communicating devices, gauges, watches, calculators, control panels, and so on. The process of its discovery demands adjustments in theory—scientific theory, but perhaps other thinking too. Thinking is altered by liquid crystallinity. These contours that are shaped by material conditions include those of thought and myth.

The state of liquid crystallinity is a curious state, in actuality and as a mode of processing existence, but it finds analogues in other forms, such as the "petrified unrest," which Walter Benjamin deemed characteristic of the late nineteenth century (the epoch more or less when liquid crystallinity was discovered) and the melancholy impotence of Blanqui and Baudelaire. Does anything connect the world of liquid crystals' discovery to the stop-start rhythm of animation, invented at the same moment, or to the jerkiness of proletarian revolutions, which "constantly interrupt themselves in their own course," as Marx put it?[6] After capitalism was installed and was already becoming sapped of any revolutionary impulses in the later nineteenth century, what was the role that liquid crystal technologies came to play actually and imaginatively in relation to capital's expansion? Did its forwarding of liquidity and crystallinity have social impact, social consequences, even if only in the imagination? Did liquidity or crystallinity win out or was there a polar pull? Are there machines or modes of production that are more or less liquid or crystalline or both at once?

Zygmunt Bauman wrote of "liquid modernity." He observes the characteristics of fluids: "extraordinary mobility," "lightness," "inconstancy," and they "neither fix space nor bind time." All these qualities are those that Baumann attributes to a late modernity that melts any remaining "patterns, codes and rules to which one could conform, which one could select as stable orientation points" and compels us to make ourselves as individuals.[7] This liquidity is, for Bauman, that of modernity, not capitalism, for that would imply something too fixed or nameable. Modernity seems vague and always reinvented, imprecise and indefinable. Yet others who have held to the concepts (and determinations) of economy have identified "the frozen time of capital," whether those others are situationist-influenced, echoing Guy Debord's phrases on the "frozen spectacle" or echoing the thoughts of a social-capitalist such as Geoff Mulgan, who fears that neoliberal capitalism will make time the most visible currency of life, for "money is frozen time; capital is frozen work."[8] What might these references to liquid and crystal states mean, beyond the metaphorical? Is there liquid thought or a crystal imagination, both of which correspond or yield to economic and political structures? Do these materials—liquids and crystals and their hybrids—shape these structures in their image, with their properties? Do these forms and forces, these material properties, seep out, extend beyond their role as materials to become the very matter of what matters? In conceptualizing them, is something lost if only the liquid flow or the crystal rigidity is stressed? Does what matters shape the contours of the world, invent new gestures and new modes of being present, new fields of action? In what ways does matter, this liquid crystal one, participate in our world of capital? And after capitalism is over, what might liquid crystal and its technologies contribute to social imagination and, indeed, social organization?

Liquid Crystal as Image

There is an old image of liquid crystal, before it was known as a phase of matter. This image is presented here as a kind of sensing or premonition of what is to come and its consequences. The image is one of liquid turned crystal and crystal amid liquid, or what should be liquid. It is a painting known in German as *Das Eismeer*, which means literally the Ice Sea or the Sea of Ice. This is the German name for a polar sea. Caspar David Friedrich's painting *Das Eismeer*, from 1824, depicts what he imagined to be the Arctic sea.[9] *The Sea of Ice* shows stretches of ice amid seawater under a frozen sky. Above the horizon there is only the tiniest hint of possible warmth, radiating from off the painting's edge. The crystals of ice appear in the image in many forms and shades, mutable as the water that makes them. In the foreground are plates and chunks of ice mixed apparently with soil, the brownish edge of land, which lies somewhere unspecified. These rusty ice blocks resemble rubble and bricks, or slabs of stone churned up in a graveyard where death occurred long ago. In the middle ground, a greyish spike of ice skewers the freezing waters. Behind this, to the left, another blue-white iceberg juts from the ocean and begins to merge with the sky and the horizon. Other spikes of ice further back have melded with the chilly blue of the sky. Some of the ice and snow is opaque, some is translucent. A boat has been ground up between the sliding plates of stony ice. Small fragments of wood, broken spars and an overturned hull, miniscule in comparison to the ice mound, poke through, smashed like the bones of a child in the hand of a giant. Depicted here is nature and its power to crush. Nature is the agent and the tiny human who is its victim is unrepresented in the scene. Life is absent. Friedrich's jagged ice pile and frozen sea is a representation of a formless upheaval, unbounded in its perversion of what might seem to be the natural order.[10] Sea that should flow is stilled. Water that should give life destroys. It may be, however, that the painter and the viewer regain some composure in the face of this devastating sublime scene, as they contemplate the encapsulation of the scene within a frame. The warm gallery Hamburg's Kunsthalle, where it is on display today, melts the iciness of the scene. The buzzing sounds of Hamburg—where the image was shown two years after it was painted and where it has found a home since 1905—drift up from the streets and in through the windows. The liquid port of the city, its trading hub, is the real life antithesis of the frozen image.

Kant, author of theories of the transcendental subject and the sublime, was also the author of "Notes on the Theory of the Winds," written in 1756.[11] These notes were an effort to explain the causes of wind directions. Kant proposes that the atmosphere is an ocean of elastic, liquid material, composed of layers of different density. Humans inhabit the seabed of this ocean of air. The direction of coastal winds depends on the contraction and expansion of air caused by differences in the rates of heating and cooling of the land and the sea waters by day and night. The trade winds, East Winds, follow the warming of the Earth. Oppositions produce weather and the winds that will aid trade. The air is a sea, and this mobile air works with the ever-undulating sea waters to produce movement. In producing movement, this system of nature allows for global trade. Such is the world thought of as a space of flow and ingress: liquidity is all. Is Kant's conception of a watery mobile cosmos a transposition of how the fluidities of trade are coming to dominate the planet? The winds are the trade winds first and foremost.

Some of Kant's writings speculate on the existence of an ice-free ocean in the far North, which would allow passage through and over the top of the world.[12] Friedrich's frozen sea is imagined as melted into its antithesis, a liquid path, in the service of movement, or captured for trade. Kant imagined something like the North-West Passage, the hoped-for trade route, which would provide a liquid journey through the ice clumps from the Atlantic to the Pacific. Such are the early bourgeois dreams of nature's complicity with human endeavors, the commercial reliance on the beneficence of the winds and flows that allow the European colonial world to draw into its orbit Africa, Asia, and the Americas.

What will be traded on these flowing seas that limn the busy ports of the world? Commodities of all types, as world trade begins in earnest from 1820 onward, at the point when, in Great Britain at least, much of the work of the first Industrial Revolution is done. The cargo ships will come to be weighed down with things extracted from far away and brought to the great cities of the world to be processed and sold. Among their number, from the 1870s, after their discovery in South Africa, are the commodities in the shape of the crystal. The diamond, a natural resource, becomes the emblem of wealth, a magical compactedness that serves as a super-fetish. Crystals are borne on liquid seas. The crystal is a commodity. For Marx the commodity is a crystal too, a crystallization of living labor. The abstraction that is human labor power forms a social substance, the value of commodities. Abstract labor turns its products—its residues, which remain use-values but are now also congealed quantities of homogenous human labor—into crystals: "When looked at as crystals of this social substance, common to them all, they are—Values."[13] Commodities are crystals, inasmuch as they are made by and of the expended energy of laborers, who have sold their vital force, which has crystallized. As Marx puts it in *Contribution towards a Critique of Political Economy*, "Use-values serve directly as means of existence. But, on the other hand, these means of existence are themselves the products of social activity, the result of expended human energy, materialized labor. As objectification of social labor, all commodities are crystallizations of the same substance."[14] Labor's energy appropriated from workers crystallizes as value. In the crystal commodity, labor is stored, congealed, objectified. The labor that made things, the motion and energy that brought about changes of state, is socially extracted, abstracted and divided in itself. It is a quantity that might be directed anywhere. For the capitalist, all that matters about the expenditure of human labor power is that it produces value, this congealed substance that forms the phantom body of the commodity, a twofold thing, compressing use-value and value, useful labor and congealed abstract labor.

In the light of realization spurred by the ever spreading darkness of Satanic mills, Friedrich's painting negates Kant's swift passage by beneficent winds, in an image of disappointment, of icing up, of blockage, of crystallization, as well as an image of how things are, how humans and nature are, in their separateness and in their antagonism, after the abstractions of Capital. Kant's promised liquidity freezes hard and suggests only impediment, dreams unfulfilled.

Envisaged on the canvas may be, on this reading, a freeze-frame of a moment in the history of abstraction. In his *Grundrisse*, written in 1857–1858, Marx states of his moment, after Capital: "Individuals are now ruled by abstractions, whereas earlier they depended on one another."[15] The abstractions are concrete enough to list: money, the commodity, exchange. These press into the textures of life, social relations, the things we do and have to do. But also, it might be said, they shape possible modes of thought. In the encounter of nature and humanity, difference, irreconcilable difference, is asserted. All freezes. All is rigidified, even though it is not in reality, but it just feels so. The sublime and, specifically, this image of the iced sea propose that there is only indifference and abstraction. The sublime is the ultimate exchange of sensuous particularity for the Idea. There is only the Idea, only the abstraction of all life into death—or its cold equivalent, the metal of money.

In Friedrich's image there is no dissolution. Even nature itself steps forward to bolster the eternalizing, abstracting victory of the Idea, to reinforce the form that is compelled out of formlessness. For what is represented here but nature's ability to make form and endlessly repeat form out of formlessness, in the formation of crystalline from fluid, the ice that outlasts time and history? To exhibit the crystal is to be able to imagine no end to now, or to deny what Marx knew and noted, in the 1867 preface to the German first edition of *Capital*: "the present society is no solid crystal, but an organism capable of change, and is constantly changing."[16] The rhetorical battle between liquid and crystal forces, between solidity and melting, is under way in earnest as capitalism effloresces. The liquidity of exchange and the freezing of time and space produce concepts that in turn melt back into our world and fix the forms of future actions. But hope insists on flow, on change and liquidity. Despair turns to the crystalline and frozen.

This history of all hitherto existing forms of capitalism could be seen as involving a mingling of the liquid and the crystal, both in acts and in thinking, that is to say, an oscillation between the two phases or a melting and a hardening of one into the other. At least, this is how it appears to us and in our language. History flows. History freezes. If it freezes, then we are cold, too cold. The world is cold. There are hotheads who will come to melt this frozen stasis. The wars are cold. The wars are hot. There are meltdowns, nuclear, economical, ecological. There is liquidity and there are frozen assets. Time slips through our fingers like water. Oh that this too solid flesh would melt, thaw, resolve itself into a dew! All that is solid melts into air, as Marx and Engels so famously put it in *The Communist Manifesto* of 1848. It might seem from this last quotation that the metaphorical relays between phases of matter appear to gather momentum under the economic system that is Capitalism. If liquidity was a trader's hope and, simultaneously, the metaphorical language of Romantic revolution (whereby current states dissolve, political renegades are liquidated, the gush of authentic sentiment overcomes the stasis of convention, and so on), is it now a capitalist necessity—along with liquid assets, the free flow of trade and labor power, the command to sink or swim in a modern global economy, a global economy that transmits images of itself globally through the energetic powers of liquid crystal?

Contemporary Liquid Crystals

The liquid crystal ball that is the Earth is ever changing, ever moving between liquid and crystal forms, metaphors, dreams. That the icy ocean thaws is, nowadays, more likely, at least at some times of the year, because of nature's shifting temperatures, which may be a result, at least in part, of human activity, in the making of the Anthropocene. This natural change generates historical—military—action, as territorial disputes occur, with new bouts of mining, orgies of primitive accumulation and dispossession.[17] Where Caspar David Friedrich's painting reported from long after the barely specified and fantasized event, our newspapers and other media report daily updates on the state of the Arctic and Antarctic regions, on the shrinkage and shifts of the ice, the current state of play with nature, the date of the death of the last polar bear, the amount of time left for what-once-was to relate in some way to what-is-yet-barely-there. Media report too on the possibility of vast resources for mining under the frozen tundra, such as those that provided the first Canadian diamonds.[18] The Arctic—like its counterpart, the Antarctic—is no longer for us a realm of eternal freezing but, rather, holds the prospect of melting without end, the transience of natural form. A measure of this change, especially the humanly induced aspects of it, is provided by polar ice. The carbon fossil fuels that powered the Industrial Age are correlated to the melting of ice at the polar points of the world. Ice cores drilled from the Antarctic continent are recordings of several thousand years of increasing carbon accumulation in the atmosphere. Inside the mind's eye the ice turns to black. It does not melt without a cost but, rather, melts never to freeze again, liquefying and flooding uncontainably.

With an improbable spanning across the liquid crystal epoch, it might be argued that present in Friedrich's *The Sea of Ice* canvas is the perfect illusion of a concocted—yet viscerally experienced—reality. This image, produced by a mechanism called oil painting, is an image of liquid and crystal. It is liquid sea and crystalline ice. Within it too, perhaps, something of the future is coiled up, in the manner of Goethe's *Urform*, conceived in relation to his botanical studies. The coolly objective modernity and perfect chimera of a concocted reality present in Friedrich's canvas reappears in the contemporary technology of the Liquid Crystal Display screen—and standing before it in the Hamburg Art Gallery a viewer may be struck by the fact that its dimensions and framing resemble nothing so much as a thirty-two-inch flat-screen TV. The painting resembles a kitsch-sublime display image on an LCD TV or a frame from a digitally post-processed eco-disaster movie (though this latter image is an image not of but *in* liquid crystals). This is the potential of liquid crystal, glimpsed in a liquid and crystal screen. Friedrich's *The Sea of Ice* is a premonition of a technological sublime that will be molded by liquid crystals in CGI and LCDs, one that disguises itself so well it appears as nature. It is an inkling of an ecological sublime—a tragic one of the Anthropocene—that finds its perfect partner in digital representation. This is liquid crystal for us. It twinkles for us every day, everywhere we look: on our TV screens, our computer monitors, in our handheld touch-screen devices. Its images today perhaps stress melting and liquidation (tsunamis, melting polar caps), rather than Friedrich's freeze up. However, the film *The Day after Tomorrow* (2004), for one, is a bombastic and globalized version of Friedrich's ice up.

As physical states and two reflexes of the dynamic sublime, the frozen and the fluid are frequently zealously rendered, or simulated more or less effectively, in CGI and mediated as narrative ciphers on the space of the screen. This narrative and technical drama of tumultuous change is represented in sudden rifts in the ice or the unstoppable roll of flooding waters, the sudden, uncontrollable movement of a character skidding down an icy chute or caught up in the inexorable force of rushing water. Of course the motivation for sublime stories about melting ice caps and icy chasms is not only technical but also political-ideological, mapping current doxa about global warming and ecological catastrophe. The devastating effects of global catastrophe in *The Day after Tomorrow* play out a human horror scenario, and the effectivity of this is reinforced formally in a dialectic of animation and its opposite—deanimation. The sudden and excessive movement of natural forces, the melting of a vast glacier, is counterbalanced by immobility—and death—as snow blankets entire cities and the banking of massive snow piles and glaciers in a sped-up Ice Age paralyzes life. In dual representation, the very stuff of animation is addressed or reflected, for the question that animation poses again and again and then answers in its various ways is, How does a concocted substance or thing that is apparently inert—frozen—begin to move, become fluid? The fluid and the frozen, the jump between these two states, is the synecdoche of computerized animation. Liquid Crystal became the matter of the screen and, as liquid and crystal, on the screen.

Like an unwilling Proteus, these elements that are liquid crystals been in their pasts theorized as quasi-life forms, as crystals were before them.[19] They have been captured in screens, in order to reveal our pasts and futures, our worlds in heightened colors. Liquid crystal's fleet mercurial motions are harnessed by CGI software and digital aesthetics. Animation in turn segues with the liquid crystal's properties: animation, in its various formats, has been about stopping and starting, about stillness impelled into life. That is what the stop-frame technique achieves. It is what the cel system and projection make possible. But now the screens themselves collaborate in this liquidity and crystallization. The permanently scanned image with a high frequency backlight is flicker-free. It can be frozen at any moment and held still like a photograph. It can flow, barely leaving traces. Animation always has been the amalgam of the crystalline and the petrified—the still, cajoled into fluidity, restlessness, movement. To this extent the new screens continue that movement, even if they more deeply integrate it as a technical, scientific logic of the machinery that conveys it.

Liquid crystal was not invented but discovered. Liquid crystal devices were invented, but long (eighty years or so) after the capacities of the phase of matter had been found. It took small research steps, worldwide, and finally some concentrated exploration in Asia to bring a liquid crystal screen into being. The shapes it then took on—ever larger screens, ever more miniaturization and flattening, ever more responsive touchscreens—are shaped by a complex coagulation of inventors' dreams, material capacities, social wishes, and in addition and sometimes, the energetic power of capital investment. Some devices fail, for a complex network of reasons, like the videophones of the 1990s. Other devices hit their moment and then shape it. It is not that capitalism gave us the iPhone and liquid crystals. Liquid crystals made a form of capitalism possible for us—we used it, in the light of the entrepreneur's visions for maximizing profit, and in line with our socially formed needs and desires. Communication is the purpose of the sector, but it is communication couched in modes of abstraction. Communication is the alibi of commerce and surveillance. We live between liquid crystalline forms of commerce and surveillance.

What might liquid crystal be that is not captured by the market and the security state?

Future Liquid Crystals

Some have fantasized a liberation—not just from but of liquid crystal—its release into the wild. There are Hito Steyerl's trashed LCD screens, which appear in the two very short video works named *Strike* from 2010 and 2012. The screen is smashed with a hammer and the colors of the pixels flash chaotically across the screen. There is also a mini-genre of videos of smashed Apple products on YouTube, uploaded by amateurs. Two photographers made an artwork of the same idea, shooting the fetish products—which had been mangled, melted, shot, hammered, run over by a train—in richly saturated colors and aesthetically posed. Graphic designer Michael Tompert had seized on the idea and engaged photographer Paul Fairchild, when his children argued over an iPod, which he, in frustration, hurled to the ground, at which point, in a kind of blood analogy, "the screen was broken and this liquid poured out of it."[20] A new beauty emerges from the shattered glass and other materials.

A history of liquid crystal displays (LCDs) has been written under the name "Liquid Gold."[21] Nowadays, it is often the liquidity that is emphasized, metaphorically, but this forgets the crystal moment, the freezing of social relations, the embedding of certain gestures and modes. Liquid modernity is the gleaming puddle on the surface, but liquid crystal capitalism is something more contradictory, producing images and forms for capital but also providing the material of its dreams, its oppositions, its breakdowns. It invades our dreams, forms our myths, our gestures and movements. The form itself necessitates a rallying between the poles of liquidity and crystallinity, not mobilizing one or the other but keeping their dynamic interplay at the fore. And dynamic interplay, their making and unmaking, is already part of their own rhythm. The liquid crystal devices smash themselves in permanent upgradings, led by a circuit of desire for the new—driven by a wish for improved functionality—and desire for profit. Liquid crystal is like the market. It is free, and it is fixed. To believe in free markets is to succumb to one idea of liquid crystal. To use the smartphone for and against the system might be another way of mobilizing its—and its matter's—contradictory nature. Capitalism did give us a smartphone, not the only one there could be, but the one that met its social moment and was shaped by it and that also shaped it.

And after this, an open question—but one indicated in my title, yet unaddressed, that might organize itself around vapors, plasma, the clouds. Or are we stuck in this phase forever, until it all melts or it all gets blocked?

We are already drawn into gaseous concerns: awareness of CO_2 emissions, fracking for shale gas, and imaging our memories that are alienated to the Cloud (the data one). Our new nature is ever regenerating, ever drawing in and on states of matter, transforming the world through energetic deployments, circuiting back, reaching tipping points, once and again.

Notes

1 For a thorough history of their discovery, see David Dunmur and Tim Sluckin, *Soap, Science and Flat-Screen TVs: A History of Liquid Crystals* (Oxford: Oxford University Press, 2011).

2 Yamiche Alcindor, "Demonstrators Stage 'Die In' at NYC Apple Store, Macy's," *USAtoday.com*, December 6, 2014, http://www.usatoday.com/story/tech/2014/12/05/protests-apple-store-new-york/19975797/.

3 Kevin D. Williamson, "A Jobs Agenda," *Nationalreview.com*, October 5, 2011, http://www.nationalreview.com/corner/279321/jobs-agenda-kevin-d-williamson/.

4 Ibid.

5 See Chad Ingram, "Beautiful Hair, Whatever the Weather," September 25, 2014, accessible at http://vimeo.com/107267546/.

6 Karl Marx, "The Eighteenth Brumaire of Louis Bonaparte," in *Marx and Engels Collected Works, Vol. 11* (Moscow: Progress, 1979), 154.

7 Zygmunt Baumann, *Liquid Modernity* (Boston: Polity, 2000), 7.

8 Geoff Mulgan, *The Locust and the Bee: Predators and Creators in Capitalism's Future* (Princeton, NJ: Princeton University Press, 2013), 224.

9 It has been displayed under various titles. In the year of its completion it was shown in Prague as "Ideal Scene of an Arctic Sea, a Shattered Ship under Piled Up Masses of Ice." That same year it was shown in Dresden as "The Sea of Ice." At other times it was known as "Ice Image: The Unsuccessful North Pole Expedition" and as "Winter Landscape with Large Ice Bergs or the Unsuccessful Hope in the Polar Sea after Perry's Journey."

10 Joseph Leo Koerner discusses the prevalence in Friedrich of "unreduplicatable chaos" in shattered ice or other natural forms and cultural-natural forms such as ruins as part of the "uniqueness" of Friedrich's nonsystematic system. See Joseph Leo Koerner, *Caspar David Friedrich and the Subject of Landscape* (London: Reaktion, 2009), 127.

11 Immanuel Kant, *Natural Science* (Cambridge: Cambridge University Press, 2012), 376.

12 Stuart Elden and Eduardo Mendieta, *Reading Kant's Geography* (New York: SUNY Press, 2011), 58.

13 Karl Marx, *Capital, Vol. 1* (New York: Modern Library, 1906), 48.

14 Karl Marx, "Contribution towards a Critique of Political Economy," in *Marx and Engels Collected Works, Vol. 29*, 271, accessible at: https://www.marxists.org/archive/marx/works/1859/critique-pol-economy/ch01.htm.

15 Karl Marx, "Foundations of the Critique of Political Economy," in *The Grundrisse (Rough Draft)* (London: Penguin Books, 1973), 164.

16 Karl Marx, "Preface," in *Capital* (New York: Modern Library, 1906), 16.

17 For a business perspective on Arctic resources, see Jeremy Bender, "Militaries Know that the Arctic Is Melting—Here's How They're Taking Advantage," *Businessinsider.com*, June 3, 2014, http://www.businessinsider.com/the-competition-for-arctic-resources-2014-6/.

18 See, for example, work on Nanisivik lead-zinc mine, Canada's first high Arctic mine, as well as the various materials relating to Chuck Fipke's Canadian Arctic™ Diamonds. At the end of 2013 the possible existence of diamonds in the Antarctic mountains was confirmed.

19 Speculations on crystal life, in one mode or another, can be found in leading evolutionary scientists of the nineteenth century, such as Pierre-Louis Maupertuis, Matthias Schleiden, Theodor Schwann, Franz Unger, Herbert Spencer, and August Weismann. With Ernsy Haeckel and Otto Lehmann and others, these ideas continue into the twentieth century. Philosophers and mystics had assumed their liveliness before this and since.

20 Tompert cited in "Destroyed Apple Products," *Designboom.com*, November 19, 2010, http://www.designboom.com/art/destroyed-apple-products/.

21 Joseph A. Castellano, *Liquid Gold: The Story of Liquid Crystal Displays and the Creation of an Industry* (Hackensack: World Scientific Publishing, 2005).

Part III

Belonging

9

Cuban Filmmaking and the Postcapitalist Transition

CRISTINA VENEGAS

A new era of United States–Cuba relations began on December 17, 2014, when Presidents Barack Obama and Raul Castro simultaneously announced that the two nations would reinstate diplomatic relations and begin negotiations to expand trade and travel. Despite the importance of this first step, the historic change so far amounts only to a hole in the Caribbean equivalent of the Berlin Wall. We are not yet seeing the end of Cuba's postcolonial/post-capitalist project because Raul Castro is committed to building "sustainable socialism." Once again, Cuba will attempt to renovate socialism, as it did during the economic collapse of the early 1990s when the government justified the incorporation of market mechanisms ironically as necessary for the salvation of socialism.

Since then, Cuba has tried to balance market- and state-controlled economic strategies while contending that it is staying the course of the Cuban Revolution.[1] Socialism in Cuba is being shaped by the temporal, organizational, and geographical parameters of capitalism. Accelerating entrepreneurial efforts, as in Havana's burgeoning restaurant sector, try to push Cuba forward, while languishing economic performance, particularly in its agricultural production, pulls backward. The oft-repeated notion that Cuba is lost in time, out of step, backward, stems from a real temporal disjunction between Cuba's decayed infrastructure and material scarcity and the unceasing production of new consumer goods in the economies of "overdeveloped" countries.[2] Territorial encroachment such as the Mariel Free Trade Zone, centered on a container port funded by international investment, jars with impoverished neighborhoods even while it is touted as a vision of economic hope. Continuation of disparities between the political rhetoric and partial adoption of capitalist practices can be anticipated even as Raul Castro's negotiating priorities appear to reduce the essence of socialist Cuba to the maintenance of state control over health, education, media, and military security. The recent thaw in Cuba–United States relations can only heighten the interplay of economic, political, and social dynamics experienced in Cuba over the last two and a half decades.

The complex processes involved include not only the practical, political, and bureaucratic aspects of making and adopting new policies, rapid technological change, and infrastructural deficiencies but also changing social relations, economic uncertainty, and cultural anxieties. A major disjuncture arises between socialist ideals and a market orientation, involving also the real complications of daily life. This is accompanied by the additional consequence of social inequality, a sacrifice acknowledged by Fidel Castro in the early 1990s in the context of the Special Period. These are the main characteristics of contemporary Cuban society. Cuba has come to occupy an indeterminate halfway space that is both capitalist and socialist—but defined by its emergence from a long socialist experience. Encroachment of market forces is allowed with a type of ideological largesse by the Cuban state as it justifies difficult compromise as a way to maintain socialist values.

This space takes center stage in fictional film narratives that illustrate mounting social discrepancies and that register the anxieties of life stretched between two ideologies. Production itself in contemporary Cuban filmmaking is filled with uncertainty as it bridges from a strong state-centered model to one that is decentralized, precarious, but thriving. Cuban film and filmmaking is focused on the negotiation of the hybrid space created between the politics of the old and the new.

The focus here is on three films that represent the thickness of contemporary Cuban experience, with the aim of examining the uncertainty produced by temporal disjuncture and the steady encroachment of capitalist values. *Melaza* (2012), *Memorias del desarrollo* (*Memories of Overdevelopment*, 2010), and *Juan de los muertos* (*Juan of the Dead*, 2011) explore loss, solitude, disappointment, and opportunism through a range of perspectives, aesthetics, and genres. The films are produced independently of the Instituto Cubano de Arte e Industria Cinematografica (ICAIC) and engage with new financing paradigms and distribution mechanisms. The stylistic heterogeneity seen in their unique signature has become characteristic of this new era filmmaking. All three filmmakers were trained in Cuba and have participated in international creative workshops. All three have found critical success at film festivals internationally, which opened up greater accessibility to transnational partnerships, prizes, and competitions that helped to leverage subsequent projects. Having come of age during economic collapse, the filmmakers make use of their intimate knowledge of material scarcity, of the reversals of socialist ideology, and the solutions devised to restore economic growth. The stories translate surreal situations generated by shortages, idleness, and despair for global and local audiences. Foreign partnerships and independence from the state production entity all help produce the films but do not safeguard them from censorship both local and institutional (although in each case the directors have prevailed). While the filmmaking participates in the difficult social and economic dynamics shaping Cuba's indeterminacy, the films themselves convey the related subjective and affective experience.

Protecting against Film Industry Capitalism

The opposition to capitalist values was a foundational principle in the re-creation of the field of culture for Cuban revolutionary society in 1959. The first policy of the revolutionary government was Law 169 of the Council of Ministers of the Cuban Republic, which established the ICAIC as the first cultural institution. As Hector Amaya argues, the law "set a discursive primer for thinking about film and art (indeed the ideas of this law would affect most cultural work) in revolutionary Cuba."[3] Film was to remain free from market coercion "in order to achieve its goal as a tool of education, reason and national pride." Moreover, the law legislated that the ICAIC "would control filmic production and distribution in internal and external markets, prepare technicians and filmmakers, and administer studios, laboratories, and any other infrastructure related to film production and distribution."[4] The aim of the institutional infrastructure created by ICAIC was—as a value of the socialist paradigm—to protect writers, producers, directors, actors, and film critics from market forces. While films and filmmakers are the focus of this essay, the same strategy guided the creation from 1959 to 1961 of several other Cuban cultural institutions. The structure of creative labor reflected the goal of social equality through salaries assigned on a minimally differentiated scale within a hierarchy that determined a system of rewards and opportunities. The distance from the market was seen as conducive to formal experimentation, which was encouraged within the institutional framework. The early accomplishments of filmmakers established the newly formed ICAIC's reputation worldwide, as socialist films embraced the construction of a new society as an alternative to the drama of colonial and capitalist exploitation.

By the late 1980s, however, the dissolution of the communist bloc and the elimination of Soviet economic support as well as internal bureaucratic struggles at the institute necessitated a very different type of engagement from the Cuban film industry. The economic fallout and the heightened political environment of the 1990s made the ICAIC vulnerable to greater state control under a weakened leadership and severe budget cuts. The material degradation of filmmaking facilities exposed the institute to the market forces that its institutional directive had tried to avoid, thus it could no longer control all aspects of the film industry. As Anne Marie Stock contends, cultural organizations established in the 1980s and 1990s such as the Escuela Internacional de Cine y Televisión (EICTV), the Asociación Hermanos Saíz, the Movimiento Nacional de Video, the Fundación Ludwig de Cuba, and the community media collective Televisión Serrana paved the way for the modes of production and circulation of films made alongside the industry.[5] The continual support of a socialist-national mode of film industry—and the acknowledgment of its aging ranks—led the new leadership of the ICAIC in 2000 to organize a nationwide search for young filmmakers to rejuvenate the pool of creative talent in order to secure the future of what was a pillar of Cuban socialist culture.[6] Filmmakers working with the support of the new cultural organizations and training institutions responded to the call, showing their films in the Muestra de Cine Joven founded in 2001. The new *tranche* of filmmakers sought out new sources of financing through international partnerships and access to digital technologies, creating a fresh and diverse corpus of work. They built on the formal training they received at film schools from national and international teachers. Their education already embodied an international perspective informing modes of work, themes, and styles of filmmaking.[7]

The deep talent and enthusiasm of the new crop of filmmakers, competition for dwindling resources, and reaction against retrenchment of the state to its own fossilized institutions produced a simultaneous response in regional projects interested in contesting the ICAIC-centric organization of film culture.[8] This has expanded film culture beyond Havana and ICAIC and led to the creation of enterprising projects such as the National Workshop of Film Critics in Camaguey province, now in its twenty-first edition. This has contributed to a reconceptualization of film culture and its multiple publics outside the capital city. The resulting alteration of the socialist-conceived cultural space has occurred without any rejection of socialist ideals or deliberate embrace of capitalist cultural values. The disintegration of the institutional form of film culture in Cuba and the energies originally located within this central concept are flowing into the nation's larger malleable space of transformation.

Institutional frameworks are key in setting the parameters of Cuba's ongoing transition. The larger changes to economic and monetary policy required of the state are refracted in the changes that ICAIC must make to its institutional framework in order to retain a Cuban film industry. Presently the activity of filmmaking as an officially recognized profession exists only for members of ICAIC. Without legal standing, filmmakers have no choice but to register the business of production in foreign countries. The scattering of sites of production is accompanied by a demand for the right to work in Cuba despite its impoverishment and offline status. Out of this has come an urgent call for a film law that would create the category of Audiovisual Creator to give non-state film production in Cuba the legitimacy now conferred on restaurant ownership, hairdressing, and so on.

Since 2008 national forums have focused on how the economic crisis has affected the arts sector, and filmmakers have organized and responded to the ongoing debates. In 2013, coming from different generations and calling themselves "Cuban Filmmakers for Cuban Cinema," they agreed on a proposal to present to ICAIC's leadership and to the Ministry of Culture. The proposal outlined recommendations for the administrative restructuring of the ICAIC. Far from rejecting the foundational role of the ICAIC and its socialist historical legacy, the filmmakers "recognize the ICAIC as the State entity overseeing all Cuban filmmaking activity; born with the Revolution and its long trajectory is a legacy that belongs to all filmmakers."[9] It is this socialist impulse around all Cuban institutions that defines the parameters of transformation and throws doubt on the inevitable contours of a capitalist destiny.

Part of the proposal addresses the economic realities of the country and the international production paradigms that have become part of Cuban filmmaking since the early 1990s, when co-productions with European and Latin American partners kept the industry afloat.[10] It argues that reform of ICAIC must be accompanied by reform of social security: presently a percentage of ICAIC project budgets include wages and vacation and social security payments; with the legalization of self-employment for filmmakers, these costs would be assumed by the independent producer. According to the Union of Writers and Artists of Cuba, the advantages of this reform would include "more sources of employment for artists, technicians, and other non-state workers," and modern production practices, greater efficiency, and budgets based on real costs rather than on those inherited from the old economic model of state subsidies.[11] Without sacrificing creativity, ICAIC would move from a space of idealism to one of realism. A film law would cover all filmmakers, whether projects are financed through the state, independently, or through international co-productions. As a result of such reforms, ICAIC would be focused on exhibition and distribution.

During this time of expansion, fractious debate, and stalling by ICAIC, filmmakers working on their own have garnered greater international exposure, found increasing support for script development in Europe and Iberoamerica, and generated international prestige for Cuba through their films.[12] The engagement in international networks of independent production by Cuban filmmakers demonstrates the influence of global media on the local space of production. The experience of participation in film festival co-production forums builds filmmakers' understanding of the role of institutional frameworks in different countries, which leads to and informs the drive for reform in Cuba.

Film laws, especially in Latin America, have been instrumental in rebuilding film industries. Institutional restructuring in Colombia and Mexico, for example, has facilitated increased production and support for script development, promotion, and training—also generating international prestige. Beyond the benefits to Cuba's extensive network of filmmakers, a Cuban film law could likewise establish a legal framework to link film production in Cuba more effectively to transnational networks of production. Mechanisms could be introduced in Cuba such as the 40 percent rebate for production budgets that forms part of Colombia's model, which has dramatically boosted the number of international productions shooting in Colombian territory.

This is not to say that film production in Cuba is not already international, impressive, and lively. The current environment may be chaotic but it is highly constructive, involving spirited exchanges of ideas and cultural products, often through informal networks of distribution. The void of bland institutional media and the limited access to online entertainment and information have been replaced by a bounty of international and local programming exemplified by the now ubiquitous *Paquete semanal* (The weekly package), a flash-drive-based peer distribution network. This distribution revolution has transformed cultural consumption on the island, and its features gesture to the forms of aggregated content distribution of large media networks outside of Cuba. It is also significant that Cuba is now allowed to exist virtually in the capitalist space as Twitter Cuba and concretely as a new trade destination for Apple Inc. Even before Cuba is broadband ready for the use of related services, the ever-expanding American media Tantalus, which also includes Netflix, is beginning to stake out Cuba's loosely organized creative distribution space. Corporate capitalism potentially stands to reap the benefits of a future negotiated outcome where so far profit making has been left to the informal Cuban enterprises such as the *Paquete semanal*. Cuba's suspended and cocooned post-capitalist existence is set for major change now that it has been designated a trading territory by the world's corporate media giants. The current political rapprochement and growing desire for all things Cuban adds to the need to build solid legal frameworks to strengthen and buttress the multiplicity of audiovisual production by Cuban filmmakers—if Cuba's place in the global media sphere is to continue to be rooted in socialist values without denying the value of a market orientation.

The participation of young filmmakers in the complex evolution of the industry shapes the landscape of creativity. They bring a freshness of perspective that addresses difficult themes in Cuban society that have typically not been represented. Not only have they revolutionized their production methods, the young filmmakers have shattered previous norms of acceptable content as they tackle the ongoing disaffection with reality. Prior to the 1990s, when Cuba was forced to grapple with market mechanisms, films—including, for example, *Lejania* (Díaz, 1985) and *Cecilia* (Solas, 1982)—revised history, dealt with ideological conflicts, and examined the revolutionary process. After the Special Period, film narratives were increasingly concerned with the individual situated amid disillusionment and fatigue where solutions to conflicts were no longer found within revolutionary ideology. New themes centered on resolving personal dilemmas in the face of an uncertain Cuban future. This move toward a focus on the self has continued, frequently providing a deeper view of the layers of contemporary Cuban society. The explicit engagement with previously taboo subject matter has led to strong local impact while the dramatic depth and confident critical stance of the films, combined with the greater number of productions, has attracted more attention and curiosity than ever from U.S. media. International critical attention and audience success means that the intricacies of Cuban concerns are circulated on a broader stage. Turning to the three first features, *Melaza, Memorias del desarrollo*, and *Juan de los muertos*, audiences all over the world can find an exploration of the cultural anxieties related to the economic difficulty, frustration at this lack of opportunities, and the experience of ideological exhaustion both individually and as a community in a post-socialist world.

Waiting for Change

In *Melaza*, a Cuba-France-Panama co-production, director Carlos Lechuga tells the story of Monica and Aldo, a young married couple living in the small town of Melaza where the sugar mill, once the lifeline of the town, has shut down. They and the few other inhabitants make the best of a harsh situation. Monica is the sole employee of the sugar mill charged with the daily test of the machinery because the mill will presumably reopen some-day. Her husband, Aldo, teaches the few remaining students to swim in an empty swimming pool. In the afternoons, he visits Monica at the mill where they make love. They share a humble, well-kept home with their pre-teen daughter, Mara, and Monica's wheelchair-bound mother. Their existence is marked by conflicts created by a failing economy, the solutions they adopt, and how they endure the consequences of their choices. Even resorting to illegal activities such as renting a room by the hour or selling meat on the black market would not sustain them and can bring steep fines or land them in jail. The situation is made tolerable only by the tenderness they have for each other, especially when they realize that a sexual favor is the only way to secure a job for Aldo. Opportunities for mobility are as scant as material goods in this rural setting, and resilience appears to be the most valuable quality to possess. The political context is underscored by repetitive and triumphalist party slogans and their dissonance with real-ity. The film comments indirectly on the redundancy of party ideology as it focuses on the travails of individuals burdened by historical contradictions.

Many co-productions turned to the use of comedy in the 1990s to address the unraveling social and ideological landscape, but Lechuga relies on drama to reflect the persistent grave economic conditions. While com-edies like Gerardo Chijona's *Perfecto amor equivocado* (*Love by Mistake*, 2004) illustrated how foreign work helped Cubans survive back home in Havana, characters in the rural setting of *Melaza* have little contact with city life let alone foreign locales. In the first half of the twentieth century the countryside was the site of a booming international—albeit exploit-ative—sugar industry. It is now a place of despair and desolation where distance from cities is part of the experience of scarcity.

Lechuga consciously avoids a gritty aesthetic focused on misery for dra-matic and aesthetic reasons. At the start of the first decade of the twenty-first century, no other sector of the Cuban economy was worse hit than agriculture, and "none collapsed more dramatically" than the sugar sec-tor. The closure of more than 50 percent of Cuba's sugar mills contributed to the tripling of lands made idle between the 1990s and the start of pol-icy changes in 2007 under Raul Castro's presidency.[13] Lechuga's choice of subject matter, the bitter reality of redundant workers and idle farmland, is unusual in Cuban feature films. He explores the social and emotional cost of survival without the cacophony of urban distractions, and his main characters purposely avoid going to Havana. Abject immersion in poverty is not the point, however, as the sugar mill he chooses appears less dilapi-dated than most and as he gives his characters a better wardrobe than they might actually afford.[14] His intended focus is the internal dilemma without the distraction of a stereotypically stark realism. The audience encounters a strangely surreal atmosphere of existential exasperation replete with discomfort and relieved by eros.

Lechuga was inspired by the work of Chinese filmmaker Jia Zhangke, particularly his film *Still Life* (2006), which comments on the temporality of development and destruction. Jia focuses on the lives of two people living in a small village being destroyed by the Three Gorges Dam construction project. The comparable reference point for Lechuga is the closure of the sugar mills. Jia Zhangke's influence is also at work in *Melaza's* representation of Cuba's ethos of transition and the temporal disjunction it produces. As they wait for development, Monica and Aldo in *Melaza* experience the same sense of suspension, lethargy, and stasis as ironically felt by the displaced inhabitants left behind by China's accelerated development. In *Melaza*, without economic development, idle lands create idle workers living in dulled anticipation of the re-start of the economy and the return of jobs. While they wait, the state's pretense of a population participating in a continuing triumphalist revolution stands in cruel contrast with the lassitude and deprivation of daily life. Deliberate slowness allows us to linger on contrasts: the beauty and bounty of the sugar cane versus material scarcity, boredom broken by spontaneous dancing, mundane repetition interrupted by lovemaking. The state justifies the wait with a false sense of imminence belied by the constant delays, deferrals, and inaction experienced in Melaza. A canned woman's voice on the roving loudspeaker hails the townspeople to unite and continue the fight against Yankee imperialism. Her plea falls largely on deaf ears. Lechuga's choice of a converted container as Monica and Aldo's house symbolizes an aspect of Cuba's tremendous insecurity. What once would have carried sugar for export has run aground without cargo, itself becoming salvage as a makeshift home. The port of Mariel and its Free Trade Zone is far away and may as well not exist.

Suspended Memories

Self-funded and made independently, Miguel Coyula's *Memories of Over-development* is the sequel to *Memories of Underdevelopment* (1968), the classic Cuban revolutionary film by Tomás Gutiérrez Alea. Both films adapt Edmundo Desnoes novels. While in Alea's film the protagonist, Sergio, remains in Cuba when his wife and friends migrate to Miami, in Coyula's film a much older Sergio has long migrated to New York City where he teaches Cuban history at a university. Turning to the depths of despair resulting from an existential crisis, Coyula's film watches the cynical Sergio fall apart from disaffection. Sergio feels anguish that his thoughts have become more real than the real world and he can no longer tell them apart. He is experiencing a creative and midlife crisis and profound ideological disillusionment. Sexist, misogynist, and perverse, Sergio claims that speaking English has turned him into a clown. Attacking vision through terrifying collages, Sergio finds his sense of emptiness ironically makes him feel transparent. Coyula positions Sergio at the center of an animated modular narrative examining the fragments of memory past and present, history and fantasy, ideology and death. When he is fired from the university for his pornographic collages, he spirals deeper into the past taking aim at political commitment, at Che and Fidel, at family memories. He begins to look for meaning elsewhere, though disenchantment is all that materializes. Bewildered, he ends up in the stark Utah countryside away from the symbols of overdevelopment—high-rise hotels and office buildings—where he appears to find solace in a desolate emotional geography. Out in the barren desert Sergio discovers the Mars Society Research Station where "astronauts" simulate a mission to Mars, and on the soundtrack we hear Bola de Nieve's "Goodbye Happiness" (Adios felicidad). Expunging almost all the familiar symbols of Cuban culture except the music on the soundtrack, *Memorias* literally and metaphorically takes us to another planetary system.

Coyula had already been trying to jettison the semiotic language of Cuban culture in *Válvula de luz* (Light valve; 1997), his second short film, where he relied on the ruins of Havana to create a post-apocalyptic setting of the island. In *Red Cockroaches* (2003), a low-budget *Blade Runner* (Ridley Scott, 1982), Havana has been replaced by New York City where *Memories* is also set. Coyula trades the crumbling buildings of Havana for the collapsing World Trade Center towers and crashing Stock Exchange of New York. Aram Vidal's *De-Generación* also examined the contradictions of capital and ideologies in a 2007 documentary where young Cubans share their opinions about the debacle of political systems, banking scandals, neoliberal fire sales throughout Latin America, growing inequality, self-absorption, and material scarcity. The intensity of their comments is reiterated in the vacated ideologies of *Memories* though Coyula's film eliminates any allegiance to realism. The cities of *Memories* are, as Sergio's confessional voice-over notes, "erections of stone and plastic." Mostly, they are reflective surfaces of consumer and political desires. *Memories* touches on different aspects of the contemporary moment of ideological collisions and capitalist encroachment in Cuba, imagining a state of suspension, considering survival, and rethinking models of living in exhausted paradigms.

Zombie Economy

A Cuba-Spain co-production, *Juan de los muertos* (Alejandro Brugués, 2011) is a commercial and calculated approach to expanding Cuban film markets. The first Cuban zombie film in four decades, it tells the story of three slackers who, when a plague of zombies takes over the island, join together to develop a business plan that will help fellow Cubans kill the zombies before the zombies kill them. Armed with lethal but primitive tools, they create a successful venture. Soon, however, the number of zombies increases—spreading the hilarity, political digs, and offensive humor that have made the film economically successful. The three slackers succeed for a while, and in the process of killing the zombies, they destroy more structures in the already crumbling city. Brugués pushes the outrageous political satire—making references to the government's obsession with blaming the United States for all of Cuba's problems, mistaking the zombies for dissidents, lampooning passive behavior as well as the characteristically Cuban wild entrepreneurial solutions to surreal problems. When the trio finally accept defeat by the zombies, three of them decide to abandon the island on a makeshift raft and head for the United States. Reiterating the opening slogan of the film our hero, Juan, calls himself a survivor: he survived Angola and the Special Period, and he'll survive whatever the zombie thing is. He thus, like Sergio in the first *Memories* of 1968, decides to stay to see what will happen.

Mockingly, the film points to uncertainty against increasing odds and to the nature of survival. The director of the film, Alejandro Brugués, talks about the film in clichéd terms too: "Cubans always turn every opportunity into a business," it's guerrilla entrepreneurship and doesn't need a capitalist environment, though that would be welcome. By using a well-worn genre formula, popular with audiences worldwide and made fresh by local humor, the producers have assured significant international profits and a broad market acceptance. Beyond *Juan*, the outward-looking Brugués is engaged in transnational productions, has directed the segment *E for Equilibrium* for the compilation horror film *The ABCs of Death 2*, and directed an episode of the *Dawn of the Dead* television series for Robert Rodriguez's El Rey Network in 2015. The commercial achievements of *Juan* have allowed him to insert himself more deeply into networks of independent production in the United States and Cuba, while demonstrating how the global media sphere makes it possible to lose national and political markers.

Looking Out, Looking In

Filmmakers belong to a new generation that also includes writers, rappers, painters, dancers, and entrepreneurs who have captured the imagination of Cuba watchers everywhere. The new paradigm of cultural and economic renewal, accumulation and circulation has been favorable to Cuban artists and musicians working internationally and to Cuban athletes. A 2014

ESPN special issue magazine proclaims that Cuba is the "next new pipe-line" in American sports—especially in Major League baseball.[15] Boosted by economic inequality, the underground economy thrives in Cuba's transitional phase, serving internet and social media use and the consumption of television, film, video games, fashion, music, and shaping new styles. With ingenuity, cash, and patience it is now possible to imagine a career abroad. The relaxation of Cuba's travel policies allows some Cubans to live elsewhere without it being a state of exile.

The number of articles about Cuba in major publications such as the *New York Times, The Guardian, Forbes, Variety,* the *Hollywood Reporter, National Geographic,* and *ESPN Sports* has grown considerably since the 1990s and especially since the rapprochement of December 17, 2014. A *New York Times Sunday Review* article from March 2014 characterizes the current situation in Cuba as part of an evolution into a modern and capitalist entity.[16] In this way the article is typical of the single-minded narratives that posit Cuba as backward and out of touch, awaiting technology, gadgets, consumer goods, and foreign investment in order to leap forward into an inevitable capitalist future. Such a future is imagined from the perspective of different stakeholders—the baseball major league owners, embargo sympathizers, curious travelers, and writers looking for new adventures and a good story. Meanwhile, the actual Cuban model defies standard definitions and merits analysis that goes beyond teleologies of capitalist progress. The simplistic vision of Cubans as hungry potential consumers desperate for iPhones does not match the reality of the Cuban economy where, for instance, the military has become a diversified conglomerate that owns an airline, hotels, hard currency stores, and technology companies that supply domestic as well as touristic demands.

Finding Capital in Socialist Remnants and National Identity

The inefficiencies and inadequacies of the socialist project have forced Cuba to open up along several dimensions of contradictory engagement, which produces the hybrid space. Cuba needs a major infrastructure overhaul to build higher internet capacity, new housing, roads, an electrical grid, and ports. Unofficial emergent capitalism cannot engage in these big projects but can and does create businesses, commercial exchanges, websites, advertising, and publications. The amount of entrepreneurial activity around supply and demand can easily give the impression that, with the removal of prohibitions, the economy would solidify into familiar capitalist forms. Confusion around the transitional dynamic formed around black markets, a double currency, mixed economic measures, changing policies, and growing inequities leads to predictions of ruin and unquestioned adoption of capitalist measures even as capitalist crises have arisen worldwide. Reflecting this confusion, growing media coverage about the changes on the island tends to assume that Cuba will become subsumed by neoliberal enterprise and development.

Cuban filmmaking reveals a more complex reality that combines elements from both socialist and capitalist models and produces new forms of engagement to fulfill social and economic needs. The opening provided by filmmaker links with transnational forces and portrayals in film of Cuban dilemmas has been positive in creative and economic terms and has also achieved positive political influence through the films' exposure of social conditions and by winning concessions regarding official censorship. Political movement is seen, too, in the proposal for a new institutional framework, which is characterized by its retention of a socialist legacy. The doubt, promise, and historical weight that imbue the remnants of the revolutionary project inspire filmmakers' narratives that contest and defend against externally generated marketing visions of Cuba. The films' international success strengthens a Cuban identity and bolsters its transnational position. The Cuban film industry thus illustrates the capacity of Cuban society to make global connections and to generate social, economic, and creative capital. Filmmaking is contributing to a new Cuban project that takes and adapts measures to suit the remaining project of self-determination, where the new generation builds capital out of socialist remnants.

Notes

1 See for instance Katherine Gordy, "Sales + Economy + Efficiency = Revolution? Dollarization, Consumer Capitalism and Popular Responses in Special Period Cuba," *Public Culture* 18, no. 2 (2006): 383–412; Anna Dopico, "Picturing Havana: History, Vision and the Scramble for Cuba," *Nepantla* 3, no. 3 (2002); Ariana Hernandez-Reguant, "Writing the Special Period: An Introduction," in *Cuba and the Special Period: Culture and Ideology in the 1990s*, ed. Ariana Hernandez-Reguant (New York: Palgrave Macmillan, 2009), 8.

2 See Miguel Coyula, *Memories of Overdevelopment* (Pirámide 2010), film.

3 Hector Amaya, *Screening Cuba: Film Criticism as Political Performance during the Cold War* (Champagne: University of Illinois Press, 2010), 8–9.

4 Ibid., 8.

5 Anne Marie Stock, *On Location in Cuba: Street Filmmaking during Times of Transition* (Chapel Hill: University of North Carolina Press, 2009), 22. She uses the term "street films" to avoid dichotomies of working either with or outside the industry.

6 Dean Luis Reyes, "After ICAIC: The Three Categorical Imperatives of Current Cuban Cinema," in *Submerged: Alternative Cuban Cinema*, ed. Luis Duno-Gottberg and Michael J. Horswell (Houston: Literal Publishing, 2013), 119.

7 Stock, *On Location in Cuba: Street Filmmaking during Times of Transition*, 4–6, 170–171.

8 Juan Antonio García Borrero, "Notes on the Contemporary Cuban Audiovisual Industry," in *Submerged: Alternative Cuban Cinema*, ed. Luis Duno-Gottberg and Michael J. Horswell (Houston: Literal Publishing, 2013), 111.

9 "Cineastas Cubanos por el cine Cubano," document submitted by filmmakers at the end of the May 4, 2013, meeting held at the Centro Cultural Fresa y Chocolate where a Grupo de Trabajo was elected. Seventy filmmakers were in attendance. The document is accessible at uneac.org.cu/.

10 Cristina Venegas, "Filmmaking with Foreigners," in *Cuba and the Special Period: Culture and Ideology in the 1990s*, ed. Ariana Hernandez-Reguant (New York: Palgrave Macmillan, 2009), 37–50.

11 UNEAC, "Relaciones de Producción: Un nuevo enfoque," March 6, 2015, at http://www.uneac.org.cu/.

12 Victoria Burnett, "A New Era's Filmmakers Find Their Way in Cuba," *New York Times*, January 4, 2013, at http://www.nytimes.com/2013/01/05/movies/digital-technology-is-making-its-mark-in-cuba.html.

13 Jorge I. Dominguez, "On the Brink of Change: Cuba's Economy and Society at the Start of the 2010s," in *Cuban Economic and Social Development: Policy Reforms and Challenges in the 21st Century*, ed. Jorge I. Dominguez, Omar Everleny Pérez Villanueva, Maya Espina Prieto, and Lorena Barbería (Cambridge, MA: Harvard University Press, 2012), 4.

14 In a post-screening question and answer session, Carlos Lechuga discusses his aesthetic choices: the town is fictitious and three different locations make up the town of Melaza. He carefully selected locations so that the mill did not appear too dilapidated and the wardrobe choices were better than what people might be able to afford. See "NG Cuba Presents MELAZA," NG Cuba: Next Generation Cuban Film Festival, Pollock Theater, University of California Santa Barbara, October 9, 2013, video accessible at https://vimeo.com/77551117/.

15 "Cuba: Opening the Next Great Pipeline in Sports," *ESPN Magazine*, February 17, 2014.

16 Damian Cave, "The Cuban Evolution," *New York Times Sunday Review*, March 2, 2014, at http://www.nytimes.com/2014/03/02/sunday-review/the-cuban-evolution.html.

10

"Neither Eastern
nor Western"

Economic and Cultural Policies in
Post-Revolutionary Iran

NIKI AKHAVAN

Emerging from slogans such as "Neither Eastern, nor Western, an Islamic Republic" and "Freedom, Independence, Islamic Republic," the post-revolutionary Iranian state has spent over three decades attempting to forge a third way distinct from the economies and values of "Western" capitalist nations on the one hand and "Eastern" socialist ones on the other. Whether cited earnestly to motivate supporters or offered cynically to justify state activities, calls for economic and cultural independence have been a consistent part of official discourses. Yet, the realities of post-revolutionary Iran have never been as clear-cut as state messaging might suggest: at best, Iran's economy is a strained mix of capitalism and socialism; confusion also reigns in the realm of cultural production, where state institutions have struggled both to attract audiences and to produce content that meets the highly politicized criteria of "cultural independence." The failure of the ruling system to introduce a sustainable third way in either the economy or the realms of media and cultural production, however, does not imply that all such possibilities have been foreclosed in Iran. Indeed, actual and potential instances of resistance to the ruling economic and political system provide glimpses of alternative structures and practices that could be used as models for transcending the Western/Eastern binary emphasized by the state.

The aim here is to provide a sketch of the Iranian state's largely unsuccessful attempts to provide viable "third" economic or cultural options by broadly considering two case studies: the revolutionary foundations and the state-run broadcasting services. As institutions that were created by the state but are effectively autonomous, the revolutionary foundations enacted the state's populist redistribution policies. Active in a range of industries, the foundations also worked as active engines in moving the economy. Yet, while such functions ostensibly allowed the state to avoid accusations of supporting either socialist or capitalist structures, the foundations have come to manifest some of the extreme characteristics of both. On the cultural front, the state's goals have proved even more elusive, particularly when it comes to media production. This is not only because of the difficulty of extracting a pure Iranian-Islamic culture from "Eastern" and "Western" influences but also because media production almost always requires interaction with foreign technologies and ideas.

To demonstrate the above, I will begin with an examination of the foundations, the rhetorical and practical needs they address in the economic and cultural arenas, and the domestic politics they have served and been shaped by. Moving from para-state institutions to a state institution, I will then consider the Islamic Republic of Iran Broadcasting (IRIB) services. Since its establishment the IRIB has contended with the challenges of drawing audiences and promoting the country's cultural independence—goals that have often seemed to be in tension with one another. I will look at some of IRIB's largely unsuccessful attempts to negotiate these dueling demands in the context of Iran's factionalized politics. I conclude by offering examples of economic structures and cultural activities that are independent of the state, showing that hope still remains for a viable "third way" in Iran.

Revolutionary Foundations and the Rhetoric of Independence

In addition to their popularity with demonstrating crowds, the revolutionary slogans of independence from the "East" and "West" were central to the rhetoric of the Islamic Republic's founder and leader, Ayatollah Khomeini, who repeatedly claimed that the revolution was for the "disenfranchised" and the "barefooted."[1] Consequently, in his lifetime and shortly thereafter (roughly the first decade of the Islamic Republic), redistributive mechanisms dominated Iran's economic policies. The two main economic goals of the new state were both to establish an economically independent system and for it to take care of the needs of its most disadvantaged members. While interrelated, these goals were also beset with tensions, namely, the challenges of achieving economic strength without falling into capitalist modes and of providing for the near complete welfare of the needy without emulating socialist structures. The parastate institutions of the revolutionary foundations appeared to be a useful mechanism for alleviating this seeming contradiction. Indeed, the revolutionary foundations (*bonyads*) were a major vehicle in the new state's endeavor of economic and cultural self-sufficiency.

The foundations are unique in their economic and social function and also have a great deal of influence over Iranian politics, particularly the two largest: the Foundation for the Oppressed and Disabled and the Martyrs Foundation. These and other similar foundations were formed right after the 1978–1979 revolution, some with funding that came from expropriating property and wealth belonging to members and supporters of the overthrown monarchy.[2] In these cases, the state justified its expropriation by claiming that the wealth recently seized had been obtained originally in an illegitimate manner, claims enabling the state both to continue to seize private property and to maintain that it defends the right to private property, thus reassuring its supporters from the religious and mercantile classes that it is not a socialist state.[3] It appears that from the earliest post-revolution years, the state was attempting to strike a delicate balance in avoiding both socialism and capitalism without offending supporters who might benefit from socialist or capitalist policies.

While they have an antecedent in religious foundations and charities prior to the revolution, the post-revolutionary foundations are distinct in a number of ways. Whereas prior to the revolution analogous religious charities and foundations were independent from the state and kept out of politics, the post-revolutionary foundations were established within a new system in which politics and religion are inextricably bound.[4] In addition, the post-revolutionary foundations also performed crucial cultural and economic functions for a state in need of practical mechanisms that did not replicate the capitalist and dependent system of the old regime but that created a new economic framework built on the principles of "independence, self-sufficiency, and distributional justice."[5]

Although most are under the supervision of the Leader (the highest political and religious position in the country), the bonyads have institutional autonomy.[6] At the same time they receive direct and indirect financial support from the state and enjoy tax exemptions and subsidized access to foreign currency and loans, among other benefits.[7] They are neither subject to state oversight (as might be the case in a centralized socialist system where the state directly controls more resources and doles out social services and payments to the needy and such) nor accountable to market forces or shareholders (as might be the case in a largely decentralized system with private ownership subject to some state regulation). This blurring of private and public enterprise and property, however, cannot be seen as a straightforward indication of the state's success in forging alternate paths that transcend socialist or capitalist systems.

From the perspective of the state, the foundations have had some successes in forging a new way forward, providing mechanisms for instituting populist policies. For reasons such as their networked connections to lower- and lower-middle-class communities, the bonyads have been particularly well suited to provide welfare services, outperforming state and NGOs in this regard.[8] To meet their original mission to support poor and disadvantaged communities, foundations have also been active in providing loans and in directly hiring individuals from the lower and lower-middle classes. Yet, these achievements have come along with political and economic consequences that call into question the foundations' standing as an example of alternative institutions that stand beyond the logics of socialism or capitalism.

While the foundations have created jobs and hired individuals from disadvantaged communities, job distribution has been politicized and used to entrench connections between the foundations and certain segments of the ruling state. Similarly, the foundations have not limited their work to the distribution of wealth and services but have greatly enhanced their own holdings. In fact, during the Iran-Iraq war, which started within a year of the official establishment of the Islamic Republic of Iran, some foundations not only began to accumulate significant amounts of wealth but actually established monopolies.[9] By the end of the 1980s, they owned hundreds of factories, construction firms, various commercial businesses, and numerous mines.[10] By the mid-2000s these holdings and the sectors in which they are active have expanded significantly, ranging from petrochemicals and transportation to tourism, and including ownership of the most popular soft drink in Iran, Zamzam soda. One foundation alone, the Foundation for the Oppressed and Disabled, is the biggest real-estate developer in the country and a major shareholder in the Iran Electronic Development Company (IEDC), which in turn is a major shareholder in the second biggest mobile phone service in the country. Numbers from the mid-2000s indicate that altogether the foundations employ up to 5 million Iranians and make up 30–40 percent of the GDP.[11]

The foundations, which were instituted as a main vehicle for transcending the politics and economies of the socialist "East" or capitalist "West," have come to represent some of the extreme characteristics of both: they are owners of vast amounts of capital and means of production while also functioning as a main hub for the distribution of funds and services. Paired with their ability to wield political and economic power, these characteristics have made the foundations the subject of much domestic debate and criticism. The internal turn against them must be seen in the context of Iran's shifting factional politics. Despite the continuing emphasis on independence and the return of populist rhetoric during the presidency of Mahmoud Ahmadinejad, Iran's economic policies have not been primarily redistributive since shortly after the death of Ayatollah Khomeini in 1989. With the war ended and the revolution's first leader deceased, growth overtook distribution in the country's economic agenda under the presidencies of Rafsanjani and Khatami.[12] Markets tightly controlled during the war economy were deregulated, and explicit condemnations of capitalism waned.

The increasing openness to free markets and the concomitant desire to attract capital required, in turn, a softening of social and cultural stances. Unlike the case with official attitudes toward capitalist economies, the shifts in the rhetoric about cultural independence have been more subtle. Reformist and other factions identified as moderate have made various attempts to tone down official pronouncements in this regard. In 1998, for example, reformist President Khatami introduced the Dialogue Among Civilizations initiative as part of a larger move for rapprochement with the West. Since his election in 2013, President Rouhani and his administration have similarly made numerous public remarks about political and cultural reconciliation. Yet hard-line elements among the ruling elite have been largely relentless in maintaining the language of hostility in continuing the call for cultural independence. At the same time, cultural independence necessitates cultural production, which in turn often requires engagement with both foreign technologies and foreign ideas. Thus, similar to the case with the Iranian economy, cultural policies are rife with contradictions and results. Given the distancing function they provide for the state, the foundations can obscure some of these tensions, but those tensions are more apparent in cases where the state has a direct role in content production and dissemination. In neither instance, however, has a successful and convincing "third way" for cultural and media independence been established.

Projects of Cultural Independence

As in their economic portfolios, the foundations have been diverse in their cultural work. A range of foundations have been active in book and magazine publications, art festivals, and exhibits, as well as the establishment of museums and other cultural spaces. While these activities have expanded over the years, the connections between foundations and both cultural spaces and cultural production go back to the earliest days of their establishment. In fact, cultural and media outlets were among the properties confiscated and turned over to the foundations. In 1980, for example, all the country's movie theaters were handed over to the Foundation for the Oppressed. In issuing his order for the expropriation of the cinemas, the attorney general stated, "The Islamic Republic seeks to eliminate fraud and corruption on all levels. Public cultural sites must be under the control of trustworthy organs so that the progress of Islam will be strengthened and these sites can be put to use to improve culture and the life conditions of the oppressed."[13] There is a direct parallel here with the stated economic aim of the foundations: on the economic front the confiscation of private property was justified in terms of the just redistribution of wealth "to the oppressed," and on the cultural front the confiscation of property as well as direct influence over production and distribution are again justified in terms of the benefit for a disenfranchised class. As with the case of the economy, the foundations have a distancing function for the state, where the state can claim not to have its fingers directly in every economic or cultural arena. So whereas the state has monopoly and direct control of the television and radio broadcasting (IRIB), it can subcontract other elements of the media-sphere to institutions that are in line with its cultural aims and can work both to guard against content that is deemed harmful and to disseminate what is deemed friendly.[14]

This conception of media as a conduit for both undermining the Islamic Republic and bolstering it characterizes the state's attitude toward a range of technologies old and new throughout its thirty-year history. A constant tension is apparent between the desire to mobilize media for state-friendly purposes and to guard against them as sites through which foreign influence can infiltrate. A contemporary example from the Foundation for the Preservation and Publication of the Values of the Sacred Defense, formed after the end of the Iran-Iraq war in 1988, illustrates how this attitude is reflected also in the activities of the foundations. The foundation's bylaws stress its mission to preserve and cultivate the values and memory of the Iran-Iraq war. They make no reference to an external cultural enemy, and both the by-laws and the foundation's early descriptions of itself are self-referential in the sense that they argue for maintaining the values and stories that sustained the nation throughout the war; the only threat to them is the nation's own forgetfulness and not an outside enemy that is working to erase them.[15] The website, on the other hand, self-consciously situates the foundation in the contemporary digital media landscape and explains the reasons for expanding its online presence by pointing to the large amounts of funding invested to undermine Iranians' identity via various new and traditional media outlets, noting that the website and the foundation's online activities aim to rectify such perceived attacks on Iranian culture and identity.[16] Furthermore, the foundation and its website are explicit that their work in cultural and knowledge production about the Iran-Iraq war is part and parcel of a larger war for cultural independence.

While the foundations' cultural and economic activities have aided the state in maintaining its revolutionary rhetoric both by supporting relevant cultural production and by claiming to continue the revolutionary missions they were given of helping the poor and needy, they cannot accurately claim to have created or maintained a culture of revolutionary resistance or independence. Indeed, even more so than the case of an economic "third way," the possibilities of cultural and media independence have proved elusive not only because of the futility of attempting to extract a pure Islamic-Iranian cultural production from a long history of interactions with both "Eastern" and "Western" ideas but also because media production almost inevitably requires interaction with foreign technologies and platforms. In short, cultural and media production are imbricated with foreign ideas and technologies. But whereas foundations may mask some of the tensions inherent in projects of cultural independence, these difficulties are more apparent in arenas where the state has direct involvement, such as the state owned national broadcasting (IRIB).

The Iranian Constitution makes several references to mass media and the IRIB specifically, tasking them with keeping the public well-informed and maintaining freedom of expression in accordance with "Islamic criteria and the best interests of the country" (Article 175). Article 3 of the Constitution, which lists the goals of the state, includes the "complete elimination of imperialism and the prevention of foreign influence." As a state institution whose head is directly appointed by the Leader, the IRIB is beholden to this task as well. Not surprisingly, the IRIB has not been successful in meeting the absolute standard reflected in this constitutional article, and from its earliest days, the IRIB has had to supplement its programming with foreign content. Some of this material—such as the films of the Italian Neo-Realists, were consistent with the state's early emphasis on the plight of the disenfranchised and, as such, were ostensibly acceptable examples of foreign influence. Yet the IRIB also broadcasts Hollywood productions (albeit in heavily edited form and in violation of copyrights). Like any other broadcaster, the IRIB faces the challenge of attracting and maintaining audiences, a challenge multiplied by the above-noted demands to take a leading role in promoting cultural independence and safeguarding from foreign influences.

A programming decision from the first decade of the IRIB illustrates how the state broadcaster has attempted to contend with these tensions. In 1986, at the height of the Iran-Iraq war, the IRIB began broadcasting the Japanese serial *Oshin*, which became a huge hit with Iranian audiences. Hamid Naficy has posited that the dearth of other quality material on the IRIB is not the only explanation for the show's popularity; rather, he argues that the show allowed Iranian audiences to identify themselves as "Asian as the Japanese" and to "escape being associated with either of the two sources of identity, now demonized: the capitalist west and the communist east."[17] Perhaps even more so than for the audience, the serial provided IRIB broadcasters with a solution to move beyond the bind of providing content that is "neither western, nor eastern." While the IRIB has since produced a number of popular comedy and drama series that have equally captivated Iranian audiences, it continues to reflect the contradictions of Iranian cultural policies and remains at the center of internal struggles over the importance and definition of independence in media and cultural production.

For example, as was the case with economic policies, attempts were made to loosen cultural policies beginning with the presidency of Rafsanjani, whose brother was the head of the IRIB. Some of the impetus for loosening these policies was economic: encouraging the participation of investors and expanding the private sector not only required less state intervention and regulation in the economy but also necessitated the toning down of pronouncements against capitalism and Western cultures more generally. These shifts partially explain changes in programming content (such as an increase in original comedy and drama productions) and programming structure (such as the introduction of commercial advertisements where they had previously not been permitted).[18] However, due to the constitutional requirement that the IRIB head be appointed by the Leader, the IRIB has remained in the hands of conservative factions and is less permeable to internal calls for change despite being the routine subject of critique from across the political spectrum. In any case, at the same time that Rafsanjani moved to loosen cultural and media policies, his own cultural minister, Ali Larijani, identified the fight against "Western cultural onslaught" as his ministry's main cultural mission, thereby rejuvenating the rhetoric of the post-revolutionary state and unleashing regulatory checks on both state and nonaffiliated cultural producers to ensure that they were not succumbing to external influences.[19] The space available here does not allow for a more detailed overview of such domestic wrangling and its impact. It will suffice to note that this internal push-and-pull around Iran's cultural and media productions has continued, resulting in contradictory policies that work to both expand and limit content.[20]

While domestic struggles have been a consistent factor influencing how media policy is shaped and received, in many ways the IRIB remains in a tighter bind than it faced in the early years following the revolution.

Although it continues to have the biggest audience share inside the country because of the high penetration of television compared to newer media forms, it has faced increasing competition from satellite channels and, to a lesser extent, from New Media outlets. In order to deal with the advent of the former in the 1990s the state adopted an approach it would later apply to the internet: it clamped down on competing technologies while attempting to enhance its own foothold and content production via those same technologies. In the case of satellite channels, the government has consistently engaged in a variety of tactics aimed at disrupting access, including periodic raids to physically remove receivers from households and jamming satellite signals. At the same time, however, it made efforts to expand state broadcasting's reach within and outside the country. The Arabic language *Al-Alam* and the English *Press TV*, for example, are satellite channels aimed at foreign audiences while the Persian language *Jam-e-Jam* channels targeted Iranians living in Europe and North America.

The launch of IRIB's Documentary Channel is among the more recent examples of the state's efforts to develop its policy of expansion and penetration. The Documentary Channel began with an initial programming schedule of five hours per day in October 2009 but was not officially launched until March 2011. It is Iran's first digitally broadcast channel, and like the IRINN news channel of the IRIB, it is broadcast to both domestic and international audiences. The Documentary Channel has many similarities to IRIB Channel 4, which is also largely devoted to documentary productions (in fact, the Documentary Channel often rebroadcasts Channel 4 programs). Despite these overlaps, the Documentary Channel has tried to claim distinction in its commitment solely to documentary programming and to cultivating Iranian documentarians. Its programming choices as well as official commentary about the channel suggest it is at least in part responding to the rising popularity of the documentary form as disseminated by the IRIB's satellite rivals from abroad. As has been the case with the IRIB more broadly, however, meeting the demand of uplifting "cultural independence" while also attracting popular audiences often have been at odds with one another. To meet the former demand in its early programming, the channel promoted the work of homegrown documentarians, in particular those whose work reflects ideological sympathy with the more conservative elements of the state. But it also aimed to lure a broader audience base with varied content, which often translated into works that fell into the foreign/and or entertainment categories.

Despite these efforts, the new channel came under almost immediate internal fire, particularly from the same conservative factions who have had direct oversight over the IRIB since its inception. The conservative Fars News Agency, which is affiliated with the Revolutionary Guard forces, for example, was among the first outlets to criticize the Documentary Channel. While the ostensible focus of the criticism was around the lack of communication about the channel's official launch, this became an occasion for criticizing the management of the IRIB in general and its past shortcomings. The Documentary Channel has also been criticized for its programming choices, with most of the objections coming from conservative voices. In keeping with its apparent programming approach of providing something for all viewers, for example, the channel included live broadcasting of soccer matches and TV shows devoted to the games. Once again Fars News led the charge, accusing the channel of violating its own mission statement. The IRIB eventually gave in to the critics, announcing in June 2012 that such programming would be available only on the Sports Channel of the IRIB.[21] Iranian filmmakers have also objected to the Documentary Channel, variously complaining that it has made unauthorized changes to their work[22] and that the programming gives preference to "second and third rate"[23] foreign documentaries rather than promoting the work of national documentarians.

Some of the most recent developments at the IRIB show that it continues to be both a site designated to lead the charge of "cultural independence" and a target of conservative criticism. Following the appointment of a new IRIB head in November 2014, for example, one of the country's largest student groups affiliated with the hard-line elements of the state issued a statement critiquing IRIB's past programming and emphasizing the broadcaster's "historic responsibility at the current juncture to maintain and enhance cultural independence."[24] In fact, this language about the IRIB's duties replicates almost verbatim Ayatollah Khamenei's own statement issued with his order to appoint the new head of the IRIB.[25] The resurgence of the rhetoric of cultural independence shows its continued importance, but it also indicates an implicit recognition that the state has failed to deliver on this revolutionary aim.

Conclusion

Calls for cultural and economic independence continue to serve as the bedrock of official discourses and policies, but the realization of this rhetoric into policy and action have proved elusive. Part of this can be attributed to the notorious infighting among Iran's political elite. Nor can international factors be ignored: the task of economic independence, for example, is difficult even for an oil rich state when it has been placed on ever-tightening sanctions since its establishment. But just as important, the state's own failures and contradictory policies within the economic and cultural realm must be blamed. Despite being the subject of numerous political speeches, treatises, and a range of other discourses produced by the state and state supporters, the concepts of cultural or economic independence remain vague, often translating into a mix of content and forms from the same economic and cultural structures that the state is ostensibly aiming to avoid. Nonetheless, state failures to achieve or even clearly define economic and cultural independence need not indicate that all hope for a "third way" is lost in the context of Iran. Indeed, examples can be found on the economic and political margins of Iranian society that act outside—if not in opposition—to state policies. Furthermore, the state's own economic and cultural policies have in many ways created the conditions that produced the possibilities for resisting the state or at least stepping outside of its confines.

On the economic front, for example, the vast gap in wealth exacerbated by the bonyads has meant a turn to work in the informal economy. Ironically, this is seen most among the lower-middle to lower classes—the segments that the main foundations were set up to support and keep within the fold. Women in particular are active in these informal sectors—such as salons run out of bedrooms, banking systems, and so on where individuals eke out a living without the constraints of the state or its affiliates like the bonyads.[26] On the cultural front, the picture is more complicated but also more exciting. Within the system enabled by the foundations, there are many examples of films and filmmakers, memoir writers, and new media content producers who provide some of the most scathing critiques of the Islamic Republic even as they produce content ostensibly in support of the state's cultural mission. Similarly, there is the work of individuals who have stepped entirely outside the "system," namely, the few who have refused both Iranian and foreign state funding or support. These works range from street art to the much touted uses of the internet for challenging the ruling system. Constrained by the demands neither of the Iranian state to produce content foregrounding cultural independence nor of foreign funders insisting on particular narratives of oppression in Iran, these few cultural producers reflect the best hope for forging new paths that are resistant to the constraints of both Iranian and foreign elements seeking to influence content.[27]

In the end, the sentiments behind the slogan "Neither Western nor Eastern" and the concomitant revolutionary promises to maintain cultural and economic independence continue to form a mainstay of official discourses, especially of the hard-line stripe. Yet in Iran it is neither capitalism nor socialism but in many ways the worst of both worlds that characterizes the economic and cultural arenas. If there is a third way to be forged, it will likely come from the informal and hidden networks of economic and cultural production.

Notes

1 Djavad Salehi-Isfahani, "Poverty, Inequality, and Populist Politics in Iran," *Journal of Economic Inequality* 7, no. 1 (2009): 6.

2 Evaleila Pesaran, *Iran's Struggle for Economic Independence: Reform and Counter-Reform in the Post-Revolutionary Era* (New York: Taylor and Francis, 2011), 35.

3 Farhad Numabi and Sohrab Behdad, *Class and Labor in Iran: Did the Revolution Matter?* (Syracuse: Syracuse University Press, 2006).

4 Suzanne Maloney, "Agents or Obstacles? Parastatal Foundations and Challenges for Iranian Development," in *The Economy of Iran: The Dilemma of an Islamic State* (New York: I.B. Tauris, 2000), 29.

5 Ali A. Saeidi, "The Accountability of Para-governmental Organizations (Bonyads): The Case of Iranian Foundations," *Iranian Studies* 37, no. 3 (2004): 480.

6 Hadi Salehi Esfahani, "Alternative Public Service Delivery Mechanisms in Iran," *Quarterly Review of Economics and Finance* 45, no. 2 (2005): 501.

7 Pesaran, *Iran's Struggle for Economic Independence*, 35.

8 Esfahani, "Alternative Public Service Delivery Mechanisms in Iran," 497–525.

9 "Iran Competition and Price: Country Briefing," American International Group, December 2014, accessible at http://www.aig.com/_2590_379135.html.

10 Ervand Abrahamian, *A History of Modern Iran* (New York: Cambridge University Press, 2008).

11 Kenneth Katzman, "Iran's Bonyads: Economic Strengths and Weaknesses," *The Emirates Center for Strategic Study and Research*, August 6, 2006, accessible at http://ecssr.com/.

12 Salehi-Isfahani, "Poverty, Inequality, and Populist Politics in Iran," 6.

13 "Tarikhe Mosadere Cinemaha Tavasote bonyad-e Mostazafan (The History of the Seizure of Cinemas by the Foundations for the Oppressed)," *The Iranian Student News Agency*, April 13, 2014, at http://isna.ir/.

14 For more on the appearance of the subcontractor state, see Kevan Harris, "The Rise of the Subcontractor State: Politics of Pseudo-privatization in the Islamic Republic of Iran," *International Journal of Middle East Studies* 45, no. 1 (2013): 45–70.

15 The by-laws of the foundation can be found at http://www1.jamejamonline.ir/newstext.aspx?newsnum=100954179979/.

16 Foundation for the Preservation and Publication of the Values of the Sacred Defense website, at http://www.khomool.ir/aboutus-fa.html.

17 Hamid Naficy, *A Social History of Iranian Cinema, Vol. 4: The Globalizing Era, 1984–2010* (Durham: Duke University Press, 2012), 137.

18 I would like to thank Khodadad Rezakhani for this example about the introduction of advertisements and the ideological shifts this reflected in terms of official attitudes toward capitalism.

19 Farhi Farideh, "Cultural Policies in the Islamic Republic of Iran," 6, at http://www.wilsoncenter.org/sites/default/files/FaridehFarhiFinal.pdf.

20 Gholam Khiabany has addressed these contradictory policies in *Iranian Media: The Paradox of Modernity* (London: Routledge, 2009), and I have specifically

traced the state's contradictory new media policy in Niki Akhavan, *Electronic Iran: The Cultural Politics of an Online Evolution* (New Brunswick: Rutgers University Press, 2013).

21 "Pakhshe mosabeghe football az shabake Mostaned montafi shod (Football Broadcasting on the Documentary Channel Cancelled)," *Alef*, June 10, 2012, at http://alef.ir/vdca0on6649nmw1.k5k4.html?159071/.

22 "Enteqad-d Farshad Farhadian az nahvey-e pakhshe filmhayash az shabake mostaned (Farshad Farhadian's Critique of How His films Are Broadcast on the Documentary Channel)," *ISNA News Agency*, September 3, 2012, at http://isna.ir.

23 "Shabak-e Mostane dar Arsey-e toleed faaliyatee nadarad (The Documentary Channel Is Not Active in Producing Documentaries)," *IRNA News Agency*, August 27, 2012, at http://irna.ir/fa/news/.

24 "Resane Melli Sahm-e Azimi dar Mobareze ba Tahajome Farhangi Darad (National Broadcasting Has a Large Role in Fighting against Cultural Invasion)," *Farsnews.com*, November 11, 2014, at http://www.farsnews.com/.

25 Khamenei's order can be found on his official website at http://farsi.khamenei.ir/message-content?id=28138/.

26 Roksana Bahramitash's research provides an extensive account of women's work in the shadow economy. See Roksana Bahramitash, *Gender and Entrepreneurship in Iran: Microenterprise and the Informal Sector* (New York: Palgrave Macmillan, 2013).

27 The case of Iranian photographer Newsha Tavakolian is instructive here. Tavakolian returned her Carmignac Foundation photojournalism award and the €50,000 she received from them after she accused the foundation of undue interference in her work. According to Tavakolian, the foundation censored her work and canned her exhibition because her work did not fit the stereotyped Western images of Iran the foundation had wanted her to produce. See "Iranian Photographer Returns €50,000 Prize." *The Art Newspaper*, September 18, 2014, at http://www.theartnewspaper.com/articles/Iranian-photographer-returns-prize/35666/.

11

Differentiating Citizenship

A. ANEESH

Over the course of the twentieth century, the notion of citizenship has become coterminous with "national citizenship"—and for good reason. National citizenship has offered an unparalleled model of inclusion and equal membership supported by schemes of citizen welfare. Among one of the major institutional accomplishments of national citizenship, as T. H. Marshall noted in his seminal account, was the gradual development of social rights in addition to political and civil ones. Marshall considered social citizenship as a welfare device through which the worst excesses of capitalism could be mitigated.[1] The second major accomplishment of the institution of national citizenship was to provide an apparent solution to the problem of social solidarity at the unwieldy scale of the nation-state by generating a new kind of legally mediated solidarity of strangers. But the institution of national citizenship is facing serious challenges in the realms of both welfare and solidarity in the twenty-first century. In a world of circulating cultures, people, and loyalties—via money, media, and migration—some of the inherent paradoxes of national citizenship have become more visible. Caught between global capitalism and still resilient communal loyalties, the contradictory pulls on citizenship are leading, I argue in this essay, to a plural, layered, and mercurial conception of belonging.

Let me begin with a link between the welfare state and national citizenship. Jürgen Habermas was one of the first to point out that the relative success of the welfare-state rendered the traditional Marxist analysis of crisis tendencies in the capitalist system outdated because the welfare compromise between the state and capital pacified the conflict lodged at the heart of capitalism.[2] For this compromise to work, a clear distinction between citizens and aliens needed to be drawn to identify worthy recipients of welfare and to reduce inequality—a necessary product of capital accumulation—through progressive taxation of the citizenry. But globalization and the increasing mobility of both capital and people across national borders appear to be recalibrating the organization of the welfare state itself in significant ways, especially at a time when capital accumulation is increasingly diverted to low tax regimes around the globe.[3] In the realm of solidarity and social integration, the nationalist imagination of community now increasingly contends with global imaginations based on human rights, diaspora, and cosmopolitanism.

Given the force of history toward globalization, a puzzle arises. What, if any, changes ensue in national citizenship? Modest evidence for the transnationalization of citizenship emerges in the rising wave of nonexclusive and non-territorial citizenships across the globe. Beyond exclusive loyalty to a single nation-state, dual and multiple citizenships have registered a tremendous surge in recent years, marking the declining significance of territorial citizenship. Indeed, the very notion of citizenship seems to have moved away from its territorial basis in recent decades, as attested by works on post-national membership, cosmopolitan citizenship, diasporic citizenship, flexible citizenship, and biological citizenship.[4] In this rich scholarly landscape, however, there is a large theoretical question that remains unanswered: if post-national or biological citizens must be citizens "of" *something*, what is that *something*? Do these newer forms of citizenship have a referent other than the nation?

A nascent political formation signals the possibility of a form of membership untied from one territory, one state, and one system of rights. In this theoretical construction, citizenship emerges as a virtual basket of rights—enforced by governments and articulated by nongovernmental organizations—in a further differentiation of the liberal rights regime. Analyzing how this regime of citizenship may be conceptualized in *thought* and how it is being realized in *practice*, in this article I engage in both theoretical construction and an empirical case study of India's recent introduction of dual citizenship.

Theoretically, the glimpses of a new regime of citizenship are already available in the existing literature. This regime is non-territorial and changes based on the context; certain rights get activated depending on one's entry into a specific affiliative setting, allowing citizenship to emerge as a variable basket of rights, differentially available in different situations. *Empirically*, the case of dual citizenship leads to the puzzle of what prompts national governments to relinquish their monopoly over citizenship and adopt a policy of dual or multiple citizenship in the era of globalization. India's recent introduction of dual citizenship offers an opportunity to analyze the context of its emergence. The political and social circumstances in which India—after decades of reluctance—began to allow dual citizenship for persons of Indian origin may at first sight appear unique to India, but policies oriented to the diaspora have soared across the world.

Even prior to the context of globalization, the idea of national citizenship harbored an incompatibility between "state" and "nation" within a modern democratic framework. On the one hand, the democratic constitutional state is conceived, normatively, as a voluntary political association of free and equal persons by their own initiative. On the other hand, this political order is also conceived as a nonvoluntary, often ethnic, membership in an ascribed nation.[5] This incompatibility between the universalism of an egalitarian legal community and the particularism of a community shaped by language, ethnicity, and history signifies the nation-state's accomplishment as well as its failure. One of the major accomplishments of the nation-state consisted in successfully borrowing the model of social solidarity from small kinship-based village communities where everyone knows each other and applying it to the larger geographical scale of nations where citizens may not know each other but still *imagine* themselves to be part of a national community.[6] But national citizenship has also been a serious failure because ethnically cohesive solidarity reminiscent of strong membership in kinship networks is nearly impossible to achieve at the national territorial scale. It is not surprising that ethnic difference, for most nation-states, emerged as a problem to be solved.[7] I highlight several paradoxes of strong citizenship, analyzing how the project of national homogeny remains forever incomplete.

Paradoxes of National Citizenship

National citizenship is traditionally characterized by strong norms of membership. Two primary criteria of membership in a modern state are ascriptive in nature, namely, *jus soli* (the law of the soil) and *jus sanguinis* (the law of blood). To be a citizen, one must either be born within a territory (*jus soli*) or be a blood relation to a citizen (*jus sanguinis*). Defining citizenship as a matter of birthright, nations have for the most part succeeded in making one's membership in a polity not a matter of decision but a matter of chance, demanding exclusive allegiance derived from the accident of birth based on territory or ancestry.[8] Strong norms of citizenship hark back to small densely knit communities of agrarian or itinerant kind. Rooted in place or kinship network or both, members in these communities lived in close proximity and tended to know each other on a personal basis. The fact of birth in a particular kinship network and/or place decided the question of belonging. The importance of place for enabling durable constructions of identity, interaction and memory is well recognized in sociology, anthropology, and philosophy.[9] The role of kinship systems is also well documented.[10] National citizenship has generally moved between ancestral and territorial forms of belonging and national citizenship.

While the strong norm of blood (*jus sanguinis*) invoked in national citizenship laws borrows from the ascriptive model of kinship systems, the equally strong law of the soil (*jus soli*) seems to follow place-based norms of village-like settlements. It would be easier, Anderson argued, if one treated nationalism "as if it belonged with 'kinship' and 'religion,' rather than with 'liberalism' or 'fascism.'"[11] But contrary to this argument, no kinship is possible at the territorial scale of the nation-state, as its members can never know most of their fellow members on a personal basis or be connected in any meaningful way. A modern nation comes to exist not because of individual interactions but because of systemic unification through print and other media, mass education, transportation, and industry in general.[12] Thus, nations become imagined communities not out of a collective desire or will but out of necessity, as it is not possible to sustain any notion of community, ethnic coherence, or place-bound interaction at the territorial scale of the nation-state.

Three paradoxes arise out of imagining a community at the national level. First, at such a geographical scale with no possibility of personal interaction among most of the members, the paradox of solidarity among strangers challenges the extension of the place-based model of solidarity to an abstract population spread over a large territory. This *jus soli* paradox raises a dilemma as to whether such a population constitutes a community at all, if the definition of "community" refers to a set of relationships marked by a high degree of personal intimacy, emotional depth, moral commitment, social cohesion and temporal continuity.

Indeed, efforts to turn this population into a community lead us to the second paradox. The *jus sanguinis* paradox pertains to the double coding of member identity as both ascriptive and voluntary. Analytically, kinship-based inclusions are ascriptive in nature whereas national citizenship is thought of as voluntary membership in a democratic constitutional state, which, according to Kant and Rousseau, is a voluntary political order where the addressees of the law may also be conceived of as its authors.[13] Consequences of this paradoxical coding of citizenship—as voluntary, formally equal, membership as well as inherited and ascribed membership based on ethnicity, language, or religion—are not merely academic in nature. They have had far-reaching effects on the ground. The combination of territorial scale and the ideal of kinship-like ethnic cohesion has given rise to "anomalous" populations in every nation, populations that do not fit the communal norm. Thus, the national territorial scale necessarily produces anomalous or minority populations that fail the criteria of single ethnicity, language, or religion. And effects of this paradox have been visible in situations where the legal equality of citizenship fails to protect ethnic and religious minorities from becoming the scapegoat for political economic turmoil.

Naturalization policies have evolved, one may argue, as one of the responses to overcome these two paradoxes. However, the earliest introduction of naturalization policies in the United States was itself marred by strong citizenship. For example, the United States confers immediate citizenship based on the *jus soli* principle, that is, one's birth in the territory of the United States. While the early polity also allowed for the naturalization of citizens not born in the United States, the principle of naturalization—a non-ascriptive method of membership—was grounded in an ascriptive model of ethnicity. The Naturalization Act of 1790 states, "Be it enacted . . . in Congress, that any alien, being a *free white person* . . . who shall have resided within the limits and under the jurisdiction of the United States for the term of two years, may be admitted to become a citizen thereof." Although the ethnic requirement was removed later on, the discourse of ascriptive belonging still haunts immigration in the United States.

The third paradox pertains to the question as to whether nation-states in the absence of kinship or place-based relationships are "national" even to begin with. John Meyer and others have pointed out over the years how all nations follow increasingly similar scripts of education, law, science, and development despite differences in ethnic, religious, or linguistic frameworks.[14] With the rise of dual and multiple citizenship formats, we witness a liberal solution to these paradoxes through a gradual loosening of citizenship norms and national exclusivity, an evolution of what I call "weak citizenship."

Weak Citizenship

There are two sets of literature that point to the emerging strength of weak citizenship and that appear to resolve the paradoxes of national citizenship: (1) cosmopolitan citizenship and (2) post-national membership. While the literature on cosmopolitanism is too vast and varied to cover here, we can look at some basic arguments, starting with those of Immanuel Kant whose clear formulation of a cosmopolitan order two centuries prior to the League of Nations and the United Nations was remarkable in extending the concept of "constitution" from the national to the global level. Kant's

genius consisted in conceptualizing the constitutionalization of international relations in a manner that allowed for the international law not to
remain merely the law of states but to become cosmopolitan law, the law
of individual persons. For Kant, while individuals remain legal subjects of
a nation-state, they also become members of a politically constituted world
republic.[15] However, constraints of history did not allow Kant to imagine
a constitution without a constitutional state or a world republic. In recent
decades, the possibility of a world republic has dwindled in scholarly analyses, which tend to question the sovereignty model of the state at the level
of the world as well as of individual countries. Many cosmopolitan theorists question the United Nation's postwar inter-state framework, which
privileges sovereign equality of nation-states. Principles of sovereignty and
noninterference, they argue, should be replaced by higher public accountability. Instead of the rights of states, the universal rights of global citizens
should become the guiding principle.[16] Millions of people, Robertson
argues, do not feel they are "bound by Article 2(7) of the UN Charter to
avert their eyes from repression in foreign countries. . . . These citizens, of
global society rather than the nation-state, cannot understand why human
rights rules should not rule."[17] After all, the horizon of the demos, democracy's subjects, was expanded from the small town to the nation-state in
the eighteenth century; there is no reason why it cannot be extended from
the nation to humankind as a whole.[18] Martha Nussbaum proposes a theory of belonging as a series of concentric circles where each circle refers to
a different kind or level of attachment, starting with self, family, group, city,
country, and humanity in general. Thus, a national citizen must also learn
to become a cosmopolitan citizen, mediating among "national traditions,
communities of fate and alternative forms of life."[19] This mediation combines two strands of cosmopolitan thinking—one that emphasizes global
obligations, the other that hails local differences—allowing for the flourishing of both on a global ethical plane.[20] Institutionally, democratic decisions
made by citizens of one state or region cannot be called truly democratic if
they affect the rights of noncitizens, people outside that community, unless
those people's voices are included.[21] Yet, some scholars question the wisdom of extending rights without accountability beyond the bounds of the
sovereign state. They argue that it may give rise to a gap between holders
of cosmopolitan rights on the one hand and those with duties on the other.
Even as the new rights remain weak, the cosmopolitan framework poses a
threat to the existing rights of democratic self-government preserved in the
UN Charter framework.[22]

However, there has emerged a second set of literature on post-national
membership that does not treat cosmopolitan citizenship as a normative
hinge or an ethical necessity of world society; rather, it documents how

the loosening of the national grip on citizenship is already happening. Yasemin Soysal identifies a nascent, non-ascriptive form of citizenship deriving from "universal personhood" rather than from "national belonging." Following the theoretical perspective of world society, this post-national membership described by Soysal traces its roots to transnational discourses on human rights that have been gaining strength since the Second World War.[23] Thus, national citizenship is losing ground, Soysal argues, to a more universal, post-national model of membership, which confers upon every person the right and duty to participate in the authority structures of a polity irrespective of his or her historical, ethnic, or cultural ties. This perspective allows us to understand how noncitizens have come to enjoy many protections previously available only to citizens.

Some scholars argue, however, that the separation between "national" and "transnational" is not as sharp as suggested in the world society perspective. Indeed, "transnational" activities of migrants are strongly oriented toward the "national" politics of both sending and receiving countries.[24] And sending and receiving states, for their part, attempt to shape the emergent "transnational social fields" by controlling, facilitating, and extending benefits and entitlements.[25] One must not exaggerate, Portes et al. caution, the language of rights or the scope of migrant transnationalism by constructing it as a challenge to the nation-state system itself.[26]

The emergence of rights-based advocacy groups and nongovernmental organizations, however, need not be considered a challenge to the state's existence; instead, one could examine it as a case of how the states are pushed to adopt a rights-based framework in their dealings with immigrants, and in adopting the legal framework of human rights the states become the sole agents of the enforcement of rights. Soysal stands on strong grounds by pointing out the documented expansion of protections for noncitizens once inside the receiving country, even though this expansion does not preclude harsher treatment by the national state at the border, which has become a highly policed zone over the years. The analogy of a soft fruit with a hard shell may appear appropriate to depict a situation where soft interiors with increasing protections fail to hide the harsher truth of unforgiving borders. Linda Bosniak takes the analogy of a soft fruit with a hard shell even further by arguing that the inside and the outside can no longer be distinguished neatly. The hard border often enters the interiors via surveillance and raids to check the legal status of the alien, who remains excluded from two of the most important rights, the right to unconditional residence and return and the right to political representation. The vision of universal personhood, Ayelet Shachar agrees, may be realized some day, but that day has not yet arrived. Indeed, we can think of post-national membership as a regime of differential inclusions, guided by different interests, where different individuals have access to different bundles of rights, depending on the country of origin and destination, ethnicity, legal status, duration of stay, familial connections, money, or primary versus secondary citizenship.[27]

In view of the above, it is not surprising that dual and multiple citizenships are still anchored in ethnicity or territory, as they often are accorded to the ethnic diaspora. The notion of "diaspora" is dependent on strong norms of citizenship, tying persons to the land of their birth and ancestry. Despite this dependence on strong norms of citizenship, however, there are certain transformations underway that, I argue, weaken these very norms. First, new forms of citizenship have increasingly become available at a distance in the wake of information and communication technologies (e.g., economic rights). Second, strong norms, in many cases, are extended to the foreign spouses of diasporic citizenry, thus further diluting the original impulse behind the law of blood and the soil. Last, new scripts of citizenship are becoming ever more complex due to the inclusion of economic motives of the state. We can capture the complexity of this transformation in terms of what I call the "virtual basket of rights."

Citizenship as a Virtual Basket of Rights

Traditionally, strong membership based on blood and the soil with perpetual allegiance to the sovereign nation has been a defining feature of citizenship, a feature that continued through the Cold War when dual citizenship and national security were seen as being in opposition to each other.[28] This was not a mere empirical fact outlined in the 1930 Hague Convention on Nationality, which instructed "every person should have a nationality and one nationality only."[29] Even in theory, dual and multiple citizenships were considered implausible. Ernest Gellner argued that a modern polity (e.g., Cyprus) could never permit two autonomous communities as easily as the Ottoman Empire tolerated a variety of communities through its *milet* system.[30] More recently Hechter argues that it is difficult for a plurality of communities to preserve their individual identity under a system of direct rule by the nation-state as opposed to indirect rule in previous empires.[31] Ernest Gellner additionally stressed that the very nature of "communities" changes with this shift in the form of rule. I have myself argued that nations are marked by the framework of "total closure," necessitating unification through constructions of national language, religion, ethnicity, or similar means.[32] In step with these observations, traditional practices of nations tended to rule out memberships in multiple other nations. How do we conceptualize, then, the rise of dual and multiple citizenships in recent decades? There are certain transformations, I argue, that allow citizenship to unhinge from its territorial and ancestral lineage toward the model of negotiated baskets of rights that tend to vary in individual settings.

The concept of the "virtual basket of rights" implies that at any point of time any individual's membership is always partial and incomplete, a basket of a limited number of rights the composition of which keeps changing depending on one's institutional and spatiotemporal location. Theoretically, this idea may claim some novelty but empirically, it has been observable for some time, though its salience may have increased in the global era.

The concept of the basket of rights may be explained through a case study: India's recent adoption and implementation of dual citizenship for its ex-citizens. Let me start by first sketching the situation of any Indian immigrant on H-1B visa in the United States. This immigrant on H-1B visa—a noncitizen and temporary US resident—enjoys multiple rights in the United States, many overlapping with those of the citizen, as Yasmine Soysal's notion of post-national membership would predict. For the sake of simplicity, let us focus on only one such right here, the right to work, which is, it turns out, not a single right universally applicable to all situations. It is a highly differentiated set of rights, much more circumscribed in spatial and temporal terms, for the H-1B visa holder than it is for citizens or for resident aliens. For the H-1B immigrant (or nonimmigrant, as one is usually called), it is not the right to work "anywhere" and "anytime." The right can be activated only on locations listed on the Labor Condition Application (LCA) accompanying the visa.[33] The right to work is also circumscribed by a temporal restriction of a maximum six-year validity period. Unlike citizen or resident alien status, the H-1B visa holder's right to work cannot be extended to the spouse who must avail him- or herself of another visa (H4), which comes with mobility rights—the right to return and reentry—for a fixed number of years but without any right to work. However, if the H-1B visa holder is able to get an institutional sponsor for his or her resident alien application (Green Card application), then he or she may gain a new set of rights quite close to those enjoyed by citizens with fewer spatiotemporal restrictions. While a resident alien must reside in the United States and must not stay outside the country for more than six months at a time, all restrictions on the right to work are lifted, and one can pretend to be a citizen—except for political rights, that is, the right to vote or hold a political office. At the same time this immigrant, still being an Indian citizen, can access many political and economic rights in India during their stay in the United States. If this individual decides to become a U.S. citizen at some point in time, the situation reverses because now one can add American political rights to one's basket but loses most economic and political rights in India. This is where India's new dual citizenship program comes in handy. One can now apply for the Overseas Citizenship of India (OCI) and gain certain economic and mobility rights in India such as the right to buy and sell property and the ability to enter and leave India without a visa—but no political rights.

In short, the concept of the "virtual basket of rights" hints at the undergoing transformation of citizenship, its move away from rigid and strong norms of citizenship to weak and varying ones, and its differentiation into finely sliced rights that can be unbundled and rebundled to fit a new situation. The transnational extension of rights to the diaspora by an increasing number of states through dual citizenship policies effects a break with the territorially rooted citizenship and the fixed basket of rights. This transformation must not be seen as a sign of progress—at least, not simply so, even if it marks a certain evolution of citizenship. The newly gained flexibility may allow highly differentiated kinds of discrimination and exclusions aimed at a specific set of citizens. For example, in Russia, citizens of most former Soviet republics have kept their mobility rights, as they do not need visas to enter Russia, but the right to work, residence permits, and political rights are for the most part not available. The case of Israel is similar in several respects. This differential basket of rights allows for flexibility for the states involved, but it can also re-create the setting in which different classes of people have different citizenship opportunities.

A further analysis of India's overseas citizenship program can shed light on the emerging landscape of dual and multiple citizenships. To research the Indian case and ascertain why India after decades of reluctance started an overseas citizenship scheme for its diaspora, my first order of business was to figure out where to study this major shift in policy. Fortunately, the Indian government had started a new ministry called the Ministry of Overseas Indian Affairs (MOIA) around the same time as it floated the dual citizenship scheme circa 2005. I decided to conduct ethnographic interviews at the ministry, where I had some contacts at the higher level of administration. In 2012–2013 I spent four months visiting the ministry, interviewing administrators and browsing through documents pertaining to citizenship and bilateral agreements between India and other countries about citizens' rights. Second, in the winter of 2013, I attended a conference in the city of Kochi called Pravasi Bharatiya Diwas (Nonresident Indian or NRI day), organized by the ministry for nonresident Indians. It was one of those events when a few thousand members of the Indian diaspora gathered at a single place. Last, I analyzed efforts by the government that preceded—and led to—the overseas citizenship scheme such as the 2001 Report of High Level Committee on Indian Diaspora.

Overseas Citizenship

The first justification for permitting dual citizenship to Indian nationals living abroad was arguably ethnic. The Report of High Level Committee on Indian Diaspora (HCID 2001) mentions that for decades there had been a considerable demand for dual citizenship by the Indian diaspora. The ethnic justification for dual citizenship was evoked in the following form: "It is so widespread that the sun never sets on the Indian Diaspora. . . . The refrain of the song, especially so far as the Indian Diaspora in North America, Europe, Australia, New Zealand, Singapore and a few other countries is concerned, is the persistent demand and expectation of dual nationality."[34] The report suggested it was time to heed those demands.

If one asks why those demands went unmet for five decades, however, the ethnic justification for granting dual citizenship loses its strength as the main determinant of the shift. In the same report another reason is forwarded, more potent from the viewpoint of the Indian government: "India has ambitious plans to increase investments in India from foreign sources by some $6 billion per year. An estimated 20 million Indians live outside of India. The law states that non-citizens cannot own property, among other things. So affluent ex-pats were unable to build hospitals, schools or corporations in India to help improve conditions and the economy. . . . India will be allowing dual citizenship for those of its people living in the United States and several other affluent countries, in an effort to spur investments in Indian markets and put to rest a longstanding irritation among ethnic Indians."[35] In short, one of the motives mentioned in the report was to supplement state welfare programs such as health and education with funds derived from the noncitizen diaspora living outside the territorial borders of India. This is one of the ways in which the organization of the welfare state is perceptibly hooking into networks of resources beyond national borders.

In the above context perhaps it is important to remember that, in 1991, the Indian government was on the verge of default on external payment liabilities. Its foreign exchange reserves had shrunk to a level where the state could barely finance three weeks' worth of imports, leading the Indian government to pawn and airlift its national gold reserves to the Bank of England as a pledge to the International Monetary Fund (IMF) in exchange for a loan to cover balance of payment debts.[36] The state's long-term response consisted in the economic liberalization of the Indian economy. The liberalization of the economy led—perhaps by the same logic—to the opening of citizenship.

Clearly, the overseas citizens' demand for transnational rights was not seen in terms of mere ethnic solidarity. Its importance was realized in terms of potential capital flows that could address some of India's welfare concerns. It is not surprising that in the first few rounds of dual citizenship rights only those Indians living in affluent countries were granted those rights, further challenging the assertion that the change was motivated by reasons of ethnic solidarity (*jus sanguinis*) alone. Indeed it could be argued that ethnicity was seen as a force to harness for increasing the inflows of capital into the country. In the first round, only those Indians living in Australia, Canada, Finland, Ireland, Italy, Netherlands, United Kingdom, or the United States of America were allowed the Persons of Indian Origin (PIO) cards. Unaware of investment motives of the state, Indians living in other countries clamored to demand the same set of rights. Yielding to the pressure India soon included many other countries such as Israel, New Zealand, Cyprus, Sweden, Switzerland, France, Greece, and Portugal. After much debate, the dual citizenship scheme was extended to the Indian diaspora in any nation *except* India's neighbors, whose populations are obviously ethnically Indian but politically unacceptable for a variety of reasons. By February 2015, the OCI category was thrown open to the citizens of most neighboring countries: Afghanistan, Bhutan, China, Iran, Nepal, and Sri Lanka. These six nationalities had previously been banned from the scheme. Pakistan and Bangladesh nationals, however, remain ineligible to apply for an OCI Card because of border-related political tensions with India.

To attract foreign exchange through remittances, India relaxed regulations and controls, introduced more flexible exchange rates through the gradual opening of the capital account, and started attractive deposit schemes earning a higher interest on investments by the Indian diaspora. The results have been impressive so far. In 1990–1991, remittances from Indians living abroad amounted to merely $2.1 billion. With economic liberalization and citizenship initiatives in place, remittances rose to $46.4 billion by 2008–2009 and $60 billion by 2011–2012.

It appears that the welfare compromise that functioned by taxing well-off citizens to support the less fortunate within its territorial borders has been extended beyond the state's border. Instead of taxation, which is obviously not possible in a transnational situation, the Indian government seeks to create and fund citizen welfare schemes with the help of nonresident Indian money. In 2008 the MOIA announced the establishment of an autonomous not-for-profit trust called India Development Foundation (IDF). An IDF brochure explained its rationale, quoting the prime minister of India: "This Foundation will serve as a credible institutional mechanism to direct overseas Indian philanthropic propensies into human development efforts in India. The Foundation will assist overseas Indians to contribute to the cause of education, health, and rural development in their erstwhile home villages, districts or states. It will also partner with credible NGOs and philanthropic organizations actively engaged in social development, thus providing a strong public-private partnership bridge between overseas Indians and their target beneficiaries."[37] One of the ways in which IDF plans to encourage development-oriented philanthropy is to register itself as a nongovernmental not-for-profit organization in other countries, which will allow it to receive tax-exempt small and large donations from the Indian diaspora scattered around the world. It may sound strange for a government to try to act as a nongovernmental organization, but the IDF is moving forward with its application for a tax-exempt status in many countries, including the United States where its 501(c)(3) application is pending. Because its promotional efforts and staff salaries will be funded by the Indian government, IDF is able to claim that donations of the diaspora will be transferred in whole to the causes they espouse. Unlike other charitable organizations, the donated funds will not be used for maintaining its bureaucracy. IDF, in its appeal to the diaspora in one of its flyers, "encourages Overseas Indians to partner in sustainable social change in India. It facilitates public-private partnerships between the overseas Indian philanthropist and credible philanthropic organizations across causes and geographies in India." Evidently, the goals of the Indian government are to go beyond economic capital and to include social and cultural capital of the diaspora as well. "When we speak of diaspora philanthropy or social entrepreneurship by the overseas Indian community," IDF's chief executive officer said to me in an interview, "our focus really is to try and draw upon this reservoir—not just in terms of diaspora philanthropy capital, but also in terms of knowledge sharing, knowledge transfer, technology transfer, driving entrepreneurship, and this is especially true of the Indo-Americans."

This endeavor to entice and integrate the diaspora into concerns of development and growth should not be understood as offering full citizenship rights to overseas Indians, however. In step with my argument about the transformation of citizenship, we can call it a mercurial bundle of rights developed for the diaspora. When the new citizenship scheme started in 1999, it found its expression in a Persons of Indian Origin (PIO) card, which came with a bundle of rights quite different from other non-resident Indians (NRIs), who still possessed an Indian passport and thus enjoyed full citizenship rights were they to return to India. PIO cardholders, on the other hand, were offered only certain mobility and economic rights such as a fifteen-year visa. They were exempt from registering at a foreign regional registration office (FRRO) and were taxed only on income earned in India. In general, they enjoyed the right to buy and sell property *except* the acquisition of agricultural and plantation properties. But the PIO card scheme came with no political rights such as the right to vote or to hold a political office in India.

To avoid the charge that the PIO card was merely a glorified visa, the Indian government floated a new scheme in 2005 called Overseas Citizenship of India (OCI), which still held back political rights but extended many others in a new basket of rights that now included a lifelong visa and permanent exemption from registration at the FRRO. It also achieved parity with NRIs in matters of intercountry adoption of Indian children, lower entry fees for visiting the national monuments, historical sites, and museums in India, employment, and entitlement to appear for the All India Premedical Test or such other tests. In addition, the OCI scheme allowed the overseas Indian's foreign spouse to apply for a PIO card, strangely allowing a non-Indian to be called a person-of-Indian origin, thus permitting a more restricted basket of rights for their non-Indian spouses. Earlier restrictions regarding the non-acquisition of agricultural or plantation properties continued in the OCI scheme.

As late as 2015 the Indian government announced the merger of the PIO and OCI schemes, allowing all individuals holding PIO card status at the time of the merger to be automatically granted the benefits, rights, and guarantees of the OCI scheme. This may be considered the most important move toward dual citizenship not just for the members of the Indian diaspora but also for their foreign spouses who would enjoy the same basket of rights. The principle of ethnicity (*jus sanguinis*) that has always guided India's citizenship regime stands amended in a serious way. Ethnicity remains important because one must still prove one's connection to Indian ethnicity by marriage but the right of blood loses its primacy. India's citizenship initiative that started with ethnicity—"the sun never sets on the Indian diaspora"—now includes non-Indian spouses, thus extending the reach of the diaspora. Yet, on the dissolution of marriage the foreign spouse may lose his or her overseas citizenship of India. While still mired in the problem of ethnic origins as well as class, the OCI scheme illustrates how practices of globalization alter the relationship of the citizen to the state through an unbundling of rights (e.g., economic, political, legal, mobility rights) differentially made available to different groups of citizens such as resident and nonresident Indians, Indians with foreign citizenship, and foreign spouses and children of Indians.

The OCI scheme is only a single case study of the large-scale shift underway in liberal regimes around the world toward a form of membership untied from one territory, one state, one ethnicity, or one system of rights. We must capture this shift, however, more in its variation than its commonalty. In a gradually forming transnational legal landscape, citizenship emerges as a virtual basket of rights negotiated between various parties, all leading to a situation where the rights basket is constituted differently in different settings.

Negotiations for the rights extended through dual and multiple citizenship schemes seem to involve many different actors, including the state, the elite diaspora, corporations, and organizations focused on development. But dual citizenship is not the only format through which certain economic and mobility rights are gained. The Indian government is also entering into bilateral agreements with other liberal regimes regarding the protection of rights for nonresident Indians irrespective of their dual citizenship status. During my research at the MOIA in 2012–2013, I came upon multiple social security agreements that India had recently entered into with Northern European countries such as France, Luxemburg, and Finland, thereby, purchasing a different set of rights in each situation for nonresident Indians who lived in those countries. These agreements cover a wide variety of topics. Let me quote only two of them:

> A Contracting State shall not reduce or modify benefits acquired under its legislation solely on the ground that the beneficiary stays or resides in the territory of the other Contracting State.

> The old age, survivors' and disability benefits due by virtue of the legislations of one Contracting State are paid to the nationals of the other Contracting State residing in the territory of a third State, under the same conditions as if they were nationals of the first Contracting State.

These bilateral agreements covered various topics such as equal treatment of nationals, taxation, employment rights, benefits, and welfare rights. Strong liberal states tend to be important in these mutual agreements by expanding the rights of its citizens or diaspora in other countries. From all the above discussion, one can glean how an individual's basket of rights changes depending on his or her entry into a different ensemble of state, territory, diaspora, ethnicity, corporations, and NGOs.

Conclusion: Mutations of Citizenship

One of the most recognizable mutations in citizenship occurred with the Universal Declaration of Human Rights, which added an entirely different dimension to the idea of membership. Any membership-based organization—whether a nation-state or a social club—is bound to be exclusive, as it provides support and services to its members to the exclusion of nonmembers. The difference between citizen and alien emanates from the exclusionary nature of all organizations. As opposed to citizen rights, however, human rights allowed all of humanity to be included, brushing aside differences based on class, blood, territory, citizenship, or any other criteria. Here we can recall Soysal's argument that citizenship increasingly derives its force from the scripts of human rights, as in many liberal democratic countries, a greater number of protections have been made available to the noncitizen, making the difference between the citizen and the alien less potent than it used to be. As many scholars have noticed, however, the difference between citizen and alien continues to be important in several respects and is not about to vanish any time soon—but the importance of the language of rights, I argue, continues to rise, even if one cannot claim that the difference between citizen and alien is disappearing under the pressure of the human rights regime. Indeed, the difference between citizen and alien does not remain absolute but becomes a sophisticated enterprise of rights negotiation whereby differences between different kinds of citizens and different kinds of aliens emerge from the actual, negotiated basket of rights.

The gradual disappearance of the fixed basket of rights may be understood in terms of the growing strength of weak citizenship. First, one may view it from the perspective of Mark Granovetter's seminal thesis, the strength of weak ties, according to which weak ties among individuals tend to demand less social involvement and thus are capable of extending one's reach beyond the clique. Strong ties, on the other hand, slow down the spread of new ideas and the reach of scientific endeavors, as cliques separated by race, ethnicity, or territory have difficulty reaching a modus vivendi.[38] Second, one may interpret the strength of weak citizenship in simpler terms: the gradual strengthening and wider adoption of weak citizenship scripts. And last, we may look at it in terms of the flexibility gained through the ability to slice and dice citizen rights in a way that allows nation-states to tailor the laws to their current needs. All three interpretations apply to my thesis, as I see that both nation-states and individuals have much to gain from the unraveling of the fixed basket of rights. Nation-states tend to regain the loyalty and, more important, the remittances and charitable contributions from the diaspora they had lost during the era of exclusive citizenship. By reintegrating the citizenry, nation-states do not have much to lose but a lot to gain in terms of investments, influence in other nations, and their bargaining position. The states are able to extend a modified form of citizenship by fine-tuning the rational scripts and configuring different bundles of rights for different groups. It would be an exaggeration to attribute too much power to the states. Through a conventional lens, it may appear that the motives of the state, corporate capital, or people have worked together to bring about the decline of exclusive national citizenship. But the emergence of rights-based transnational citizenship may be part of a gradually emerging global social formation informed by mobility and communication. In this perspective, the states are not necessarily the architects of the emerging regime; indeed, global scripts of rights-based inclusion affect nation-states by influencing their national policies. By adopting, extending, and enforcing the rights-based citizenship model, the states may be mere brokers of the late modern force of history where everything solid—blood or soil—melts into air.

Notes

1 Thomas H. Marshall, *Citizenship and Social Class* (London: Cambridge University Press, 1950).

2 Jürgen Habermas, *Legitimation Crisis* (Boston: Beacon Press, 1975).

3 Castles et al., *The Oxford Handbook of the Welfare State* (Oxford: Oxford University Press, 2010); Paul Pierson, *The New Politics of the Welfare State* (Oxford: Oxford University Press, 2001).

4 Yasemin N. Soysal, *Limits of Citizenship: Migrants and Postnational Membership in Europe* (Chicago: Chicago University Press, 1994); Andrew Linklater, "Cosmopolitan Citizenship," *Citizenship Studies* 2, no. 1 (1998): 23–41; Michael S. Laguerre, *Diasporic Citizenship: Haitian Americans in Transnational America* (New York: St. Martin's Press, 1998); Aihwa Ong, *Flexible Citizenship: The Cultural Logics of Transnationality* (Durham: Duke University Press, 1999); Adriana Petryna, *Biological Citizenship: Science and the Politics of Health after Chernobyl* (Princeton: Princeton University Press, 2002).

5 Jürgen Habermas, "The European Nation-State: On the Past and Future of Sovereignty and Citizenship," *Public Culture* 10, no. 2 (1998): 397–416.

6 Benedict Anderson, *Imagined Communities: Reflections on the Origin and Spread of Nationalism* (New York: Verso, 1991).

7 A. Aneesh, "A Bloody Language: Clashes and Constructions of Linguistic Nationalism in India," *Sociological Forum* 25, no. 1 (2010): 86–109; Arjun Appadurai, *Fear of Small Numbers: An Essay on the Geography of Anger* (Durham: Duke University Press, 2006); Craig Calhoun, "Nationalism and Ethnicity," *Annual Review of Sociology* 19 (1993): 211–239.

8 Ayelet Shachar, *The Birthright Lottery: Citizenship and Global Inequality* (Harvard University Press, 2009).

9 For sociology see, for example, Georg Simmel, "The Metropolis and Mental Life," in *The Blackwell City Reader*, ed. Gary Bridge and Sophie Watson (Malden, Wiley-Blackwell, 1903); Thomas F. Gieryn, "A Space for Place in Sociology," *Annual Review of Sociology* (2000): 463–96. For anthropology see, for example, Marc Augé, *Non-Places: Introduction to an Anthropology of Supermodernity* (New York: Verso, 1995); Steven Feld and Keith H. Basso, eds., *Senses of Place* (Santa Fe: SAR Press, 1996); Akhil Gupta and James Ferguson, *Anthropological*

Locations: Boundaries and Grounds of a Field Science (Berkeley: University of California Press, 1997). For philosophy see, for example, Martin Heidegger, "Building Dwelling Thinking," in *Poetry, Language, Thought* (New York: Harper and Row, 1971), 145–161; Gaston Bachelard, *The Poetics of Space* (New York: Orion Press, 1964); Michel de Certeau, *The Practice of Everyday Life* (Berkeley: University of California Press, 1984).

10 Claude Lévi-Strauss, *The Elementary Structures of Kinship* (Boston, Beacon Press, 1969); Alfred Reginald Radcliffe-Brown and Cyril Daryll Forde, eds., *African Systems of Kinship and Marriage* (New York: International African Institute, 1950).

11 Anderson, *Imagined Communities,* 5.

12 Ibid.; Ernest Gellner, *Nations and Nationalism* (Oxford: Blackwell, 1983).

13 Kant and Rousseau quoted from Habermas, "The European Nation-State."

14 George Krücken and G. S. Drori, *World Society: The Writings of John W. Meyer* (New York: Oxford University Press, 2009).

15 Immanuel Kant, *Kant: Political Writings* (Cambridge: Cambridge University Press, 1991).

16 Andrea Bianchi, "Immunity versus Human Rights: The Pinochet Case," *European Journal of International Law* 10, no. 2 (1999): 237–277; Joseph A. Camilleri and Jim Falk, *The End of Sovereignty: The Politics of a Shrinking and Fragmenting World* (Cheltenham: Edward Elgar Press, 1992); Daniele Archibugi, "Cosmopolitan Democracy and Its Critics: A Review," *European Journal of International Relations* 10, no. 3 (2004): 437–473.

17 Geoffrey Robertson, *Crimes against Humanity: The Struggle for Global Justice* (New York: New Press, 2006), 99.

18 David Beetham, *Democracy and Human Rights* (Cambridge, England: Polity, 1999).

19 Martha Nussbaum, "Patriotism and Cosmopolitanism," in *The Cosmopolitan Reader,* ed. Garrett Wallace Brown and David Held (Malden: Polity, 2010), 155–162.

20 Kwame Anthony Appiah, *Cosmopolitanism: Ethics in a World of Strangers* (New York: W. W. Norton, 2006).

21 Archibugi, "Cosmopolitan Democracy and Its Critics: A Review," 437–473; David Held, *Democracy and the Global Order: From the Modern State to Cosmopolitan Governance* (Stanford, CA: Stanford University Press, 1995).

22 David Chandler, "New Rights for Old? Cosmopolitan Citizenship and the Critique of State Sovereignty," *Political Studies* 51, no. 2 (2003): 332–349.

23 Soysal, *Limits of Citizenship.*

24 Rainer Bauböck, "Towards a Political Theory of Migrant Transnationalism," *International Migration Review* 37, no. 3 (2003): 700–23.

25 Thomas Faist, "Transnationalization in International Migration: Implications for the Study of Citizenship and Culture," *Ethnic and Racial Studies* 23, no. 2 (2000): 189–222.

26 A. Portes, L. E. Guarnizo, and P. Landolt, "The Study of Transnationalism: Pitfalls and Promise of an Emergent Research Field," *Ethnic and Racial Studies* 22, no. 2 (1999): 217–237.

27 Linda Bosniak, *The Citizen and the Alien: Dilemmas of Contemporary Membership* (Princeton: Princeton University Press, 2008); Shachar, *The Birthright Lottery.*

28 Peter J. Spiro, "Dual Nationality and the Meaning of Citizenship," *Immigration and Nationality Law Review* 18 (1997): 491.

29 League of Nations Treaty, *Convention on Certain Questions Relating to the Conflict of Nationality Laws,* The Hague, April 12, 1930, accessible at http://www.refworld .org/docid/3ae6b3b00.html.

30 John Breuilly, "Introduction," to Ernest Gellner, *Nations and Nationalism* (Oxford: Blackwell, 1983).

31 Michael Hechter, *Containing Nationalism* (Oxford: Oxford University Press, 2000).

32 A. Aneesh, "A Bloody Language: Clashes and Constructions of Linguistic Nationalism in India," *Sociological Forum* 25, no. 1 (2010): 86–109.

33 The Labor Condition Application (LCA) is a prerequisite to H-1B approval. The LCA (US Department of Labor Form-9035) contains basic information about the proposed H-1B employment such as rate of pay, period of employment, and work location. It also contains four standard attestations or promises that the employer must make. (1) It is paying (and will continue to pay) the H-1B employee wages that are at least the actual wages paid to others with similar experience and qualifications for the specific job; or the prevailing wage for the occupation in the area of employment is based on the best information available. (2) It will provide working conditions for the H-1B employee that will not adversely affect the working conditions of workers similarly employed in the area. Working conditions commonly refer to matters including hours, shifts, vacation periods, and fringe benefits. (3) There is no strike or labor dispute ongoing at the place of employment. (4) It has provided notice of this filing to the bargaining representative (if any); or if there is no such bargaining representative, it has posted notice of filing in at least two conspicuous locations at the place of employment for a period of ten business days.

34 Clause 36.5, HCID, *Report of High Level Committee on India Diaspora* (New Delhi: Ministry of External Affairs, 2001).

35 HCID, *Report of High Level Committee on India Diaspora* (New Delhi: Ministry of External Affairs, 2001).

36 Kaushik Basu, "Structural Reform in India, 1991–1993: Experience and Agenda," *Economic and Political Weekly* (1993): 2599–2605.

37 *The India Development Foundation of Overseas Indians* (New Delhi: Ministry of Overseas Indian Affairs), December 1, 2008, accessible at http://www.cgisf.org/ page/display/294/14/.

38 Mark S. Granovetter, "The Strength of Weak Ties," *American Journal of Sociology* (1973): 1360–1380.

12

Gaming the System

Imperial Discomfort and the
Emergence of Coyote Capitalism

BERNARD C. PERLEY

As my mother, a tribal elder from Tobique First Nation, and I were driving past the Tobique First Nation bingo hall and casino operation at the end of an evening bingo event, we observed all the people leaving the hall.

"It looks like there was a good bingo crowd," I said.

"Yes, but most of them are losers," my mother responded.

"Then, why play?" I asked.

"You can't win if you don't play," she quickly replied.

Tobique Gaming Center is a modest metal building located at the entrance of Tobique First Nation, New Brunswick, Canada. The Tobique Gaming Center website boasts bingo jackpots of $1,000 (Canadian dollars), a Soaring Eagle Poker Room, and the Two Rivers Restaurant.[1] The Gaming Center is located on Tobique First Nation, a Maliseet community that has a population of approximately fifteen hundred people.[2] The patrons who frequent the casino/bingo hall come from the surrounding rural communities of Victoria County, New Brunswick, Canada, and from across the United States–Canada border in northern Aroostook County, Maine. The regional economy is predominantly public services, agriculture, and timber-related industries.[3] Tobique Gaming Center is a small operation that draws its patronage from a rural and depressed economy.

All the Bells and Whistles

Lights were flashing all around us. Music blared and bells were ringing and clanging from thousands of video slot machines. The lights and sounds illuminated and rippled through the four of us as we stood bewildered in the center of Mohegan Sun Casino in Uncasville, Connecticut.[4] The four of us, visitors to the Mohegan homeland, are all American Indians—two Tuscarora, one Mohawk, and one Maliseet. We were not entranced by the glittering and flashing lights of the noisy slot machines. Instead, we were captivated by the motions of an animatronic wolf.[5] We watched as it moved its head from side to side and after a few moments up and down. At one point, if you stand in the right place, the wolf will look directly at you. We watched for twenty minutes as the wolf went through its entire cycle of wolf animatronics. Meanwhile, hundreds of people were depositing thousands of dollars into the video slot machines. The four of us were not there to gamble. We were attending and presenting papers at the Native American and Indigenous Studies Association (NAISA) conference hosted by Mohegan Sun Casino.

Coyote Capitalism

These two vignettes are ethnographic representations of two very different American Indian casino operations. They differ in locale, scale, and patronage. They do have critical similarities. They both reflect alternative means of generating capital for their respective communities that may not at first glance seem to be traditional subsistence strategies. By doing so, they also represent what I am terming "coyote capitalism" as a response to Western strategies of capital accumulation and wealth distribution. To understand the coyote perspective it must be remembered that the traditional economies of American Indian communities were dramatically altered, if not eradicated, by over five hundred years of colonial processes of oppression, dispossession, and assimilation. American Indians were forced to find alternative subsistence strategies that would retain crucial aspects of their traditional values while creatively exploring innovative approaches for asserting their economic sovereignty. Indian Gaming has become one of the greatest American Indian economic success stories in the late twentieth and early twenty-first centuries. That success is coyote capitalism in practice. Coyote capitalism is the historically informed American Indian participation in global markets characterized by culturally grounded practices of economic development, cultural revitalization, and global cosmopolitanism. The greater the economic success of coyote capitalism, however, the greater the "imperial discomfort" for non-Indian critics. Imperial discomfort is the unsettling recognition of colonial wrongs against indigenous peoples that colonial settler societies experience through their everyday relations with indigenous peoples in contemporary colonial states. Outward manifestations of discomfort can be as obvious as criticism of indigenous peoples, the perpetuating of gross stereotypes of indigenous peoples, and legal machinations denying indigenous peoples their sovereignty. Subtler forms of imperial discomfort are hidden in plain sight—such as the total dismissal or disregard of indigenous peoples in colonial states, the willful ignorance of colonial histories, and the failure to become informed of the complex histories entangling colonial and indigenous peoples. American Indian casinos offer a critical perspective on both coyote capital and imperial discomfort. The casinos bring together both constituencies—indigenous peoples and nonindigenous peoples—in a common space of interaction. While non-Indian consumers invest in the fantasy playgrounds through games of chance, they also contribute to American Indian projects of self-determination and sovereignty. The casino patrons' experience of imperial discomfort is hidden through self-deception, because they are cognizant of the public discourses surrounding controversies regarding Indian casinos, yet they push those discourses to the background as they "play to win." One obvious form of imperial discomfort can be readily discerned in non-Indian critics as they condemn Indian gaming as crass commodification of ethnic identity. Critically, both forms of imperial discomfort are also naturalized forms of colonialism. "Naturalized colonialism" is the everyday assault on indigenous peoples by colonial/settler societies that go unnoticed by those societies.[6] In this essay I explore the tensions between coyote capitalism and imperial discomfort to argue that American Indian economic success represents indigenous economic sovereign praxis against ongoing imperial/colonial oppression of the American Indian First Nations of North America in the twenty-first century.

Critical Capital and Indigenous Economies

At the Mohegan Sun Casino, the convergence of American Indian scholars and gamblers from New York, Boston, and all the metropolitan areas in between seem incongruous at first glance, but the anomaly is momentary because the gamblers arrive every day at all hours of the day and night while the scholars were there for only a few days. Generally, the Mohegan tribe of Connecticut (the owner-operators of the Mohegan Sun Casino) will be viewed as merely creating a new form of entrepreneurial capitalism. John L. Comaroff and Jean Comaroff, for example, refer to this as Native American "ethno-preneurism." Their analysis, however, is an unfortunate exercise in naturalized colonialism that reads like a colonial/settler society apologist's survey of American Indian gaming. The Comaroffs disparage American Indian gaming development initiatives as "commodifying descent, American-style." The authors amplify this disparagement by proposing "seven dimensions of the identity business" to expose the commodification of ethnicity as "the occult power of capital to manufacture identity." Unfortunately, their analysis ignores much of the casino activities that go unnoticed by casual critics and gamblers alike.[7]

My work on language endangerment and language revitalization in American Indian communities has given me opportunities to see another side of the casino business that is overlooked by popular representations, casual scholars, and critics. The Comaroffs deserve credit for at least considering indigenous economic strategies as survival strategies. However, their disparagement of indigenous economic development strategies reflects an irresponsible critical analysis that perpetuates naturalized colonialism by failing to take into account the distribution of wealth across indigenous communities who have been successful in establishing gaming operations that are profitable in both "real" and symbolic capital. That failure is symptomatic of imperial discomfort, a discomfort that is also a condition of globalization.

The current era of globalization has been described as an era unprecedented in human history, in which the speed of global flows of ideas, economies, cultures, and populations traverse borders, oceans, and imaginaries.[8] This era has been championed as an era of global economic growth and improvement in global health and quality of life.[9] The optimistic view is often couched in Simon Kuznet's phrase "Growth is the rising tide that lifts all boats."[10] Too often, popular discourses extolling the benefits of globalization have marginalized if not ignored the detrimental effects that globalization has meant for indigenous peoples and how global economic growth and its attendant ideology continue to perpetuate colonialism in naturalized and nonreflexive ways.

The promise of globalization is echoed in actions of nongovernmental bodies as humanitarian agents that, as Marc Abélès puts it, "hear the echo of rejected humanity, those who seem abandoned on behalf of modernity." These rejected populations "are truly there, they keep knocking on the doors of the universe of the rich only to be generally rejected with a violence of which we are aware. And the place that nongovernmental organizations [NGOs] occupy in public space depends foremost on the action that they carry out to ensure the survival of these rejected humans."[11] Abélès enthusiastically articulates the optimistic view of NGOs: "The end of the twentieth century will be remembered for the progressive rise to power of a broad movement that came to counterbalance the most harmful effects of globalization."[12] One such counterbalancing move by a significant NGO is the adoption of the *Declaration of the Rights of Indigenous Peoples* by the United Nations in 2007. The UN *Declaration of the Rights of Indigenous Peoples* brought the lingering inequalities and suppression of indigenous lifeways into the global conversation on development and social justice in hopes that indigenous peoples across the globe may become the beneficiaries of international efforts recognizing their inherent indigenous rights as distinct from universal human rights. Some scholars have reported some success stories for indigenous development initiatives.[13] Other scholars have taken those success stories and criticized indigenous entrepreneurs for successfully participating in global market expectations.[14] Those critics condemn indigenous communities for profiting from their ethnic, cultural, and environmental popularity in the global market for indigenous art, performance, tourism, and other commodities. These critics analytically err by either making cursory acknowledgments or completely ignoring the historical conditions that force indigenous communities to market ethnicity, culture, and landscape.

Indigenous entrepreneurs who practice coyote capitalism will never perfectly emulate "anglo-capital" to the satisfaction of nonindigenous critics, because the colonial and settler society capitalists have historically imposed (and continue to impose) severe constraints on indigenous economic development efforts. The predictable outcome is that "ethno-capital" will always be susceptible to denigration from colonial/settler society critics. For example, the Comaroffs use clever terms such as "ethno-preneur" and "ethno-capital" to describe indigenous economic development projects, but unfortunately the clever descriptors also disparage indigenous economic strategies as either misapplied or deficient in their practice of "anglo-preneurship" and "anglo-capitalism." Rather than denigrate ethno-capital as an imperfect reflection of anglo-capital, we should appreciate the coyote ethos (or trickster ethos).[15] It is this ethos that underlies the creative and emergent aspect of indigenous self-determination.[16] Contemporary enactments of the coyote ethos and American Indian economic development recall, as Philip Deloria puts it, the "social fluidity characteristic of Native societies in the first periods of colonial disruption" and the adjustments made in the wake of colonial imposition of "more rigid social and political identities: treaties codified tribal units, and the federal government began identifying and tracking members associated with discreet territories." As Deloria describes it, "Indian people shapeshifted from suits to headdresses to buckskins and back to suits as suited their needs." Coyote capitalists take advantage of the opportunities to exercise their sovereignty as they participate in the global markets through culturally grounded practices of economic development, cultural revitalization, and global cosmopolitanism. Due to the shape-shifting nature of coyote capitalism in the twenty-first century, it probably never will be a perfect reflection of anglo-preneurism or anglo-capital. The essential difference between coyote capitalism and other forms of capital development is "the opportunity to work within tribal structures that linked together land, identity, legal rights, and government visibility."[17] To understand the importance of how coyote capitalism developed into an Indigenous praxis for sovereignty and survival, a brief history of economic, cultural, and social erasure of indigenous worlds by colonial and neocolonial regimes will put self-determination and coyote capitalism in proper context.

Globalization for American Indians started in 1492. If we want to understand the successes as well as the tragedies associated with globalization we need to look to American Indian history over the last five hundred years. That history presents both continuity and innovation in American Indian economic development across sovereign domains such as economies, languages, cultures, and landscapes. The last five hundred years is coyote capitalism on the global scale. Echoing this perspective Peter Sloterdijk, in his grand narrative of globalization and capital, argues that a middle stage for globalization can be demarcated as the period between 1492 and 1945. He describes this period as "terrestrial globalization" in which globalization was "realized practically through Christian capitalist seafaring and politically implanted through the colonialism of the Old European nation states" and is alternatively known by historians as the "age of European expansion."[18] Sloterdijk identifies this period as "world history" and characterized as "one-sidedness in action," "Eurocentrism," and the work of an "arrogant centre." He adds, "We will characterize this epoch as the time of the crime of unilateralism—the asymmetrical taking of the world whose points of departure lay in ports, royal courts and ambitions of Europe."[19] Sloterdijk describes the United States as a colonial society with deep "historico-theological deliriums."

> America rose from the Atlantic like an auxiliary universe in which God's experiment with mankind could be started from scratch—a land in which arriving, seeing, and taking seemed to become synonymous. While, in the feudalized and territorialized Old Europe, every strip of arable land had had an owner for a thousand years, and every forest path, cobblestone or bridge was subject to age-old rights of way and restrictive privileges in favor of some princely exploiter, America offered countless arrivals the exciting contrasting experience of a virtually lordless land that, in its immeasurability, wanted only to be occupied and cultivated so as to belong to the occupier and cultivator. A world in which the settlers arrive before the land registers—a paradise for new beginners and strong takers.[20]

The last sentence is developed later as an argument for the "moral gap" where "the agents of expansion, in the American West and the rest of the globe, exculpated themselves in their interventional acts through an implicit theory of the moral gap: there are seemingly times in which action must be ahead of legislation."[21] Such moral gaps can be found in colonial capital cataclysms in the colonization of the Americas. The remainder of this essay will identify four such cataclysms, while explaining where the fugitive modes of coyote capitalism emerge from them.

Colonial Capital Cataclysm I: Empire

"In fourteen hundred and ninety-two Columbus sailed the ocean blue." It seems we all learned that rhyming couplet sometime during our elementary education. It is usually associated with a segment on "the discovery of America." We learned about the brave mariners led by the determined and heroic Christopher Columbus as they sailed in three tiny ships across uncharted waters. These are the stories of legend, of heroism, of new worlds. Yet, the heroic narratives require some foil to make the deeds of the heroes appear heroic. What did Columbus find when he discovered America? If you ask American Indians, they will tell you "Columbus discovered he was lost!" However, if you read Columbus's journal he provides a personal account of all the dazzling wonders before him and his mariners. Among the wonders were the indigenous peoples. Columbus makes some complimentary remarks, but they are couched in "historico-theological deliriums" of his time. Take for example his observation of the indigenous people on October 12, 1492:

> In order to win their good will . . . because I could see they were a people who could more easily be won over and converted to our holy faith by kindness than by force, I gave some of them some red hats and glass beads that they put round their necks, and many other things of little value, with which they were very pleased and became so friendly that it was a wonder to see. . . . They ought to make good slaves for they are of quick intelligence since I notice they are quick to repeat what is said to them, and I believe that they could very easily become Christians, for it seemed to me that they had no religion of their own. God willing, when I come to leave I will bring six of them to Your Highness so that they may learn to speak.[22]

Columbus's first impulse is to "free" the Indians, convert them to Christianity, and give them "things of small value." The most troubling statement comes toward the end of the excerpt. With those sentiments Columbus set the agenda to deny the American Indians their religions, their freedom, and their languages. The beginning of over five centuries of colonialism can be traced back to Columbus's initial representations in his journals. Those representations will be echoed in imperial policies, colonial practices, and literary fictions.

I purposely read the Columbus journals as proto-ethnographies alongside the writings of Barolomé de las Casas.[23] One las Casas text in particular represents ethnographic accounts of the Spanish cruelty against the indigenous peoples of the New World. *A Short Account of the Destruction of the Indies* was a text intended "to press upon the reader the immediacy of the American experience, the importance of 'being there,' and of being there with innocent intentions."[24] This early ethnographic account was to serve two purposes. First, it was to correct false reports regarding the nature of Indian societies that colonial sympathizers relayed to the Spanish court. Second, it was designed to prompt the Crown into actions to protect the Indians from the cruelty of Spaniards. Las Casas writes:

> It was upon gentle lambs, imbued by the Creator with all the qualities we have mentioned, that from the first day they clapped eyes on them the Spanish fell like ravening wolves upon the fold, or like tigers and savage lions who have not eaten meat for days. The pattern established at the outset has remained unchanged to this day, and the Spaniards still do nothing save tear the natives to shreds, murder them and inflict upon them untold misery, suffering and distress, tormenting, harrying and persecuting them mercilessly.[25]

The rest of the *Account* describes the atrocities from Hispaniola to the Kingdom of New Granada. The accounts are graphic and tragic and deliberately so. The text became the foundation for the "Black Legend," described by Pagden as "a distorted Protestant-inspired record of Spanish atrocities and cruelties which was to darken every attempt to exonerate Spanish imperial ventures from the sixteenth to the eighteenth centuries"[26] A sixteenth-century Dutch edition of the *Account* included illustrations by the Flemish engraver Theodor de Bry. The text together with the illustrations are the basis for the "Black Legend" but also the historical documentation of the underlying ideologies of the colonial capital cataclysm unleashed upon the Indians by Spanish imperial agents.

Capital Cataclysm II: Manifest Destiny

U.S. history is a record of internal colonialism against the American Indians, couched in a "historico-theological delirium" expressed as

Manifest Destiny. Sloterdijk describes "the basic American experience" as "the ease with which possession can be taken of land and resources. This produced—along with numerous other social characters—a world-historically unprecedented type of peasant who no longer resided on a lord's property, but rather managed his new, self-owned soil as an armed land-taker in his own right and a farmer under God." This American experience is representative of the "possession as law" doctrine:

> The taker-entrepreneurs on the colonial fronts act, to speak in Kantian terms, under the maxim that is usually more suitable for the definition of crime than that of a noble participation in the exploration of the world: for, by seeking to become owners of goods by pure taking, they elude the impertinent demands of fair exchange. Their consciences are barely ever damaged by this, as history shows, as they invoke the right of the supreme moment: in this instant, justice must lie in the appropriation itself, not in fair trade and mutual acknowledgement.[27]

That supreme moment was America's expansion westward. The historico-theological justification came in the form of Manifest Destiny.

John O'Sullivan, a journalist, is credited with making the phrase "Manifest Destiny" part of the American justification for taking land in the name of God and country, when he famously said, "And that claim is by the right of our manifest destiny to overspread and to possess the whole of the continent which Providence has given us for the development of the great experiment of liberty and federated self-government entrusted to us."[28] O'Sullivan's public support for American expansion—as expressed in Manifest Destiny and its variants—follows on the Jacksonian era of expansion. President Andrew Jackson realized American expansion by forcibly removing the five civilized tribes (Cherokee, Choctaw, Chickasaw, Creek [Muscogee], and Seminole) from their homes and traditional lands in the American Southeast. Despite assuming all the outward appearances of being civilized, the five tribes were denied their lands, their property, their sovereignty, and their dignity as they were forced to march to Oklahoma. The capital investments the five civilized tribes had made on their traditional lands in the form of houses, government structures, buildings, and industries were utterly destroyed or were appropriated by Jacksonian colonizers as part of American expansion in the antebellum United States. O'Sullivan would add to his visionary mission of American expansion with self-congratulatory rhetoric in his article "The Great Nation of Futurity":

> The far-reaching, the boundless future will be the era of American greatness. In its magnificent domain of space and time, the nation of

many nations is destined to manifest to mankind the excellence of divine principles; to establish on earth the noblest temple ever dedicated to the worship of the Most High—the Sacred and the True. Its floor shall be a hemisphere—its roof the firmament of the star-studded heavens, and its congregation an Union of many Republics, comprising hundreds of happy millions, calling, owning no man master, but governed by God's natural and moral law of equality, the law of brotherhood—of "peace and good will amongst men."[29]

His evocation of "peace and good will amongst men" will be repeated in the most cruel of circumstances on December 29, 1890. In what many historians regard as the last of the Indian wars when the West was truly won by American colonial expansion, the massacre of over three hundred Sioux by the American cavalry seemed to be the fulfillment of Manifest Destiny. Dee Brown describes the aftermath of the massacre:

When the madness ended, Big Foot and more than half of his people were dead or seriously wounded; 153 were known dead, but many of the wounded crawled away to die afterward. One estimate placed the final total of dead at very nearly three hundred of the original 350 men, women, and children. The soldiers lost twenty-five dead and thirty-nine wounded, most of them struck by their own bullets or shrapnel . . .

The wagonloads of wounded Sioux (four men and forty-seven women and children) reached Pine Ridge after dark. Because all available barracks were filled with soldiers, they were left lying in the open wagons in the bitter cold while an inept Army officer searched for shelter. Finally the Episcopal mission was opened, the benches taken out, and hay was scattered over the rough flooring.

It was the fourth day after Christmas in the Year of Our Lord 1890. When the first torn and bleeding bodies were carried into the candlelit church, those who were conscious could see Christmas greenery hanging from the open rafters. Across the chancel front above the pulpit was strung a crudely lettered banner: PEACE ON EARTH, GOOD WILL TO MEN.[30]

Three years after the Wounded Knee massacre, in 1893 Frederick Jackson Turner would deliver his seminal "frontier" thesis to the American Historical Association in Chicago. Turner drew his thesis from the 1890 census in which the findings report such fragmentation of the frontier that they proclaimed there was no longer a frontier line. Notably the 1890 census was taken in June 2, 1890. According to the census there were 248,253 American

Indians in the United States. By December 29 of that same year the number had dropped by another 300. Despite the end of the American frontier and despite the claim that Wounded Knee represented the end of the Indian wars, America would continue its assault on American Indians through additional capital cataclysms.

Capital Cataclysm III: Capitalism

The attempts by the five civilized tribes to emulate the civilized ways and attributes of their colonial neighbors earned them the "civilized" descriptor. However, being civilized did not prevent them from the colonial appropriation of their lands, wealth, livelihoods, and sovereignty in the 1830s. Over one hundred years later, the horrors endured by the five civilized tribes would be visited upon the American Indians again in the form of the various termination acts passed by U.S. Congress. Again, land and wealth were at issue. Among the first American Indian nations to be terminated was the Menominee of Wisconsin. The responsible agency for termination was the 83rd Congress in June 1954. The opening text of the Act is as follows:

> *An Act To provide for a per capita distribution of Menominee tribal funds and authorize the withdrawal of the Menominee Tribe from Federal jurisdiction.*
>
> *Be it enacted . . .* that the purpose of this Act is to provide for the orderly termination of Federal supervision over the property and members of the Menominee Indian Tribe of Wisconsin.

While the opening of the act identifies the Menominee as the beneficiary of termination, the most chilling aspect is found in Section 3:

> SEC. 3. At midnight of the date of enactment of this Act the roll of the tribe maintained pursuant to the Act of June 15, 1934 (48 Stat. 965), as amended by the Act of July 14, 1939 (53 Stat.1003), shall be closed and no child born thereafter shall be eligible for enrollment.[31]

The remainder of the act outlines the "final closure of the roll of the tribe and the final roll of the members," the control of "services in the fields of health, education, welfare, credit, roads, and law and order," the transfer of "the title to all property, real and personal, held in trust by the United States for the tribe," to ensure that "individual members of the tribe shall not be entitled to any of the services performed by the United States for Indians because of their status as Indians, all statutes of the United States which affect Indians because of their status as Indians shall no longer be applicable to members of the tribe."[32] What could be behind the U.S. decision to unilaterally declare the Menominee no longer a tribe?

In 1934 Congress passed the Wheeler-Howard Act of 1934, better known as the Indian Reorganization Act. This was "to conserve and develop Indian lands and resources; to extend to Indians the right to form business and other organizations; to establish a credit system for Indians; to grant certain rights of home rule to Indians; to provide for vocational education for Indians, and for other purposes."[33] The years following the Wheeler-Howard Act were a period of reorganization of American Indian communities, many of which began to thrive under their new tribal organizations, constitutions, and economic development programs. Some became so successful that many congressional members decided that those communities did not need government assistance or protection and that the members of those communities were ready to be relieved of the burden of federal management of Indian Affairs. However, many congressional leaders saw a different reason for terminating Indian tribes.

In 1948 the Hoover Commission, acting on behalf of Congress, states: "the basis for historic Indian culture has been swept away. Traditional tribal organization was smashed a generation ago . . . assimilation must be the dominant goal of public policy."[34] In short, the strategy was to limit government assistance to American Indians by assimilating them into the greater American polity. The congressman behind the termination act, Senator Arthur V. Watkins of Utah, had declared the termination act an emancipatory project "following in the footsteps of the Emancipation Proclamation ninety-four years ago, I see the following words emblazoned in letters of fire above the heads of the Indians—'THESE PEOPLE SHALL BE FREE!'"[35] Not only did Watkins perpetuate Columbus's promise to free the Indians, he also had a skewed sense of American Indian realities and his perception of the consequences of termination may have had ulterior motives. The rhetoric of congressional supporters of termination reflects America's historico-theological delirium. The moral gap is still present in this new period of capitalist assimilation. Watkins's emancipatory zeal resulted in the termination of over 109 tribes, the loss of at least 1,362,155 acres of Indian land, and the termination of 11,466 individuals.[36]

The Menominee of Wisconsin was not only the first but also one of the largest tribes to be affected by termination. Senator Watkins's plan was directed toward the Menominee who had been successful in managing their tribal services and businesses. Wilkinson writes: "by the time of the termination bill the Menominee, almost unique among tribes, were able to pay for most of the social programs normally funded through the BIA. The Menominee's economic situation, however, was brittle."[37] During the public hearings for Menominee termination, Senator Watkins visited the

Menominee reservation and reportedly "told the tribal members that they were going to be terminated whether they liked it or not, that they would be allowed no more than three years to prepare a plan for termination, and that unless they agreed to termination, their own tribal funds [from the federal claims case] would not be released."[38] The coercive and unilateral power wielded by Senator Watkins to terminate the Menominee became a disaster for both the Menominee and the federal government. Historian Colin Calloway succinctly describes the aftermath of the Menominee Termination Act:

> They reorganized the tribe as a corporation, Menominee Enterprises Incorporated, to manage the lands and lumber mill formerly owned and operated by the tribe, and the reservation became a county. Nevertheless, the impact of termination was devastating. The once-thriving tribal lumber industry was deprived of federal contracts at a time of a nationwide slump in housebuilding. Menominees had to sell land to pay taxes. Hospitals closed and health problems increased. A plan to save the government money cost more than ever in the form of welfare payments.[39]

The costs to all tribes who were terminated included:

1. Fundamental changes in land ownership patterns were made.
2. The trust relationship was ended.
3. State legislative jurisdiction was imposed.
4. State judicial authority was imposed.
5. All exemptions from state taxing authority were ended,
6. All special federal programs to tribes were discontinued.
7. All special federal programs to individuals were discontinued.
8. Tribal sovereignty was effectively ended.[40]

The Wheeler-Howard Act, as the catalyst for the American Indian economic initiative and success, was instrumental for many tribes to realize unprecedented degrees of self-determination since the arrival of colonial/settler societies. However, the irony for those tribes who were successful in engaging in capital relations in America was to find that their success only brought them to the attention of termination advocates. All the capital gains were immediately lost without consultation, without consideration of consequences, and without any consideration for tribal sovereignty. The costs of termination are devastating for those tribes who were terminated; but for all tribes in the United States "termination stands as a chilling reminder to Indian peoples that Congress can unilaterally decide to extinguish the special status and rights of tribes without Indian consent and without even hearing Indian views."[41] The backlash from the various termination acts led to the reinstatement of the Menominee in 1973. An additional consequence of the disastrous termination acts was the unified American Indian movement to resist such unilateral decisions by the U.S. government, a new move toward self-determination. American Indian self-determination develops at the same time America was exercising its historico-theological delirium of American global exceptionalism. Manifest Destiny goes global.

Capital Cataclysm IV: Globalization

While American Indians exercised self-determination within the colonial conditions of the United States, American leadership turned its attention to global markets. Sloterdijk argues that terrestrial globalization ended "with the establishment of the gold-based world monetary system by Bretton Woods in 1944." Sloterdijk's characterizes his third stage of globalization as a de-spatialized globe where "being human becomes a question of spending power, and the meaning of freedom is exposed in the ability to choose between products for market—or to create such products oneself."[42] Sloterdijk projects an optimism for his third stage of globalization as the hopeful constellation of human modalities among which "its moral crux is the transition of the ethos of conquest to the ethos of letting oneself be tamed by the conquered."[43] Has that third stage of globalization arrived? Sloterdijk's terrestrial globalization epoch (1492–1944, his second stage globalization that he also refers to as the Modern Age) "reads like a giant indictment of imperial incorrectnesses, infringements and crimes, and the only solace offered by a study of its contents is the thought that these deeds and misdeeds have become unrepeatable. Perhaps terrestrial globalization, like world history as a whole, is the crime that can only be committed once."[44] I appreciate Sloterdijk's optimism, but his own understanding of American exceptionalism on the global stage suggests that his optimism is misguided. "As if in some scene from the early modern age, the U.S.A. sends its fleets to drive world-taking forward as a naval power; like a modern colonial power, it uses aerial and ethereal weapons to win out in asymmetrical warfare against hopelessly inferior opponents; like a neo-apostolic bringer power, it makes use of the right to invade that follows from the knowledge that they must bring God's gift to mankind—in the present case it is termed democracy—to unwilling recipients, by force if necessary."[45] However, there is one area where Sloterdijk's own delirium might be on target. Indian gaming is the site where the "conquered" tames the "conquerors"—or is it?

The Indian Gaming and Regulatory Act (IGRA) of 1988 was a response from Congress to reverse the ill will of the termination acts of the 1950s and 1960s and to assure American Indian communities of federal support for economic self-determination efforts. Not all political leaders approved of American Indian gaming. There was outrage that American Indians could enjoy some kind of special status separate from regulation by state governments. Congressman Norman Shumway of California claimed that "Indian communities have taken unfair advantage of the unique jurisdictional status of their reservations by establishing large-scale gambling operations. . . . The Indian nations' unique position in the federal system . . . have made the Indians a separate, unaccountable segment of society who claim many rights but deny accountability for commensurate responsibilities." Another criticism of Indian gaming is expressed by Congressman James Bilbray of Nevada: "The States have a constitutional responsibility to protect their citizens from harm, here in the form of fraudulent manipulation by the operators of the games and of victimization by criminal elements that may infiltrate the legal games operated on Indian lands."[46] These two concerns were addressed in the final legislation:

SEC 3. The purpose of this Act is—
1. to provide a statutory basis for the operation of gaming by Indian tribes as a means of promoting tribal economic development, self-sufficiency, and strong tribal governments;
2. to provide a statutory basis for the regulation of gaming by an Indian tribe adequate to shield it from organized crime and other corrupting influences, to ensure that the Indian tribe is the primary beneficiary of the gaming operation, and to assure that gaming is conducted fairly and honestly by both the operator and the players; and
3. to declare that the establishment of independent Federal regulatory authority for gaming on Indian lands, the establishment of Federal standards for gaming on Indian lands, and the establishment of a National Indian Gaming Commission are necessary to meet congressional concerns regarding gaming and to protect such gaming as a means of generating tribal revenue.[47]

The ironies involved in IGRA are twofold. First, the second proviso claims to shield American Indian communities "from organized crime and other corrupting influences." The irony is that American colonization of American Indian lands is a long history of organized crime and corrupting influence. Second, the establishment of the federal regulatory authority and the

National Indian Gaming Commission is a direct contradiction of the federal support for self-determination. Anishinaabe scholar Gerald Vizenor identifies this second irony as a potential threat to tribal sovereignty:

> The white people are throwing money at the tribes once more . . . millions of dollars are lost each month at bingo, blackjack, electronic slot machines, and other mundane games of chance at casinos located on reservation land. The riches, for some, are the new wampum, or the casino coup count of lost coins. The weird contradiction is that the enemies of tribalism have now become the sources of conditional salvation. . . . This preposterous carnival of coup coins has transformed tribal communities. The reservation governments throw nothing back to the states in fees or taxation, and that is one of the serious concerns of tribal sovereignty.[48]

Vizenor's concerns are not to be dismissed. He echoes "congressional concerns" regarding the returns from casino operations and how that wealth will be distributed. Vizenor expresses his concern that "Future generations of the tribe may wonder what became of the billions and billions of dollars that were lost, and lost, and lost at the postindian pancasinos on reservations." Vizenor does offer one solution: that "tribes could name ambassadors to various nations and establish presence as a sovereign government," leading to "the liberation of hundreds of stateless families in the world," such as Kurds, Tibetans, Haitians, and traditionally tribal families.[49]

Vizenor's critical reflection about Indian gaming operation and the nature of the distribution of wealth continues to be debated where new Indian casinos are being proposed. Vizenor is correct to point out that the agreements between American Indian Nations and state governments—as well as regulation by the federal government—do indicate "limited" tribal sovereignty. His suggestions for moral traditions will be fulfilled through less conspicuous activities and ironies than those he proposed.

Self-Determination and the Rise of Coyote Capitalism

Sloterdijk projects a third stage of globalization as the hopeful constellation of human modalities among which "its moral crux is the transition of the ethos of conquest to the ethos of letting oneself be tamed by the conquered."[50] Perhaps we have entered a third stage of globalization. Non-Indian patrons investing their earnings in American Indian casinos are allowing themselves to be "tamed by the conquered." American Indian economic self-determination can take on many forms. The coyote ethos permits adaptation in terms that are indigenous and grounded in traditional practices and precepts. Coyote ethos is a shape-shifting stance that presents one perspective to outside observers while engaging in integrated assertions of self-determination across many domains of indigenous life. Projects such as bison ranching by the Cheyenne River Sioux of South Dakota,[51] the ambivalent success of eco-tourism of the Maasai of Tanzania,[52] and the success of the Mohegan Sun Casino are all practices of coyote capitalism where indigenous reinvestment of capital gains for the return of symbolic capital—in the forms of language and cultural revitalization, economic self-determination, and assertions of sovereignty—is often at odds with expectations from neoliberal principles of anglo-capitalism.

The Language of Symbolic Capital

I have firsthand experience in observing and participating in indigenous investment of symbolic capital. My research on language revitalization at Tobique First Nation focused on community investments of symbolic capital into language and cultural revitalization as a strategy to forestall the extinction of Maliseet language and culture.[53] The investment of monetary capital figured to be an important resource for planning, programming, and production of materials for language and cultural revitalization. Over the last decade and a half, it has become clear to me that monetary capital investment was not enough to keep language and culture a vital aspect of Maliseet daily life. Language revitalization required a great deal of symbolic capital to prompt community members into using their languages and cultural traditions in their everyday community activities. This is an ongoing process of economic, cultural, and linguistic self-determination. It is too soon to assess the success of these investments, but the good news comes in the increasing numbers of projects initiated by growing numbers of ethno-preneurs dedicated to leveraging both symbolic capital and monetary capital into the future solvency of the various domains of Maliseet economies—political, cultural, linguistic, and monetary.

An additional example of language and investments of symbolic capital is the "awakening" of the Miami language. Daryl Baldwin, a Miami language activist, suggested that the "academics" were wrong to describe the Miami language as "extinct."[54] He preferred to think of the Miami language as sleeping. And if the language is sleeping, then the Miami people can awaken it. Baldwin's innovative approach led to the creation of a summer language camp, a Miami research center at Miami University of Ohio, and a growing community of language learners.[55] The process required considerable symbolic capital from Baldwin and the Miami Nation of Oklahoma to solicit monetary capital from the tribal government and Miami of Ohio

University to create a multifaceted program of Miami language awakening. This is in stark contrast to linguists who saw no capital to be gained from an extinct language.

These examples of the Maliseet and the Miami are indicative of the innovative and unexpected approaches to language, culture, and economics that make coyote capitalism a significant process for indigenous self-determination. Both cases may not seem to implicate processes of globalization, but the long colonial process of linguistic colonialism had rendered the Maliseet language as "severely endangered" and the Miami language as "extinct."[56] Furthermore, the global discourses on language endangerment and extinction had all but relegated the Maliseet and Miami languages to the status of hopeless cases. The audacity of the Maliseet and Miami communities in challenging prevailing wisdom creates opportunities for creative solutions to imminent or proclaimed extinction of language, culture, and identity. Both communities coordinate symbolic capital and monetary capital as everyday practices of coyote capitalism. These are smaller-scale examples of capitalism. Mohegan Sun Casino provides a case where the promise of coyote capitalism to fulfill the moral traditions can be observed on a larger scale.

Globalization and the Promise of Coyote Capitalism

Mohegan Sun is a sight to behold. American Indian themes are distributed throughout the complex, from the abstracted "natural" lobby to the "rocky tumble" of the avenue of trendy restaurants and shops to the elaborately decorated "Earth," "Sky," and "Wind" casinos where animatronic wolves observe gamblers and scholars alike. The Mohegan Sun complex dazzles and delights all gamblers with the promise of the full richness of monetary capital—while paying dividends to American Indian scholars in the returns of symbolic capital. But what does the animatronic wolf have to do with coyote capitalism? One obvious answer is the investments made by non-Indian patrons in Indian casinos. Perhaps this is an aspect of Sloterdijk's optimistic program for his conception of the third stage of globalization, where "the moral crux is the transition of the ethos of conquest to the ethos of letting oneself be tamed by the conquered."[57] So, as four American Indian scholars watched the animatronic wolf, hundreds of gamblers were investing thousands of dollars in the Mohegan Sun Casino, which in turn made it possible for indigenous scholars to have critical conversations about indigenous states of affairs. Causal critics and commentators view American Indian casinos as crass commodifications of ethnicity because they expect indigenous economies to be perfect emulations of anglo-capital. From the indigenous perspective, the goal is not to emulate anglo-capital in all its excessive glory. Rather, the goal is to tap into anglo-capitalism in order to promote the return of indigenous symbolic capital. Those returns include my participation in a NAISA conference at Mohegan Sun, my enjoyment of a reception dinner for American Indian scholars at the Pequot Museum, and giving a keynote presentation at an American Indian language revitalization conference at the Yavapai Nation's Fort McDowell Casino at Fort McDowell, Arizona. All three venues are casinos operated by American Indian tribes. Each one supported American Indian language and cultural scholarship and revitalization projects. Each one contributed to the dissemination of critical indigenous commentaries and practices that benefit communities not directly affiliated with the casino or resort. Casual analysis of popular media reports and other texts will not provide the necessary knowledge to understand that there is more to American Indian casinos than the accumulation of monetary capital. The investment of monetary capital into language and cultural revitalization programs distributes the returns of symbolic capital back to indigenous communities. At Mohegan Sun, while nonnative gamblers invest their money in video slot machines, immersed in the creature comforts of gambling and with all the bells and whistles, the critical work of indigenous language and cultural revitalization, critical scholarship, and everyday practices of self-determination goes on in the background.

Global Capital Crisis and Coyote Capitalism

The global financial crisis of 2008 was instrumental in foregrounding economic theories and practices in popular imaginations and conversations. *Capital* was not just an abstraction for specialized knowledge brokers and policy makers. As Thomas Piketty observes in his popular treatise on capital:

> Indeed, the distribution of wealth is too important an issue to be left to economists, sociologists, historians, and philosophers. The concrete physical reality of inequality is visible to the naked eye and naturally inspires sharp but contradictory political judgments. . . . there will always be a fundamentally subjective and psychological dimension to inequality, which inevitably gives rise to political conflict that no purportedly scientific analysis can alleviate. Democracy will never be supplanted by a republic of experts—and that is a very good thing.[58]

The global financial crisis of 2008 affected all classes from the very poor to the very rich. Furthermore, the crisis highlighted how the experts got it wrong. Ironically, just before the 2008 crisis, the "experts" (the "quants" in particular) were celebrated in popular media—from television interviews and reports to news articles—for their innovative analyses of financial markets, and their skills were confirmed by the escalating wealth produced by their exotic financial tools. Those exotic tools failed to promise "to lift all boats" as the global financial crisis crashed world economies into global recession. In the midst of the crisis, there was great fear and uncertainty among experts and consumers alike as to whether the crisis would mitigate and whether recovery was possible. The global reach of the crisis reinforced the perception that capital had become a key condition of globalization.[59] This global imaginary also affirmed Hardt and Negri's postulated "multitudes" as one global citizenry oppressed by the machinations of *Empire*.[60] Piketty also underscores that the growing wealth gap privileges the quantification of the fundamentally "subjective and psychological dimension to inequality."[61] The emancipatory aspirations of Hardt and Negri as well as Piketty have limited salience for indigenous peoples. Indigenous peoples continue to suffer from the colonial appropriation of indigenous capital— in all forms, including material and immaterial, human and nonhuman, as well as in symbolic capital. Emancipatory commentators proclaim critical intervention on behalf of oppressed peoples, but their efforts fall short as long as the colonial wrongs against indigenous peoples go unacknowledged. Perhaps Sloterdijk is right; maybe it is time for the conquerors to be tamed by the conquered.

"You Can't Win If You Don't Play"

I descended by escalator into Potawatomi Casino. The escalator slowly moved me past historical photographs of Forest County Potawatomi people displayed along the walls of the escalator passage. As I approached the end of the descent, I could hear the ringing, clanging, and electronic music coming from hundreds of slot machines. The escalator spilled me out into an open public foyer where casino guests can choose their gambling venue. I walked into the cacophony of blinking slot machines displaying bright graphics of fantastic images of exotic peoples and places from the past as well as from contemporary popular culture. The slot machines projected ancient Egyptians, mythical fairies, and heroic figures from the *Lord of the Rings* movies. I marveled at the four seasons pseudo natural décor of the ceiling hovering above the phantasms of electronic wizardry. I walked through the four seasons and observed hundreds of patrons as they deposited tokens into the slot machines. The patrons were mostly white, elderly or late-middle-aged men and women. The expressions on their faces seemed devoid of life as the lights from the slot machines illuminated them in eerie glows of flickering promise. I moved through the comatose crowd, and not once did I hear the winning clamor of a payout signaling the fulfillment of casino promise. The longer I stayed in the midst of the slot machines and their attendant investors the more I appreciated the ironies of coyote capitalism. I also am reminded of my mother's bingo philosophy, "You can't win if you don't play." Was that a payout I just heard?

Coyote capitalism is never what you think it is. This phenomenon is an emergent process, historically informed indigenous responses to participation in global markets characterized by culturally grounded practices of economic development, cultural revitalization, and global cosmopolitanism. At best we can attempt to capture indigenous economic strategies as Indigenous peoples go "after capital" according to the constraints of the global economy. In such cases, success is measured by how much capital profitable ventures can bring to indigenous communities. We can also describe and record indigenous investments of capital gains from economic and development projects as processes that bring significant returns in the form of symbolic capital to indigenous communities engaged in such investments.[62] The symbolic capital derived from such investments can be unexpected and innovative developments in culture, environment, and self-determination. These unexpected and innovative aspects of capital investment and symbolic returns are the shifting contours of coyote capitalism. Key to understanding coyote capitalism is recognizing that the phenomenon is always emerging, which requires a critical focus on indigenous practices of leveraging the tensions of relative value between monetary capital and symbolic capital as strategies of self-determination, in anticipation of multiple forms of capital returns while participating in the global economy.

My own recent work has pointed out that such criticism fails to appreciate the coyote (trickster) ethos that underlies the creative and emergent aspect of indigenous self-determination.[63] Self-determination is also an emergent process that includes symbolic capital development projects initiated by indigenous communities—such as language and cultural revitalization, ecotourism, gaming and related services, and indigenous arts performances. Grounding indigenous self-determination in the coyote ethos provides an indigenous perspective on the cultural, social, and ethnic benefits that are gained from profits of market capitalism. Furthermore, the coyote ethos of indigenous self-determination reveals the benefits of successful coyote capitalism projects for larger issues of sustainable futures of global economies, environments, and cultures.

Notes

1 See Tobique Gaming Center, at http://tobiquegaming.ca/, accessed January 18, 2015.

2 Population is listed as 1,443 on December 31, 2011, by Aboriginal Affairs and Northern Development, Government of Canada, at http://www.aadnc-aandc .gc.ca/eng/1100100017100/1100100017101/.

3 See the Aroostook County website at http://www.aroostook.me.us/. See also http://en.wikipedia.org/wiki/Victoria_County,_New_Brunswick/, and *New Brunswick Regional Profiles: Highlights and Updates. Northwest Economic Region*, Province of New Brunswick (no date given but statistics are drawn from data published in 2012 and 2013).

4 "Become immersed in the bells and whistles of the more than 5,000 slot machines that will thrill your senses." Mohegan Sun website, at http://www.mohegansun .com/playing/slots.html.

5 Videos of one of the animatronic wolves are viewable on YouTube.

6 Bernard C. Perley, "New Life for Historical Documents: Native American Linguistic Repatriation in the American Northeast" (unpublished document).

7 John L. Comaroff and Jean Comaroff, "Commodifying Descent, American-Style," in *Ethnicity Inc.* (Chicago: University of Chicago Press, 2009), 60–85 (quotes 65, 69).

8 Arjun Appadurai, *Modernity at Large: Cultural Dimensions of Globalization* (Minneapolis: University of Minnesota Press, 1996).

9 Dan Smith, *The Penguin State of the World Atlas*, 9th ed. (New York: Penguin, 2012).

10 Kuznet quoted in Thomas Piketty, *Capital in the Twenty-First Century* (Cambridge, MA: The Belknap Press of Harvard University, 2014), 11.

11 Marc Abélès, *The Politics of Survival* (Durham: Duke University Press, 2010), 160.

12 Ibid., 161.

13 Jessica R. Cattelino, *High Stakes: Florida Seminole Gaming and Sovereignty* (Durham: Duke University Press, 2008); Shane Greene, *Customizing Indigeneity: Paths to a Visionary Politics in Peru* (Stanford: Stanford University Press, 2009); Dorothy L. Hodgson, *Being Maasai, Becoming Indigenous: Postcolonial Politics in a Neoliberal World* (Bloomington: Indiana University Press, 2011).

14 Comaroff and Comaroff, *Ethnicity Inc.*, 60–85; Karen Engle, *The Illusive Promise of Indigenous Development* (Durham: Duke University Press, 2010).

15 Philip Deloria, *Indians in Unexpected Places* (Lawrence: University of Kansas Press, 2004), 235.

16 Bernard C. Perley, "'Gone Anthropologist': Epistemic Slippage, Native Anthropology, and the Dilemmas of Representation," in *Anthropology and the Politics of Representation*, ed. Gabriela Vargas-Cetina (Tuscaloosa: University of Alabama Press, 2013); Bernard C. Perley, "Living Traditions: A Manifesto for Critical Indigeneity," in *Global Histories and Contemporary Experiences*, ed. Laura R. Graham and H. Glenn Penny (Lincoln: University of Nebraska Press, 2014), 32–54.

17 Deloria, *Indians in Unexpected Places*, 235.

18 Peter Sloterdijk, *In the World Interior of Capital* (New York: Polity, 2013), 9.

19 Ibid., 10.

20 Ibid., 117.

21 Ibid., 118.

22 B. W. Ife, *Christopher Columbus: Journal of the First Voyage (Diario del primer viaje) 1492* (Wiltshire: Aris and Phillips, 1990), 29–31.

23 Perley, "New Life for Historical Documents: Native American Linguistic Repatriation in the American Northeast."

24 Anthony Pagden, introduction to *A Short Account of the Destruction of the Indies,* by Bartolomé de las Casas (New York: Penguin, 1992), xxx.

25 Bartolomé de las Casas, *A Short Account of the Destruction of the Indies* (New York: Penguin, 1992), 11.

26 Pagden, introduction, xiii.

27 Sloterdijk, *In the World Interior of Capital,* 118.

28 Trevor B. McCrisken, "Exceptionalism: Manifest Destiny," in *Encyclopedia of American Foreign Policy,* 2nd ed. (New York: Charles Scribner's Sons, 2001), 68.

29 John L. O'Sullivan, "The Great Nation of Futurity," *The United States Democratic Review* 6, no. 23 (1839): 426–430 (quote, 427), text may be accessed at http:// ebooks.library.cornell.edu/.

30 Dee Brown, *Bury My Heart at Wounded Knee: An Indian History of the American West* (New York: Sterling Innovation, 2009), 523–524.

31 Francis Paul Prucha, *Documents of United States Indian Policy,* 2nd ed. (Lincoln: University of Nebraska Press, 1990), 234.

32 Ibid., 234–236.

33 Ibid., 222.

34 Charles Wilkinson, *Blood Struggle: The Rise of Modern Indian Nations* (New York: W. W. Norton, 2005), 64.

35 Ibid., 69.

36 David H. Getches, Charles F. Wilkinson, and Robert A. Williams Jr., *Cases and Materials on Federal Indian Law,* 3rd ed. (St. Paul: West Publishing Co., 1993), 235.

37 Wilkinson, *Blood Struggle: The Rise of Modern Indian Nations,* 71.

38 Verne Ray quoted in ibid., 72.

39 Colin G. Calloway, *First Peoples: A Documentary Survey of American Indian History,* 2nd ed. (Boston: Bedford/St. Martin's, 2004), 407.

40 Getches, Wilkinson, and Williams, *Cases and Materials on Federal Indian Law,* 235–236.

41 Ibid., 230.

42 Sloterdijk, *In the World Interior of Capital,* 12–13.

43 Ibid., 14.

44 Ibid., 119.

45 Ibid., 239.

46 Wilkinson, *Blood Struggle: The Rise of Modern Indian Nations,* 335.

47 Prucha, *Documents of United States Indian Policy,* 316.

48 Gerald Vizenor, "Casino Coups," *Manifest Manners: Postindian Warriors of Survivance* (Hanover: Weslyan University Press, 1994), 139.

49 Ibid., 148.

50 Sloterdijk, *In the World Interior of Capital,* 14.

51 Sebastian Felix Braun, *Buffalo Inc.: American Indians and Economic Development* (Norman: University of Oklahoma Press, 2008).

52 Hodgson, *Being Maasai, Becoming Indigenous: Postcolonial Politics in a Neoliberal World.*

53 Bernard C. Perley, "Managing Language as an Integrated Cultural Resource," in *Companion to Cultural Resource Management,* ed. Thomas F. King (Malden: Blackwell, 2011); Bernard C. Perley, *Defying Maliseet Language Death: Emergent Vitalities of Language, Culture, and Identity in Eastern Canada* (Lincoln: Nebraska, 2011); Bernard C. Perley, "Last Words, Final Thoughts: Collateral Extinctions in Maliseet Language Death," in *The Anthropology of Extinction: Essays on Culture and Species Death,* ed. Genese Sodikoff (Bloomington: Indiana University Press, 2012).

54 Miami Nation of Oklahoma, *myaamiaki eemamwiciki: Miami Awakening,* Sandy and Yasu Osawa, dir. (Upstream Productions, 2008), video.

55 Daryl Baldwin and Julie Olds, "Miami Indian Language and Cultural Research Center at Miami University," in *Beyond Red Power: American Indian Politics and Activism since 1900,* ed. Daniel M. Cobb and Loretta Fowler (Santa Fe: School for Advanced Research Press, 2007).

56 UNESCO, "A Methodology for Assessing Language Vitality and Endangerment," *Unesco.org,* March 12, 2003, accessible at http://www.unesco.org/new/en/culture/themes/endangered-languages/language-vitality/.

57 Sloterdijk, *In the World Interior of Capital,* 14.

58 Piketty, *Capital in the Twenty-First Century,* 2.

59 Manfred B. Steger, *Globalization: A Very Short Introduction* (Oxford: Oxford University Press, 2003).

60 Michael Hardt and Antonio Negri, *Empire* (Cambridge, MA: Harvard University Press, 2000); Michael Hardt and Antonio Negri, *Multitudes: War and Democracy in the Age of Empire* (New York, Penguin, 2004); Michael Hardt and Antonio Negri, *Commonwealth* (Cambridge: The Belknap Press of Harvard University Press, 2009).

61 Piketty, *Capital in the Twenty-First Century,* 2.

62 Pierre Bourdieu, *Distinction: A Social Critique of the Judgment of Taste* (Cambridge: Harvard University Press, 1984).

63 Bernard C. Perley, "Living Traditions: A Manifesto for Critical Indigeneity," in *Performing Indigeneity: Global Histories and Contemporary Experiences,* ed. Laura R. Graham and H. Glenn Penny (Lincoln: University of Nebraska Press, 2014).

NOTES ON CONTRIBUTORS

NIKI AKHAVAN is assistant professor of media studies at the Catholic University of America and author of *Electronic Iran: The Cultural Politics of an Online Evolution* (2013). Her research interests include new media and transnational political and cultural production, international cinema and national identity, documentary and social change, state-sponsored and oppositional propaganda, and postcolonial and critical theory. She is currently researching a new project on media, state, and militarization in Iran.

A. ANEESH is associate professor of sociology and global studies at the University of Wisconsin–Milwaukee, and author of *Virtual Migration: The Programming of Globalization* (2006). His scholarship intersects a plurality of research realms: globalization, migration, science, and technology. He has co-edited two publications, *Beyond Globalization: Making New Worlds in Media, Art, and Social Practices* (2011) and *The Long 1968: Revisions and Perspectives* (2013), and he authored a forthcoming book, *Neutral Accent: Global Language, Labor, and Life* (2015). Currently he is working on a project on citizenship.

IVAN ASCHER is assistant professor of political science at the University of Wisconsin–Milwaukee. He holds a PhD in political science from the University of California, Berkeley (2007). Before arriving at UWM, he was assistant professor at the University of Massachusetts, Amherst. Ascher's teaching interests include modern political and social theory, and he is currently writing about the continued relevance of Karl Marx and Max Weber for a critique of contemporary capitalism. He is also interested in the crisis of the university in the age of instrumental reason.

MARCUS BULLOCK is professor emeritus of English at the University of Wisconsin–Milwaukee and an honorary research associate in the Department of Comparative Literature and Folklore Studies at the University of Wisconsin–Madison. He is co-editor of the Harvard University edition of *Walter Benjamin: Selected Writings* and has published books and essays

primarily in the area of Weimar-era German literature and poststructural-
ist theory and film. His most recent edited book, with Peter Paik, is *Aftermaths: Exile, Migration, and Diaspora Reconsidered* (2008).

KENNAN FERGUSON is associate professor of political science at the University of Wisconsin–Milwaukee, where he is also director of the Center
for 21st Century Studies. He is the author of three books: *The Politics of
Judgment: Aesthetics, Identity, and Political Theory* (2nd edition, 2007);
William James: Politics in the Pluriverse (2007); and *All in the Family: On
Community and Incommensurability* (2012). Professor Ferguson also holds
various editorial and professional positions including co-editor of the
series Modernity and Political Thought (Rowman and Littlefield) and co-
editor of the *Blackwell Encyclopedia of Political Thought*.

ESTHER LESLIE is professor of political aesthetics at Birkbeck,
University of London. Her books include *Walter Benjamin: Overpower-
ing Conformism* (2000); *Hollywood Flatlands: Animation, Critical The-
ory, and the Avant Garde* (2000); *Synthetic Worlds: Art, Nature, and the
Chemical Industry* (2005); *Walter Benjamin* (2007); and, most recently,
Derelicts (2013), a study of the effects of war on the critical writings of
Benjamin, Adorno, Schwitters, and others. She is currently working on
a book on liquid crystals.

GEOFF MANN is associate professor of geography at Simon Fraser University, in Burnaby, British Columbia, Canada, where he directs the Centre
for Global Political Economy. His books include *Our Daily Bread: Wages,
Workers and the Global Economy of the American West* (2007) and *Disassembly Required: A Field Guide to Actually Existing Capitalism* (2013). He
is currently finishing a book on the many lives of Keyensianism. His writing has appeared in several journals, including *New Left Review, Historical
Materialism*, and *Antipode*.

BERNARD C. PERLEY is associate professor of anthropology at the University
of Wisconsin–Milwaukee. He has published an ethnography entitled *Defying Maliseet Language Death: Emergent Vitalities of Language, Culture, and
Identity in Eastern Canada* (2011). His current research interests include a
critical analysis of global indigenous practices of repatriating various fields
of sovereignty and self-determination such as language, culture, identity,
governance, and economics. He builds on that research by identifying
indigenous strategies of exercising self-determination as an expression of
traditional practices of a trickster (or coyote) ethos in dealing with settler
society, state structures, and institutions.

PATRICE PETRO is professor of English and film studies at the University of Wisconsin–Milwaukee, where she also serves as vice provost and director of the Center for International Education. She is the author, editor, and co-editor of eleven books, most recently *Teaching Film* (Modern Language Association of America, 2012); *Idols of Modernity: Movie Stars of the 1920's* (2010); *Rethinking Global Security: Media, Popular Culture, and the "War on Terror"* (2006), and *Aftershocks of the New: Feminism and Film History* (2002). She is past president of the Society for Cinema and Media Studies, the United States' leading professional organization of college and university educators, filmmakers, critics, scholars, and others devoted to the study of the moving image.

ANDREW ROSS is professor of social and cultural analysis at NYU and an activist in the debt resistance movement. A contributor to *The Nation*, the *Village Voice*, the *New York Times*, and *Artforum*, he is the author of many books, including *The Celebration Chronicles: Life, Liberty, and the Pursuit of Property Value in Disney's New Town* (1999); *No Collar: The Humane Workplace and Its Hidden Costs* (2004); *Fast Boat to China: Lessons from Shanghai* (2006); *Nice Work if You Can Get It: Life and Labor in Precarious Times* (2010); and *Bird on Fire: Five Lessons from the World's Least Sustainable City* (2011). His most recent book, *Creditocracy and the Case for Debt Refusal* is available from OR Books.

JEFFREY SOMMERS is associate professor of Africology and global studies at the University of Wisconsin–Milwaukee where his work focuses on political economy and public policy. He is also visiting faculty and curator of the Andre Gunder Frank Memorial Library at the Stockholm School of Economics in Riga and an affiliated researcher at Linkoping University's Institute for Research on Migration, Ethnicity and Society. He is a frequent contributor to global media outlets such as the *Financial Times*, the *Guardian*, the *European Voice*, *Asia Times*, *TruthOut*, and others, and he is co-editor and contributing author to the volume *The Contradictions of Austerity: The Socio-Economic Costs of the Neoliberal Baltic Model* (2014).

CRISTINA VENEGAS is associate professor and chair of the Department of Film and Media Studies at the University of California, Santa Barbara. Her research focuses on the history and politics of Latin American film and media, regional and transnational media formations, and political culture. She is author of *Digital Dilemmas: The State, the Individual, and Digital Media in Cuba* (2010) and is working on a new book entitled *Region and Media across the Americas*, which explores the spatial and ideological contours of media's territorial geographies shaped by political, economic, and cultural interactions.

SHERRYL VINT is professor of science fiction media studies at the University of California, Riverside, and co-director of the Program in Science Fiction and Technoculture Studies. She has published widely on science fiction and co-edits the journals *Science Fiction Studies* and *Science Fiction Film and Television*. Her book publications include *Bodies of Tomorrow* (2007) and *Animal Alterity* (2010), and her current research project, *The Promissory Imagination: Speculative Futures and Biopolitics*, reads science fiction in the context of biopolitical theory.

INDEX

Available titles in the New Directions in International Studies series:

Tasha G. Oren and Patrice Petro, eds.
Global Currents: Media and Technology Now

Peter Paik and Marcus Bullock, eds.
Aftermaths: Exile, Migration, and Diaspora Reconsidered

Rebecca Prime
Hollywood Exiles in Europe: Blacklisted Filmmakers in Postwar Europe

Freya Schiwy
Indianizing Film: Decolonization, the Andes, and the Question of Technology

Cristina Venegas
Digital Dilemmas: The State, the Individual, and Digital Media in Cuba